W9-BEZ-364

Magna Carta

The Foundation of Freedom
1215–2015

Magna Carta

The Foundation of Freedom
1215–2015

Nicholas Vincent

THIRD MILLENNIUM
PUBLISHING, LONDON

Magna Carta: The Foundation of Freedom 1215–2015
© Third Millennium Publishing Ltd

First published in 2014 by Third Millennium Publishing Ltd,
a subsidiary of Third Millennium Information Ltd, in association with
the Magna Carta Trust 800th Anniversary Commemoration Committee
(Chairman Sir Robert Worcester KBE DL)

Second edition 2015

Third Millennium Publishing Ltd
2–5 Benjamin Street, London ECIM 5QL, United Kingdom
www.tmiltd.com

ISBN: 978 1 908990 28 0 (HB)
      978 1 908990 48 8 (PB)

All rights reserved. No part of this publication may be reproduced or
transmitted in any form or by any means, electronic or mechanical now
known or hereafter invented, including photocopying, recording or any
storage or retrieval system, without permission in writing from the publisher

Principal author and general editor: Nicholas Vincent
Contributing authors: Justin Champion, Richard Goldstone,
Joyce Lee Malcolm, Anthony Musson, Miles Taylor

Editor and project manager: Neil Titman
Design and layout: Ian Denning
Art director for Third Millennium: Matthew Wilson
Production: Bonnie Murray
Picture research: Patrick Taylor
Proofreading: Neil Burkey
Indexing: Gerard M-F Hill

Reprographics by Studio Fasoli, Italy
Printed and bound in Slovenia by Gorenjski Tisk on
acid-free 150gsm matt art paper from sustainable forestry

Set in Adobe Garamond

In the list of picture credits opposite, every effort has been made to contact
the copyright owners of all images featured in this book. In the case of
an inadvertent omission, please contact Third Millennium Publishing Ltd
at the address quoted above

178 **Alamy/CSI Productions**; 49 (R) **Alamy/David Lyons**; 142 (B) **Alamy/Everett Collection Historical**; 136, 143 (T) **Alamy/Heritage Image Partnership Ltd**; 181 (R) **Alamy/Homer Sykes**; 146 **Alamy/The National Trust Photolibrary**; 44 (T) **Alamy/nagelestock.com**; 135 **Alamy/North Wind Picture Archives**; 93 (L) **Alamy/Photos 12**; 154 **Alamy/PjrTravel**; 50 **Alamy/Prisma Bildagentur AG**; 92 (L) **Alamy/Maurice Savage**; 181 (L) **Alamy/US Air Force Photo**; 169 **Architect of the Capitol**; 18, 29, 41 (R), 42 (R), 53, 91, 105, 122, 158 (T), 172 (L) **The Art Archive**; 75 (R) **The Art Archive/A Dagli Orti**; 26 (*Bodley Rolls 3 rows 14–15*), 101 (*MS Hatton 10 f.43r*) **The Art Archive/Bodleian Libraries, The University of Oxford**; 46 (R), 113 **The Art Archive/British Library**; 38 (L) **The Art Archive/CCI**; 125 (L) **The Art Archive/Culver Pictures**; 129 **The Art Archive/DeA Picture Library**; 23 (L), 94, 115 **The Art Archive/Eileen Tweedy**; 49 (L) **The Art Archive/Kharbine-Tapabor**; 40, 54 (B), 63 **The Art Archive/Manuel Cohen**; 57 (L) **The Art Archive/Mondadori Portfolio**; 133 (L) **The Art Archive/Superstock**; 39 **Avco Embassy/The Kobal Collection**; 43 (T), 93 (R) **Bibliothèque nationale de France**; 175 **Bloomberg via Getty Images**; 81 (R) (*MS Ch. Glouc. 8*), 100 (T) (*MS Rawl. 612B f.7r*) **The Bodleian Library, University of Oxford**; 107 (R), 109, 118 (L), 138, 176 (R) **Bonhams Auction House**; 104 **Boston College Law Library, Daniel R Coquillette Rare Book Room**; 32 (L) **Bridgeman Images/Musée de la Tapisserie Bayeux**; 35 **Bridgeman Images/Fitzwilliam Museum, University of Cambridge**; 64 (L) **Bridgeman Images/Photo © Neil Holmes**; 126 **Bridgeman Images/Ken Welsh**; 111 **Bridgeman Images/© Collection of the Earl of Leicester**; 125 (R) **Bridgeman Images/Peter Newark American Pictures**; 127 **Bridgeman Images/Newberry Library**; 124 **Bridgeman Images/Photo © John Noott Galleries**; 88 **Bridgeman Images/Private Collection**; 96 **Bridgeman Images/Palazzo Schifanoia**; 144 **Bridgeman Images/The Stapleton Collection**; 20 (L) **Bridgeman Images/Universal History Archive/UIG**; 139 **Bridgeman Images/Palace of Westminster/John Bethell**; 68 **Simon Brighton**; 45 (R) **Britain Express**; 2, 15, 24 (T), 27, 30, 31 (both), 32 (R), 36, 41 (L), 48 (L), 52 (both), 57 (R), 61, 66, 69, 76, 77, 80 (R), 83 (both), 90, 97, 98, 99, 100 (B), 140 (R), 167, 182, 188 **British Library**; 156 (R) **British Pathé**; 120 **Capitol Collection, Washington**; 62 **Jim Champion**; 60, 75 (L), 81 (L), 82 (T) **Master and Fellows of Corpus Christi College, Cambridge**; 23 (R), 28 © **English Heritage**; 156 (L) **Eric Chaim Kline Bookseller**; 46 (L) **Chapter of Durham Cathedral**; 70 © **Fine Art Photographic Library/CORBIS**; 12 **Franz Jantzen, Collection of the Supreme Court of the United States**; 130, 150, 168 (both), 173, 177 **Getty Images**; 170, 182 **Getty Images/AFP**; 55 (R) **Getty Images/Print Collector**; 162, 179 (R), 180 (L) **Getty Images/Time & Life Pictures**; 74 **The Hereford Mappa Mundi Trust and the Dean and Chapter of Hereford Cathedral**; 158 (B) **TP Holland**; 34 (L) © **The J Paul Getty Trust**; 152 **Library and Archives, Canada**; 48 (R), 79 **Lincoln Cathedral**; 24 (B) **Jim Linwood**; 106 **London Collection, Bishopsgate Institute**; 22 (L), 128, 142 (T), 143 (B) **Mary Evans Picture Library**; 118 (R), 164 **Mary Evans/©Illustrated London News Ltd**; 149 **Mary Evans Picture Library/© The March of the Women Collection**; 131 (R) **Massachusetts Archives**; 25 (R), 38 (R), 47 (R), 55 (L), 64 (R) **Matthew Wilson**; 25 (L) **Medway Archives and Local Studies Centre**; 47 (L), 95 **The National Archives' Image Library**; 14, 102, 110, 117 (both), 140 (L), 141, 147 © **National Portrait Gallery, London**; 179 (L) **National Portrait Gallery, Smithsonian Institution**; 6–7 © **National Trust Images/Andrew Butler**; 85, 165 **Parliament House, Canberra/Brenton McGeachie**; 145 **People's History Museum**; 172 (R) **Ronald Reagan Library**; 176 (L) **Science Museum/Science & Society Picture Library**; 78 **Salisbury Cathedral/Photo © Ash Mills**; 86, 89 **Master and Fellows of St John's College, Cambridge**; 17, 43 (B), 65 © **Trustees of the British Museum**; 157 **Universal Pictures/The Kobal Collection**; 22 (R) © **University of Aberdeen**; 119 © **University of Manchester**; 133 (R), 134 (both) **US National Archives and Records Administration**; 42 (L) © **Dr Stuart Whatling**

Contents

'The barons having obtained a great piece of their purpose (as they thought) returned to London with their Charter sealed, the date whereof was this: "Given by our own hand in the meadow called Kuningsmede or Runnymede, betwixt Stanes and Windsor, the fifteenth of June, in the eighteenth year of our reign." Great rejoicing was made for this conclusion of peace betwixt the King and his barons, the people judging that God had touched the King's heart and mollified it, whereby happy days were come for the realm of England…'

Raphael Holinshed, *Chronicles* (1577)

Foreword

The Rt Hon. Lord Dyson

I am delighted to provide a foreword for this magnificent book, which celebrates the eight hundredth anniversary of one of the world's most defining and influential documents, Magna Carta.

The Charter was a remarkable document for its time: it went far beyond the nature of the immediate dispute between King John and the barons, and much further than a range of real, contemporary concerns – although it addressed those too.

It was designed to govern the relations between successive monarchs and their most powerful subjects eternally. However, it has become one of the foundation stones supporting the freedoms enjoyed today by hundreds of millions of people in more than one hundred countries.

It enshrined the rule of law in English society, limited the power of authoritarian rule and for centuries it has influenced constitutional thinking worldwide. Its direct influence can be traced in many other documents preserving personal liberties today, most notably the Constitution of the United States of America.

In 1965 Lord Denning, one of the most celebrated English judges of the twentieth century, described Magna Carta as 'the greatest constitutional document of all times – the foundation of freedom of the individual against the arbitrary authority of the despot'.

One of the remarkable features of Magna Carta is the way in which its historic role is so little appreciated and understood in the nation of its birth. I am always struck by the knowledge and veneration that people from other nations have towards Magna Carta, particularly in the United States. In contrast, the impression is that for many Britons it is a historic footnote to be counted alongside other notable events such as the Battle of Hastings or the defeat of the Spanish Armada. It has a far greater significance for all of us and how we live our lives.

The increased focus on Magna Carta as we mark its eight hundredth anniversary is a special opportunity to increase public knowledge and appreciation for the events that unfolded on the meadows of Runnymede in the thirteenth century, and their resonance and continuing importance in the twenty-first.

This impressive volume will play an attractive part in educating and informing the world about Magna Carta, and it gives me great pleasure as Chairman of the Trust to write this foreword.

The Rt Hon. Lord Dyson
Master of the Rolls and Chairman of the Magna Carta Trust

Magna Carta

The Foundation of Freedom
1215–2015

Chapter One

Bronze doors of the Supreme Court, Washington, DC, designed by Gilbert and John Donnelly, Sr, sculpted by John Donnelly, Jr, cast in Long Island and installed in 1935. The panels depict key incidents and personalities in the development of the rule of law, notably Justinian in the top left panel, Edward Coke and James I in the second row on the right, and, bottom right, King John attaching his seal to Magna Carta with a seal press.

Introduction

Nicholas Vincent

The greatest constitutional document of all times – the foundation of the freedom of the individual against the arbitrary authority of the despot.

Lord Denning (1899–1999)

Magna Carta is the most famous document in the history of England, perhaps in the history of the world. It has been cited in parliamentary, congressional and constitutional debates more frequently than any other text, save only for the Christian Bible. Written on a single sheet of parchment and proclaimed under the authority and seal of England's King John, it sets out in roughly 3,500 words of medieval Latin a programme for the reform of English government. Issued in 1215, reissued in 1216, 1217 and 1225, this programme very swiftly came to be identified as a guarantee of 'liberty'. By 1218, it was being described as the 'Great' (*Magna*) Charter. By 1279, when the archbishop of Canterbury demanded that a copy of it be publicly displayed and annually renewed in every major English church, it already enjoyed totemic status. It played a part in the constitutional struggles of the later Middle Ages. Thereafter, it survived to be cited as a touchstone of 'liberty' in the great quarrels between King and Parliament, in the English Civil Wars of the 1640s, and again in the Glorious Revolution of 1688. By modern commentators it has been credited with placing England's sovereigns, and by extension the rulers of all states governed according to English legal tradition, under the 'rule of law'.

As this suggests, Magna Carta was widely broadcast beyond the English realm. In 1217, its privileges were extended to Ireland. Proclaimed in northern France, they played no small part in the constitutional struggles of the early fourteenth century between French kings and their subjects claiming protection under the particular regional customs of Normandy. With the spread of English law

thereafter, Magna Carta was exported to England's dominion in Wales and later co-kingship with Scotland. By 1606, with the granting of English common law to the colonists of Virginia, it had reached America. It played a part in the debates that led to the American Revolution of the 1770s, and to the French Revolution a decade later. Following British victory against Napoleon, it was to Magna Carta that the world looked for an explanation of why Great Britain had escaped the political turmoil that engulfed the rest of Europe. Seeking to emulate such success, in 1814 the French, and after 1830 the Belgians, awarded themselves *chartes constitutionelles* deliberately modelled upon the principle, if not the practice, of 1215. In India, in New Zealand, in Canada and in South Africa, Magna Carta was cited, throughout the nineteenth century, by the representatives of 'native' peoples determined to share in freedoms claimed by their colonial oppressors. Phrases, first drafted for the Charter of 1215, were rehearsed in the 1628 Petition of Right, the 1789 Declaration of the Rights of Man and the United Nations' 1948 Universal Declaration of Human Rights.

Not surprisingly, Magna Carta continues to be treated with awe and wonder. Lord Denning (1899–1999) proclaimed it 'the greatest constitutional document of all times – the foundation of the freedom of the individual against the arbitrary authority of the despot'. G. M. Trevelyan (1876–1962) declared it to be 'the first great step on the constitutional road'. Yet Trevelyan's praise was already, as early as the 1920s, tempered with caution. Magna Carta, Trevelyan realized, had been totemized to such an extent and from so early a date that it could represent all things to all men. Left and right, radical and ultra-

*G. M. Trevelyan,
pencil portrait by
Francis Dodd, 1933.*

conservative, politicians of every conceivable hue could claim support for their cause from an eight hundred-year-old document drafted to meet quite other needs. As Trevelyan put it:

> Pittites boasted of the free and glorious constitution which had issued from the tents on Runnymede, now attacked by base Jacobins and levellers; Radicals appealed to the letter and the spirit of 'Magna Charta' against gagging acts, packed juries and restrictions of the franchise. America revolted in its name and seeks spiritual fellowship with us in its memory.

What then was (and remains) the 'real' Magna Carta? Its title means merely 'the Great Charter', a 'charter' being any letter or proclamation, generally written on a single sheet of parchment, awarding rights or property. In this particular instance, it describes a parchment document, roughly one and a half feet square, issued in June 1215 by King John under the royal seal, proclaiming the King's intention to reform his government and to make peace with his rebellious barons. As a peace treaty, Magna Carta endured for less than twelve weeks. In theory, it was condemned to oblivion as early as September 1215. In practice, it survived. Revised and reissued, it evolved into a bargaining counter used by kings, throughout the thirteenth century, to promise good government in the future to subjects protesting against bad government in the present or past. As such, it bought successive kings respite from criticism, and consent to royal taxation. What had begun as a distinctly anti-royal settlement thus evolved into a tool of royal manipulation, proof that kings ruled with the full authority of the law. As we shall see, Magna Carta was neither the first English royal statute, nor the first attempt to bind an

English king to what would later come to be described as the 'rule of law'. Its provisions did little in practice to stem the royal abuse of power. It was nonetheless treated in statute books, from the thirteenth century onwards, both as an established reality and as the very earliest statement of English legal tradition.

As this suggests, as early as the thirteenth century, the history of Magna Carta was compounded of legend and paradox. Magna Carta both restricted the King yet proclaimed the King's right to rule. It sought to place the King under the rule of law, yet it helped define law itself as something made (and therefore alterable) by kings. Such paradoxes continued to multiply. In the seventeenth century, Magna Carta was used by the opposition to Charles I to demand that the King be bound to the law and to an ancient, though unwritten, 'constitution'. Yet when the parliamentary opposition triumphed, its principal leader, Oliver Cromwell, having defeated and beheaded the King, went on to deride Magna Carta as a mere gust of hot air. 'Magna Farta', Cromwell insisted, threatened to set up Parliament and the judges as a tyranny even greater than that of the Stuart kings. Magna Carta was used in America and France, from the 1770s onwards, to justify revolution. Yet, at precisely this time, it was this same Magna Carta that was believed by British conservatives to bolster the power and legitimacy of the anti-revolutionary British Crown. Nineteenth- and twentieth-century radicals appealed regularly to the spirit of Magna Carta. Yet it was also fetishized by imperialists who proclaimed it one of the bulwarks of an Anglo-Saxon 'race', manifestly destined to world domination.

Such trends perhaps reflect the fact that Magna Carta is a document more often cited than read. Anyone who takes the trouble to read the text of the 1215 Charter (see page 183) will find there relatively few legal principles but a great deal of thirteenth-century facts. In many cases such facts are of only doubtful relevance to our modern age. It is in many ways easier to define what Magna Carta omits than what it includes. It says nothing, for example, of democracy. It nowhere refers explicitly to the rule of law. It not surprisingly omits any mention of the writ of habeas corpus (itself a seventeenth-century innovation). It does not in any way codify or set out in writing the essential laws of England, either criminal or civil. It embodies no political manifesto. It does not even promise explicitly that the King will rule better in future than he has ruled in the past. What it offers instead, in the King's

THE·ROYALL OAKE OF BRITTAYNE

A parody against Oliver Cromwell, here shown pulling down a tree bearing a series of British symbols, including 'Magna Charta', from The Compleat History of Independency, *1661.*

name, is to restore and uphold the traditional customs and liberties of England's Church and free men. As such, it declares itself a settlement relevant to only a small part of the English nation, those above the level of the peasantry, perhaps only ten or twenty per cent of the realm's population.

To a modern audience, the Charter's attempts to define custom can themselves appear extremely strange. We are taught that Magna Carta is 'the great cornerstone in England's temple of liberty' (as Jerome K. Jerome put it, writing for a popular audience in 1889). But what place in liberty's temple can there be for such provisions as clauses 50 and 51 (promising the forced repatriation of immigrants), or clause 10 (restricting the ability of Jews to profit from commercial enterprise)? What possible connection can there be between the rule of law and clause 33, forbidding the construction of fish weirs on the rivers Thames and Medway? Several clauses have nothing to say of law, but instead concern the making of peace with Scotland, Wales and the English barons. A lot more contain distinctly 'medieval' terminology ('scutage', 'halberjet', the writ of 'praecipe' and so forth), with no apparent relevance to modern life. Even in its definitive form, as reissued and revised in 1225, Magna Carta has bequeathed only thirty or forty words to modern English law. Of the clauses of the Charter as originally issued, only three and a half still operate as statute (parts of clause 1 on the Church, clause 13 on the rights of the city of London,

and clauses 39 and 40, on the general rights of free men). The rest were repealed, between 1828 and 1966, in a series of campaigns intended to rid the statute book of redundant legislation. The majority of its clauses were written out of English law during the reign of Queen Victoria, at precisely the same time that Magna Carta itself was being demythologized by the first generation of truly professional English historians.

Why, then, do Magna Carta and its memory continue to resonate throughout the English-speaking world? There are two chief reasons. The first is that Magna Carta, for all of its limitations, does indeed represent the first effective attempt to bind an English sovereign in obedience to the law. Many such attempts had been made in the past. In 1100, 1135, and again in 1154, kings had been obliged to promise that they would rule well. But they had sooner or later wriggled their way out of all such promises. In 1215, King John did his best to wriggle out of the promises of Magna Carta. He was prevented from doing so. The barons rebelled. The Charter itself could be interpreted as sanction for their rebellion. In 1216, and again thereafter, it was reissued by King John's son and grandson as a manifesto of royal determination to rule properly and in obedience to the law.

The second reason for the continued veneration of Magna Carta lies in the text itself. Buried amidst the feudal jargon are phrases that still resound. Those who made the Charter were expert in the terminology of the law, and could sum up complicated ideas in simple but definitive terms. Clauses 39 and 40 provide a powerful example:

No free man will be taken or imprisoned or disseised or outlawed or exiled or in any way ruined, nor shall we go or send against him, save by the lawful judgement of his peers and/or by the law of the land. To no one shall we sell, to no one shall we deny or delay right or justice.

From these two clauses stretches the path not only to rule by law, but to the prohibition of arbitrary arrest, the accountability of the State to its subjects, the obligation of government to strive after efficiency for the public good, even the very specific right to trial by jury of one's peers. Even here, however, we are a long way removed from Lord Denning's 'foundation of the freedom of the individual'. How are we to traverse the vast distance between 1215 and the present-day understanding of Magna Carta? Indeed, how did King and barons first come to issue Magna Carta in 1215? What was their understanding of the law? How did their understanding differ from ours, or from that of the intervening eight centuries of politicians, historians and constitutionalists, English, American or otherwise? What does Magna Carta have to teach us both about the foundations of the Anglo-Saxon common law tradition, and about the prospects of that tradition and the whole concept of 'freedom' or 'liberty' in the twenty-first century?

In what follows, half a dozen experts have been invited to explain Magna Carta's background, context and posterity. We shall begin with English law as recorded in the six hundred years before Magna Carta. What role did the concept of liberty play within this system? How did it impact upon the rule of the Plantagenet kings, the dynasty from which King John sprang, and their own very peculiar tradition of royal rule? From there, we shall explore the immediate background to 1215, in the troubled reign and personality of King John. We shall attempt to explain how Magna Carta came to be made, issued and, in the aftermath, preserved. We shall then turn to its posterity in the later Middle Ages and beyond. How did it come to be interpreted as the very foundation stone of English law? How did it cross the Atlantic to America, and with what consequences? What did early modern, or Victorian, interpreters make of it, and why did it remain so central to constitutional debates not only in England, but in America and across

the British empire? By 1900, most of the individual clauses of Magna Carta had been repealed. Yet the Charter itself lived on. It remains significant both in the spirit, as a guarantee of liberty, and in physical reality, as an artefact lovingly collected, preserved and celebrated across the English-speaking world. Here too, chapters in the present book offer guidance to the meaning of Magna Carta to the twentieth and twenty-first centuries. Finally, and in an attempt to think forwards into an uncertain future, a distinguished modern interpreter of the law offers his own reflections on what Magna Carta may continue to mean to generations of humanity as yet unborn.

Law, politics and history have always been interdependent. Our first obligation must therefore be to explain the origins of this symbiosis, far back in the dim and distant past. In due course, we shall have to travel back in time more than two millennia, to the very earliest emergence of law as a defining characteristic of human society. However, let us begin our journey in a period slightly less remote. In 1810, England stood virtually alone against the threats posed by Napoleonic France. England's King, George III, had recently lost his American colonies to revolutionaries proclaiming their adherence to a newly drafted American Constitution. From across the English Channel, Englishmen had witnessed the fall of the French King and his beheading at the hands of revolutionary assemblies proclaiming their right to 'liberty, equality and fraternity'. George III's ministers were aware that in places such as Holland, Prussia and the Papal States, in most cases in direct imitation of France, cries were being raised for 'liberty' to be guaranteed by written constitutions setting out the proper foundations of law and the relationship between government and the governed. In both France and Prussia, and in an attempt to sweep away the dead lumber of the feudal past, law had come under intense scrutiny. Vast swathes of ancient or obsolete legislation, local, regional and national, had been collected and in due course codified: reduced to a single body of law that could claim consistency, reissued under the authority of the present age. Similar things had been attempted in the distant past, most famously in sixth-century Constantinople, where the Roman Emperor Justinian had commissioned a codification of the laws of earlier emperors, the so-called *Corpus Iuris Civilis*. Between Justinian and the *Code Napoléon*, however, stretched thirteen centuries in which laws, although regularly made, had been only

Print by Thomas Rowlandson contrasting French revolutionary fury with the sanity of British liberty symbolized by, among other things, 'Magna Charta' in Britannia's hand.

haphazardly collected, publicized or obeyed.

It was in this context that royal commissioners charged by King George III with the preservation and publication of English records set about the collection of materials that, in due course, were to grow into a mighty series of nine folio volumes, the *Statutes of the Realm*. This enterprise was both official and deliberately conservative. If the French could run mad for a new revolutionary constitution, then England's political sanity would be preserved by respect for the good old laws of the English past. What should most concern us here is that the makers of George III's great *Statutes of the Realm*, still the most ambitious attempt ever made to assemble English law into a single published collection, chose to begin their edition with Magna Carta.

In presenting Magna Carta at the head of all subsequent English law, George III's Record Commissioners could claim ancient and long-established precedent. Across the Middle Ages, the many thousands of so-called books of statutes, collections made by and for lawyers, intended as professional training manuals and textbooks, had begun with Magna Carta. George III's commissioners thus helped enshrine a myth already ages old. Magna Carta, their edition proclaimed, was the very bedrock and foundation of English law. It was in effect England's first constitution. In reality, of course, it was nothing of the sort.

Had George III's commissioners paid rather more attention to the language of the text that they themselves were the first properly to edit, they would have realized that Magna Carta was not intended at the time as 'constitutional' in any significant or revolutionary sense. On the contrary, and in so far as it offered any clues as to its abstract purpose, King John's Charter of 1215 claimed to be an attempt at the repair or improvement (in the Latin preamble *emendatio*) of the King's

realm. This it offered to achieve through the writing down of a series of 'liberties'. Such 'liberties' promised to the Church and to the free men of the realm are repeatedly referred to throughout the document (cc.1, 13, 52, 56, 59, 60–1, 63). On one occasion, clause 13 upholding the liberties of London as of all other English towns, they are described specifically as 'ancient liberties and free customs'. Custom itself is mentioned repeatedly (cc.2, 4, 13, 41, 48, 60), on occasion described as 'ancient' (c.2) or 'ancient and good' (c.41). The need to respect the traditions of antiquity is further stressed in at least three other clauses (cc.23, 25, 46). The concept of liberties reappears in the Charter's final and in many ways summative clause (c.63), guaranteeing 'all the aforesaid liberties, rights and concessions'. 'Rights' (in Latin *ius*, or plural *iura*) are themselves mentioned on at least four occasions (cc.1, 23, 52–3, 59, 63), in one instance (c.23) coupled with the idea of ancient or established custom. Other operative words include the concept of good practice (*rectus*, in the sense of doing what is right), and justice (*iusticia*, cc.40, 52–3, 57), brought together most famously in clause 40 where the King promises never to sell, to deny or to delay what is 'right or just'. We might note, meanwhile, that the word 'law' (Latin *lex*) is referred to relatively sparingly, sometimes as 'the law of the realm' or 'the land' (cc.39, 42, 45, 55–7), elsewhere used adjectivally to qualify judgement, or those assisting in judgement, as 'lawful' (c.4, 26, 52, 56–7). In none of these instances does Magna Carta itself claim to 'make' new law.

Readers, now as in the thirteenth century, must beware of the Latin language in which Magna Carta was written. Latin has a tendency sometimes to elide, sometimes to distinguish, concepts that in modern English take on rather different meanings. Even so, and with apologies for the necessary linguistic technicalities here, enough should be apparent from the wording of the Charter to demonstrate that what King John offered to do in 1215 was not to create a written constitution but to defend and uphold law, liberties and customs already considered 'just', 'good' and perhaps above all 'ancient'. Magna Carta was intended not to make new laws but to ensure that respect was paid to the good old laws of the past. To this extent, it was not the foundation of English law but an attempt to preserve or restate something regarded as much more ancient and binding. What, then, were those ancient laws, liberties and customs that Magna Carta claimed both to restore and to protect?

EDWARD

Edward the Confessor sending Earl Harold (later King Harold II) to Normandy, from the Bayeux Tapestry, c.1075.

Chapter Two

Law before Magna Carta: The Anglo-Saxon Law Codes and Their Successors before 1215

Nicholas Vincent

The king, who is the vicar of the highest King, was established for this, that he rule and defend the earthly kingdom and people of God and above all the Holy Church from all wrongdoers, and destroy and expel evildoers. If not, he loses the name of king …

Interpolations to the London copy of the *Leges Edwardi Confessoris* (c.1210)

The rule of law in Antiquity

Men have been ruled by laws since the first emergence of human society. Laws themselves are the subject of some of the most ancient of human writings, in the cuneiform clay tablets of ancient Babylon or Egyptian hieroglyphs. At least two of the first five books of the Jewish Old Testament, the so-called 'Pentateuch', are given over to the written record of laws supposedly bequeathed to the Jews by God speaking through the patriarchs and prophets. The kings and city states of ancient Greece made laws. So did the Roman emperors, claiming powers originally invested in the Senate. Law, in all of these traditions, was seen as fundamental, both to society and to the social enforcement of virtue.

The Emperor Justinian, in the sixth century, codified a vast body of such laws into his *Corpus Iuris Civilis*, ever afterwards the portal by which later kings or peoples approached the legislation of the classical

A vision of ancient law: Gustave Doré's engraving of Moses descending from Mount Sinai, 1866.

Tacitus and 'barbarian law'

It was not just Jews or Romans who proclaimed obedience to law. The Roman historian Tacitus, writing in the first century AD, claimed to record at least some of the customs of the barbarian tribes living east of the Rhine. His descriptions of tribal society are not to be trusted in detail, any more than we would today trust an outside sophisticate's descriptions of the tribal 'laws' of 'Red' Indians or Australian 'aboriginals'. Nonetheless, in general point of principle, Tacitus was surely correct to distinguish between barbarian law, preserved by oral and tribal tradition, and Roman imperial statute proclaimed in writing. The Germanic tribes, according to Tacitus, ruled through kinship networks gathered together at tribal assemblies. Here law was upheld but not written down. When, three hundred years later, these same Germanic tribes burst their bounds and seized control of what had previously been Roman territory, they abandoned neither their own assemblies nor the laws of Rome.

Early 20th-century drawing of a Germanic tribal assembly depicted on the Column of Marcus Aurelius, Rome, 2nd century AD.

past. Like the 'law' of the Jewish Old Testament, the *Corpus* was intended to refine a great chaos of miscellaneous rulings into a single body of 'law'. Without such law, it was widely agreed, there would be mere anarchy. It was the duty of kings and legislators to seek out good laws, just as it was the duty of philosophers or natural scientists to probe the deeper mysteries of time and creation. The more presumptuous of ancient rulers might claim to make their own laws. Most preferred merely to restate, rediscover or mend laws that were believed to be dictated by the gods or inherent to human society. According to the Roman jurist Ulpian, law was 'what nature teaches all animals': a concept of 'natural law' that existed in Western thought long before its rediscovery by Locke and philosophers of the seventeenth century. The gods themselves might change their minds. What, after all, was the coming of Christ but a sign of God's desire for a new covenant and understanding with mankind? As a result, laws could evolve, and legal experts grow rich exploiting the loopholes and disparities between precept and practice. In doing so, however, like Isaac Newton later revealing the 'laws' of the physical universe, they operated within a solid-state system. The law itself could not be contradicted, save at the very gravest peril to mankind.

The fall of the Roman empire gave birth to what we today term 'the Middle Ages'. It also led to the deliberate preservation of Roman law.

*The divine plan
to which all laws
must answer: God
as architect of the
universe, frontispiece
of a medieval picture
Bible from Paris,
c.1220–30.*

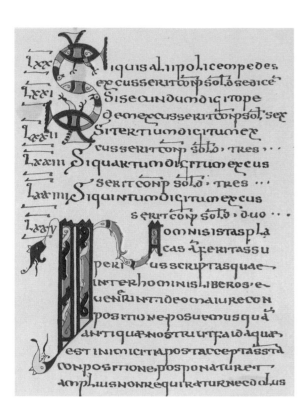

Page from the Edict of Rothair, a compilation of Lombard law, 643.

Kings and laws in etymology

Isidore of Seville, the great sixth-century dictionary-maker, whose definitions of Latin vocabulary remained influential throughout the Middle Ages, derived the word 'king' (in Latin *rex*) from the verb 'to rule' (*regere*). In this understanding, only those who 'ruled', i.e. who proclaimed and enforced laws, had the right to be considered truly 'royal'.

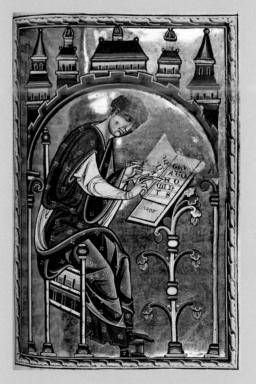

Isidore writing on the nature of the world, illumination from the Aberdeen Bestiary, 12th century.

Modern historians continue to dispute the relative proportion of Germanic or Roman law to be found in the 'codes' by which the Franks, the Visigoths, the Lombards and other post-Roman 'Germanic' peoples proclaimed their laws. The so-called 'Salic Laws' of the Franks, for example, turn out on examination to be not so much German law imported from east of the Rhine but a restatement, in post-Roman terms, of edicts and decrees issued by the later Roman emperors. What is not in dispute is that the barbarian peoples who succeeded the fall of Rome believed in law. Law, indeed, was essential to their collective existences. The very idea of a nation, people or *gens*, as a society governed by one law, and of their king as lawmaker and defender of his people, was inherent in this early medieval impulse to set down law in writing.

The law codes that survive to us from this time are themselves heavily influenced by another development whose impact had been felt within the Roman empire only within the last hundred years of Roman imperial rule. Previously treated as a dangerous and revolutionary cult, Christianity had been adopted since the 320s as the official religion of the Roman emperors. As a result, it achieved a status and charisma in which the barbarian successor kings were keen to share. Christianity was a religion both of the written word (the Bible) and of writing that itself was very largely given over to the reporting of law, both Jewish and as revealed by Christ. The New Testament included the great series of letters attributed to St Paul in which Paul

grappled with the problems of accommodating the early Christian Church to the laws both of the Jews and the Romans. No one who had read St Paul could be in any doubt that the laws of God were not necessarily those either of Caesar or of the Jewish prophets. As a result, the conversion of barbarian kings and their peoples to Christianity led to a speedy acquaintance both with the technology of writing and with the laws, various and often conflicting, of the classical, barbarian, Christian and Judaic pasts.

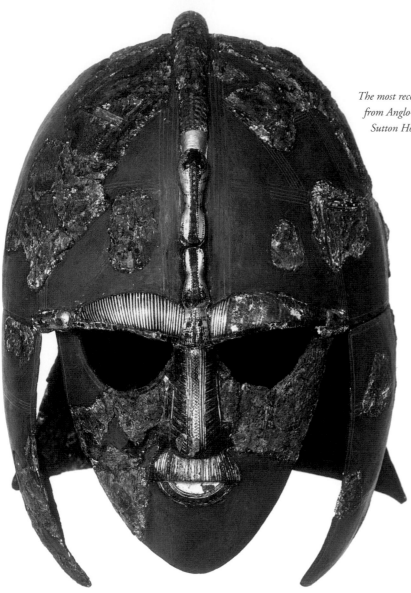

*The most recognisable symbol of power
from Anglo-Saxon England: the
Sutton Hoo helmet, 7th century.*

Germanic law. At the same time, certain places of peace – the assembly meetings or 'courts' in which kings themselves resided, the roads by which those attending such courts journeyed to and from the King – became the subject of special, royally guaranteed protections. In a world of mead halls and feastings, in which it was all too easy for drunkenness to slide over into violence, the protection of the peace of the King's hall was an especial priority. Certain persons, themselves judged incapable of meeting violence with violence, were placed under an added degree of protection, in particular women, priests, the young and the infirm.

In order to preserve the peace, kings were obliged to shed blood. Maiming, castration, blinding, and in ultimate extremity the capital punishment of offenders were an essential corollary of power, reserved for use against those who preferred violence to the lawful settlement of disputes. Despite the unhealthiness of much of the modern obsession with 'medieval' torture, there is no doubt that the medieval punishment of crime was severe: hanging, beheading, burning, the

The roots of early English Law

How did such concepts of law first reach England and those particular 'Germanic' tribes, the Angles, Saxons and Jutes, who had crossed to Britain, from the fourth century onwards, in pursuit of land and plunder? Such peoples were long accustomed to the settlement of disputes, most often through feuding between families or kinship clans. The slaying of a kinsman or the theft of property, as in many societies today, risked an escalating pattern of violence and revenge. Law, either of the community or increasingly of the kings who emerged to represent and govern the community, offered a means of resolution here. Through the payment of money or other goods in compensation, feud could be averted and the injured parties appeased. In all of this, kings and lawmakers could claim to be acting in the interest of peace, itself a concept central both to Roman and to Christian ideas of the right ordering of society. As a result, the establishment of fixed monetary payments, intended to guarantee the King's peace, became a central function of Anglo-Saxon as of wider

*Reconstruction of Saxon Yeavering in Northumberland, a royal
hall depicted as it might have been in the early 7th century.*

Left: The sword of justice and the gallows, in an 11th-century Old English Hexateuch. Below: Alfred the Great, statue by Count Gleichen at Wantage, unveiled in 1877.

the very earliest English laws take the form of a code, said to have been committed to writing by Aethelbert King of Kent, traditionally dated *c.*594, opening with a series of fixed monetary penalties decreed as compensation. Damage to property belonging to God or the Church was to incur a twelvefold penalty. Damage to the property of those summoned to the King was to be repaid at twice its cost, with a further fifty-shilling payment to the King. A freeman who stole from the King was to pay nine times the damage in compensation; a killing on the King's estate was to be compensated with a fifty-shilling payment, and so forth, through more than eighty clauses that attempt to deal with an enormous range of eventualities. How much should be paid if a man were unlawfully castrated, if a handyman's eye or foot were struck off, if a man should lose a thumb or a thumb-nail, a middle or a little finger? Judged by modern conceptions of the law, Aethelbert's code reads more like the small print to a personal injuries insurance policy than as a comprehensive statement of legal principles.

Though questions remain concerning the authenticity of Aethelbert's code, certain of its features were to remain typical. To begin with, Aethelbert's law was written not in Latin (the language of the Roman empire and later of the Church) but in the Anglo-Saxon vernacular, essentially a German dialect. It survives only in a much later copy. It claims not so much to make new law as to define customs already in place. It seeks to cover all eventualities, both probable and improbable. It lays great emphasis upon preserving the peace and upon the King as chief peace-maker. It assumes the circulation of money, and that monetary payments could be negotiated, if necessary under royal supervision, to avert the dangers of unlicensed or unlimited feuding between families or clans.

These same features can be found in the law codes attributed to later kings of Kent, and subsequently to Ine, King of Wessex (*c.*694). After a hiatus of nearly two hundred years, they reappear in the law code attributed to Alfred the Great (d. 899) itself claiming to be a deliberate gathering together or 'codification' of early Saxon and Danish law. Similar features characterize all subsequent codes attributed to Anglo-Saxon kings,

hurling of criminals from cliffs. The sword of justice was wielded by kings who themselves dispensed ultimate punishment by the gallows, a mechanism judged appropriately public to display the consequences of base felony. In all of this there was an assumption that only through the threat of greater violence could the violent be deterred. This in turn helped establish a further characteristic of medieval law. Law today is the preserve of professionals, of police authorities, lawyers and judges acting on behalf of communities or litigants themselves only vaguely familiar with the laws that such professionals enforce. This was not the medieval way. In the absence of policing or professional law courts, long before the emergence of the modern machinery of justice, and with extreme violence as the only recourse against criminality, each community and every local warrior or lord was obliged to possess a basic understanding of law. To punish the guilty, to counsel dependants, to display a fitness to rule, kings, like the lords or the communities they ruled, required a degree of legal expertise that we would today consider exceptional. This was a society already hard-wired with law. If we regard Magna Carta as an attempt to bind the King to a tradition of pre-existing law, then Magna Carta's roots were planted deep in the communal and for the most part unwritten understanding of what was or was not lawful.

As for the writing down of such traditions,

Aethelbert's code: an authentic document?

Aethelbert's code survives to us in only one copy, made at least five centuries after its issue, for the monks of Rochester (part of the so-called *Textus Roffensis* of the 1120s). Much debate surrounds both its authenticity and its form. Aethelbert was the first English king to convert to Christianity, an event famously recorded by the eighth-century historian, the Venerable Bede. Bede also tells us that Aethelbert made laws for his kingdom. But does Aethelbert's code as it survives really report these laws? Is it perhaps a later attempt to flesh out Bede's report, or does it represent a body of pre-Christian, Germanic law which was only subsequently brought into line with Christian principles, for example by its opening insistence that compensation to the Church be paid at a much higher rate than compensation to the King?

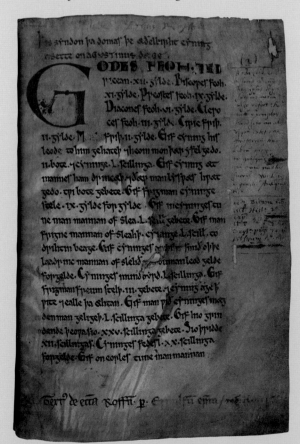

Opening page of the Textus Roffensis, *1122–4.*

The tribal divisions of Anglo-Saxon England.

the last of them issued by King Cnut forty or so years before the Norman Conquest of 1066. Through the influence of the Church, and in several instances in law codes clearly written by bishops and churchmen rather than by the King's secular officials, law itself developed a degree of sophistication. Alfred's laws open with a long preamble borrowed from the Bible, recounting the role of Moses in the Old Testament lawmakings of the Jews and declaring that a king's subjects owe obedience to their temporal lord. They also carefully distinguish between the customs of the various parts of England and in particular between those regions placed under the law of Wessex and those under the law of the Danes. Similar distinctions between the laws of Wessex, Mercia, Kent or the Danish-held parts of northern England occur in subsequent codes. Through to the time of Magna Carta and beyond, the body of English royal law applicable to all has to be offset against regional customs more or less compliant with a national norm. Meanwhile, the laws of King Athelstan (d. 939) and his brother King Edmund (d. 946), introduce moral injunctions that go beyond the simple regulation of feuding, that provide for the needs of the poor, and that predict much future lawmaking by contrasting the lawlessness of the present age with the peace that God had ideally decreed. The laws of King Edgar (d. 975) establish uniform standards of coinage, weights and measures. By the time of King Cnut (d. 1035), it had become accepted that the role of the King was, first and foremost, to protect his people by restating and reissuing the good old laws of his royal predecessors. Cnut claimed to have reissued the laws of Edgar. Cnut's successor, Edward the Confessor, before being accepted as King, is said to have been obliged to reissue the laws of Cnut. Even so, basic principles persisted. Law was written in the vernacular. It sought to be comprehensive even at the expense of clarity. It was chiefly concerned with the preservation of peace, the regulation of feuding, and the establishment of penalties for crimes that would otherwise provoke violent revenge from kinsmen.

Freedom and law enforcement in Anglo-Saxon society

So much for law. But what of 'liberty', by many modern authorities assumed to be the guiding principle both of Magna Carta and of Anglo-Saxon legal tradition? 'Liberty' is today a word that implies freedom from control: the right or privilege to resist unjust oppression. In the Middle Ages, long before the French revolutionary endorsement of *liberté, egalité et fraternité*, its meaning was rather different. As used in Magna Carta, the concept of 'liberty' seems often to imply not just some insubstantial absence of compulsion but an entirely substantial bundle of rights, often equated with the greater 'liberties' such as the archbishopric of Canterbury, the jurisdiction of the city of London, or the lordships of earls and bishops into which the realm of England was divided. Here the concept of 'liberty' shades uncomfortably into the

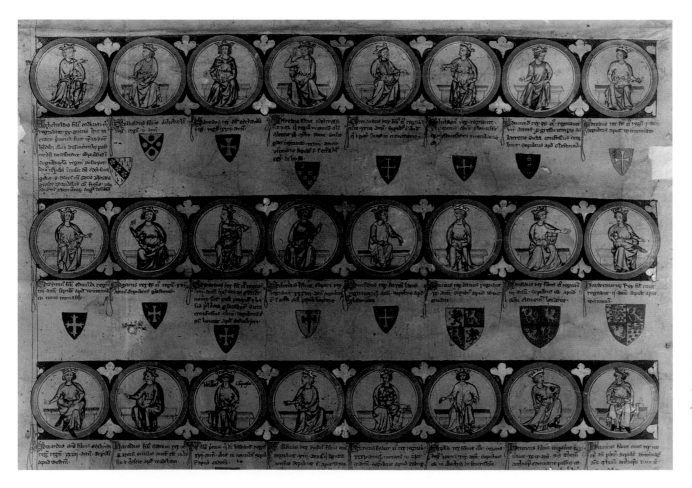

The succession which lay at the heart of early English lawmaking: a 14th-century genealogical roll (section listing the kings from Aethelwulf to Henry the son of Henry II).

The King as lawmaker answerable to divine authority:
Edgar offering a charter of ecclesiastical reforms to Christ,
illumination from the New Minster Charter, c.966.

idea of a private lordly jurisdiction standing apart from 'state' control, not so much as a guarantee of personal freedom, but as a sanction for the sort of power that we might otherwise describe as a private 'lordship' or jurisdictional 'franchise'. How did this paradox originate? The word liberty had first been coined by the Greeks, to describe immunity from taxation. The Romans adopted the idea, but in the process changed its meaning so that it now implied the negation of slavery. In Roman law, a freed man enjoyed 'liberty' in that he ceased to be the personal property of someone else. This version of liberty was adopted into the language of Anglo-Saxon royal charters, from the eighth century onwards, to refer to the 'liberties' of particular subjects, most often of the greater cathedral or monastic churches, guarantied against the more predatory aspects of royal lordship or *dominium*. From this, it was a short step to the equation of liberty with franchised right.

We are a long way here from the modern meaning of 'freedom' that, to the Middle Ages, would have carried unwelcome connotations of chaos. What was being guaranteed by Anglo-Saxon kings to their greater churches, and ultimately to the 'free' men of the realm, was a degree of 'liberty' from what contemporaries would have recognized as 'tyranny'. Having no sophisticated machinery of state, but a highly developed sense of the Christian duty of obedience to kings constituted by God, the Middle Ages necessarily invested 'liberty' with meanings different from those that the word enjoys today. We are nonetheless, as early as the reign of King Offa (d. 796), confronted with language that, four centuries before Magna Carta, suggests a sophisticated understanding of the political significance of law. We also find ourselves in a world in which the Church already laid claim to a role as liberty's chief protector.

The Anglo-Saxon administration of law and government was far cruder than that we would expect of a modern state. Violence and theft were brought within the Anglo-Saxon law codes, but property disputes were regulated by the King principally in so far as they might involve unlawful dispossession and therefore provoke feuding. Land law, testamentary law, commercial law, as we would today understand such concepts, clearly existed in Anglo-Saxon society but to a large extent were governed by unwritten custom, beyond the range of the surviving royal codes. The codes themselves were only semi-official rulings, surviving haphazardly, in many cases more significant as

statements of royal or ecclesiastical ideology than as descriptions of what happened in practice when a crime was committed. Kings had to be seen to make laws, and law was inscribed in writing precisely so that it might be seen. Whether such laws were enforced or obeyed was another matter altogether. Certainly, they covered only a small part of what we would today consider the orbit of the law.

Even so, the administrative machinery of Anglo-Saxon England was far more advanced than that of most other parts of tenth- or eleventh-century Europe. England was a wealthy land, lying on the North Sea trade routes, directly in the path of Danish and Scandinavian marauders who from the eighth century onwards threatened the authority of Kentish, Mercian and West Saxon kings. In response to such 'Viking' raids, King Alfred (d. 899) and his successors had attempted to raise taxes to pay for armies and defences that themselves led to the emergence of tax-gathering administrations. England was divided into a series of administrative units – vills, hundreds and shires

Rochester Castle, a potent symbol of the new royal control exercised by the Normans.

– each of which had a responsibility for defence and hence for the maintenance of its own peace. Officials, such as the shire reeves (later 'sheriffs') or hundred bailiffs emerged to administer this system. Such men were required not only to know the law but on occasion to enforce it. In the meetings of hundreds and shires, where justice was administered, there was a need for men (we will later know them as 'jurors') who could testify to past and present events, and for officials, answerable to the King, to ensure that right was done. Such local officials (we will later call them 'justices' or 'judges') had on occasion to be distinct from the shire reeves, since it was often the deeds of shire reeves that they were required to judge. Both Edgar and Cnut insisted that no appeal could be made to the King unless a suitor had failed to obtain justice locally. This in turn implies a routine of local law enforcement. What we have here, albeit in embryo, are the origins of the future law courts and judiciary.

But in embryo only. Lawmaking and law enforcement remained *ad hoc* affairs in which might was a great deal more persuasive than right. There was no effective policing system save for the operation of community self-defence forces, albeit that here too England could boast institutions as sophisticated as anything to be found elsewhere in northern Europe. Certainly by the early eleventh century, all the free men of England, according to laws promulgated by Cnut, were assigned to groups of ten or so households, in southern England known as tithings, in the Danelaw called 'frankpledge'. Between them, such groups were accountable for any crimes committed by their members. Frankpledge did not create a police force. It did, however, extend ideas of law enforcement and mutual accountability beyond the kin or family to far wider social units. England was subject to frequent invasions and in the eleventh century to at least three changes of dynasty – from the West Saxon line of King Aethelred to the Danish King Cnut, from Cnut back to the West Saxon Edward the Confessor, and in 1066 from Edward's successor, Harold, to the Norman, William 'the Conqueror'. In terms of law, these dynastic upheavals might have proved disastrous. In practice, they served to re-emphasize the need for legal continuity. Cnut was persuaded by his new English subjects to swear to uphold the laws of Edgar. Edward swore to uphold the laws of Cnut. After 1066, so it was widely believed, William the Conqueror swore, both before and after his coronation, to uphold the laws of Edward the Confessor.

The Norman revolution

The Conquest changed many things. Where previously the Anglo-Saxon kings had claimed authority from God to legislate over a realm that in no sense 'belonged' to them as personal property, William the Conqueror's victory placed every acre of land in England directly at the King's disposal, to grant away or retain as he saw fit. Hastings itself was viewed by contemporaries as a divine punishment for the sloth and sinfulness of the Anglo-Saxons: a great trial by battle, in which the English were judged to have lost the support of God. The word 'feudalism' has in recent decades fallen out of favour with historians. It nonetheless remains a convenient term with which to describe the revolution effected after 1066, in which the King was transformed from chief peace-maker into effective proprietor of the realm. Henceforth, all estates were held from the King. Some were held directly by great barons and churches, others indirectly by knights and lesser men, rewarded with smaller portions of land in return for service to their lords who in turn served the King. Since the priority after 1066 was the preservation of Norman military control, most such service became defined in military terms, as the obligation to supply a fixed number of knights to a lord and ultimately to the King's army.

Paradoxically, although the Conquest transformed the basis of property-holding in England, it did more to embed than to destroy the

VBI HAROLD:SACRAMENTVM:FECIT: HIC HAR
VVILLELMO DVCI:-

The Bayeux Tapestry legitimizing Norman rule: Harold swears the oath to William he would subsequently break.

pre-existing traditions of English law. The King now 'owned' his realm by right of conquest. But conquest had to be justified. Clearly it had been granted to the Normans by God. Clearly, too, the last of the Anglo-Saxon kings, Harold Godwinson, could be vilified by Norman propagandists as an oath-breaker and usurping tyrant whose unlawful seizure of power had been punished by the Norman scourge. Similar lines of argument had been deployed, four centuries earlier, by the Venerable Bede to justify the Anglo-Saxon conquest of England from British tyrants and usurpers. To this extent, Norman propaganda could present the events of 1066 not so much as the conquest but as the 'liberation' of England. At the same time, in justifying the Norman claim to serve as the lawful and legitimate successors to the 'good' Anglo-Saxon kings of the past, William the Conqueror and his propagandists were obliged to deploy arguments themselves based upon respect for law. According to this argument, Edward the

Confessor had nominated William of Normandy as his legitimate successor. With God's help, William had triumphed over the tyrant Harold. So far so good. But in adopting this line of justification, Norman kings placed themselves under a duty of obedience to English law that they might otherwise, as conquerors, have sought to repudiate. Henceforth kingship itself was caught in an uneasy tension between claims based on law and those founded on the brute force of conquest.

England's new Norman conquerors had somehow to accommodate themselves to a centuries-old tradition of English law. The process was piecemeal, and remains poorly documented. From around 1100, however, we begin to receive our first clear proofs that English law was once again operating with a degree of routine. We also obtain our first glimpses of a Norman king issuing written legislation for his English subjects. The Domesday survey of 1086, from which Domesday Book emerged, was itself testimony to the survival of Anglo-Saxon traditions

*Seal of Henry I, depicting
the king armed and
on horseback.*

Royal seals: the paradox of kingship

The seals used to authenticate English royal charters after 1066, including the seal of King John applied to Magna Carta, embody the paradox of legal claims and violent conquest inherent in Norman rule. On one side, the King is displayed as an agent of God's law, enthroned in majesty, carrying the orb and sceptre of good government. On the other he appears on horseback, sword in hand, charging into battle, the violent instrument of God's law.

of law and local government. The vast array of details reported in Domesday, in effect listing the ownership and profits of every estate in England, could not have been recorded had it not been for the survival of hundred and shire courts in which records were kept and inquests conducted. From the opening decades of the twelfth century, we have a small handful of law books in which attempts were made to transmit, and in the process often to transform Old English law codes. From both Rochester and London, we have collections of Anglo-Saxon laws that remain our principal source of knowledge of the Old English codes from Aethelbert onwards. It is worth remarking that both London and Kent (in which Rochester lay) jealously preserved their own legal peculiarities, standing apart from the regional or national norms derived from Wessex or the Danelaw. To this extent, what we know of the Anglo-Saxon 'national' law comes to us, paradoxically, only from the fringes of legal tradition.

Return to the Anglo-Saxon codes: the *Quadripartitus* and *Leges Edwardi*

From the second decade of the twelfth century, we also have a collection that survives in half a dozen copies but that, unlike the London or Rochester law books, seems to have continued to circulate through to the year 1200 and beyond. This sought to translate into the Latin of the educated post-Conquest elite the Old English texts of Anglo-Saxon law. Its Latin translations vary considerably in accuracy and reliability. In many instances they nonetheless remain our only means of access to texts first composed in Old English, whose contents would otherwise have vanished without trace. They are preceded in the surviving manuscripts by a preface setting out what the collection's author believed to be the purpose of his collection, and they are followed by a series of more modern statements of law, the most important of which claims to record the laws of King Henry I (r. 1100–35), the so-called *Leges Henrici Primi* (*c.*1115). The preface, following in the tradition of earlier legislators such as King Edmund, dwells at length on the fallen state of English society, upon the need to eradicate sin and hence to restate good laws fallen into abeyance. The *Leges Henrici Primi* that follow after the translations of the Anglo-Saxon codes, whatever else they may be, are most definitely not an official, royally sponsored codification of English law. Rather, and again very much like the Anglo-Saxon codes, they seem to strive after comprehensiveness even at the expense of clarity. They are principally concerned with offences for which monetary compensation was due. To this they add a concern for correct legal procedure and the operations of justice, apparently at a fairly local level. They perhaps represent the work of a legally trained author accustomed to pleadings in the hundred court. The *Leges*, combined with the preface and Latin translations from Old English codes, are known collectively (and extremely misleadingly) as the *Quadripartitus* or 'fourfold' (in reality at most two or threefold) book of law. Assuming a single author for this work, likely candidates include either the archbishop of York or the bishop of Exeter, both of them closely attached to the King's chancery or writing office.

As this contested attribution should make plain, *Quadripartitus* is very far from being a clear or definitive digest of English law. It was never officially recognized let alone officially issued by any English

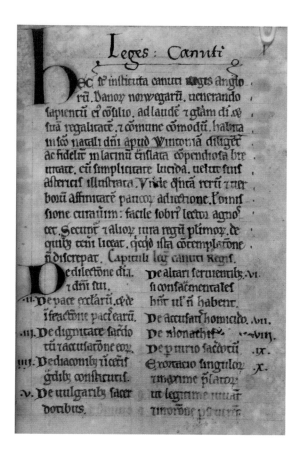

The alleged laws of Cnut, in a late 12th-century legal encyclopedia.

king. Its text was frequently miscopied, altered or confused in transmission. It nonetheless represents an attempt to merge the laws of Antiquity with those of the present. To this extent, it is to be associated with further post-Conquest attempts to preserve, or if necessary to invent past laws. Some of these attempts took the form merely of glossaries offering bilingual and on occasion trilingual translations of Old English legal vocabulary, supplied with Latin and sometimes French equivalents. Others are more ambitious. Amongst these, the most influential were the so-called *Instituta Cnuti* (a purported translation of laws attributed to Cnut, in reality in many instances newly invented), and the *Leges Edwardi Confessoris*.

The *Leges Edwardi* circulated during the course of the twelfth century in at least twenty manuscripts. They seem to have been composed at some date in the 1130s or 40s, claiming to offer a summary of the laws in force on the eve of the Norman Conquest of 1066. According to the author's preface, these laws had been confirmed by William the Conqueror, four years after Hastings, at a great assembly to which were summoned twelve men from every county, competent and sworn to report 'the rules of their laws and customs, omitting nothing nor altering anything deceitfully'. What follows is a travesty: an ahistorical conflation of legal traditions, some of them pre-Conquest, many of them (including regulations on the relations between Christians and Jews only introduced to England after 1066) of much more recent vintage. The *Leges Edwardi* are infuriatingly selective and wholly inaccurate as a record of 'real' pre-Conquest law.

They are nonetheless of great significance. They reveal that, as late as the 1140s, English law was still in a state of flux, as a French-speaking elite struggled to make sense of much older English traditions. They prove that authority was sought from the past. To be effective, law had not only to be properly administered. It had also to be respected. Such respect could only be guarantied for laws believed to represent ancient tradition, passed down from Antiquity, in this instance from the last sainted King of Anglo-Saxon England.

The *Leges Edwardi* have a direct and pressing significance for anyone interested in the history of Magna Carta, since the barons and bishops who in 1215 negotiated Magna Carta believed that they were demanding not some revolutionary new settlement, but the restoration of the good old laws of King Edward. A contemporary chronicler writing at Waverley Abbey in Surrey reports specifically that, in 1215, 'there arose a great quarrel between the King and the barons of England, who sought from him the laws of St Edward and the liberties

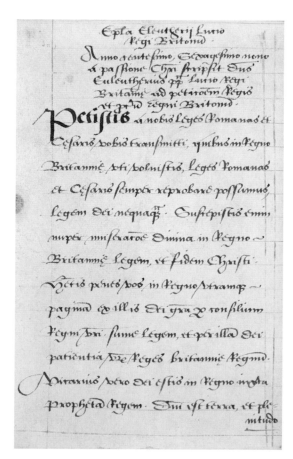

Fake epistle from Pope Eleutherius to King Lucius of the Britons, contesting his plan to introduce Roman law, a text appended to the Leges Edwardi *in the same encyclopedia.*

Latin text of the Coronation Charter of Henry I, from a bifolium also containing the coronation charters of Stephen and Henry II.

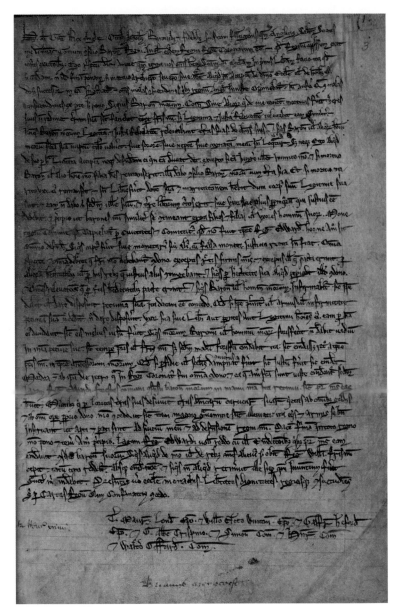

and free customs of other later kings'. There can be little doubt that the *Leges Edwardi* were themselves amongst the textual authorities employed by those who, in 1215, demanded that King John amend his ways and restore the law to its pristine purity. Was it not the *Leges*, at least in the form in which they circulated in London, a few years before Magna Carta, that declared that 'right and justice ought to rule in the realm rather than the perversities of will', and that 'law is always made by right, but will and violence and force are not right'? Even if the *Leges* had remained entirely unknown to those who sought an end to King John's abuses, there can be little doubt that the idea of law as something inviolable, passed down from Antiquity, was present in the minds of the barons of 1215. For evidence here we need to turn from apocryphal texts such as the *Leges Edwardi* to what little we know for certain of the lawmaking and legislative activities of England's post-Conquest Norman kings.

Henry I and the Coronation Charter

The makers of Magna Carta undoubtedly had access to a text, long familiar to historians, that itself represents one of the principal records of lawmaking in England in the century after 1066. William the Conqueror bequeathed no genuine statutes to posterity, and only a tiny number of letters to his officials that can be interpreted as specifically

The only extant depiction of Westminster Abbey (then St Peter's Abbey) as it was at the time of William I's coronation in 1066, from the Bayeux Tapestry.

'legal' decrees. The legislative record of his son and successor, William Rufus, is even more obscure. However, in 1100, following Rufus's death, the youngest of the Conqueror's sons, King Henry I, came to the throne by no means as the sole or strongest candidate. He was therefore obliged to make concessions to his future subjects. These concessions were embodied in a so-called 'Coronation Charter', supposedly issued before Henry's crowning at Westminster Abbey. Following in the footsteps of both Cnut and Edward the Confessor, who are said to have sworn to uphold the laws of earlier English kings as a precondition of their own coronations, Henry I now took the further momentous step of committing such a promise to writing. In a document of approximately a thousand words, carefully preserved thereafter in ecclesiastical and other archives, the King declared the

The 'Unknown Charter'

Another copy of Henry I's charter survives in Paris. Because it was rediscovered there only in the late nineteenth century, it is generally (though by now misleadingly) described as the 'Unknown Charter'. Having recited the text of Henry I, it immediately goes on to list a series of provisions that 'King John has conceded', opening with a promise that the King 'will arrest no man without judgement nor accept any payment for justice nor commit any unjust act', the origins of two of the most important clauses decreed at Runnymede. This 'Unknown Charter' is clearly a memorandum of negotiations between King and barons in or shortly before 1215, conducted on the basis of Henry I's Coronation Charter, in due course to grow into the finished agreement sealed as Magna Carta.

circumstances of his crowning 'by the mercy of God and with the common counsel of the barons of the realm of England'. Having first declared the Church 'free' from all financial oppressions, Henry's charter proceeds to promise the abolition of 'all evil customs by which the realm of England has been oppressed'. In particular, the heirs to barons and other great men should have their inheritances on payment of 'a legitimate and just' sum of money to the King. Heiresses should be free to marry, subject to the King's approval, itself mediated through baronial advice. Debts owing to the King's late brother, William Rufus, were in most instances to be pardoned. Above all, the good practices of the past should be restored. Thus money should be minted as in the time of King Edward the Confessor. Certain judicial fines should be regulated 'according to the law of King Edward', and this same 'law of King Edward' should be restored to the King's subjects together with whatever reforms had been made to it by William the Conqueror.

What we have here is a standard political technique: an attempt to buy popularity and favour through deliberate blackening of the reputation of a previous regime, coupled with promises to rule according to the good old traditions of the past. Similar manifestos had been broadcast by Roman emperors, by the kings of Judea as reported in the Old Testament, and, as we have seen, by earlier English kings. What is remarkable about the negotiations of 1100 is not that they were undertaken but that they were committed to writing, carefully preserved, and thereafter used as a precedent to bind future kings in obedience to the law. Both of Henry I's immediate successors as King – Stephen in 1135 and Henry II in 1154 – issued coronation charters, less elaborate than that of Henry I, but nonetheless repeating

the promise, first recorded in 1100, to govern according to precedent, as Henry II's charter puts it 'granting … all those concessions, gifts, liberties and free customs that Henry (I) my grandfather granted and conceded', and remitting 'all those bad customs which he abolished and remitted'. In the months immediately prior to the making of Magna Carta in 1215, we are specifically informed by the chroniclers that Henry I's Coronation Charter was brought out of the archives by no less a figure than the archbishop of Canterbury, Stephen Langton. It was thereafter employed to bind King John to the good laws of Henry I, and hence to those of Edward the Confessor as supposedly confirmed in 1100. We still possess what may well have been the very copy of Henry I's Coronation Charter, carried onto the field of Runnymede in 1215 by Langton and the English barons. It survives as a small booklet, today in the British Library, offering Latin texts of the coronation charters of Henry I, Stephen and Henry II, together with vernacular French translations that themselves suggest a meeting of barons and other laymen more confident in their own Anglo-Norman language than in the Latin of the Church.

There is thus a direct connection between Magna Carta and Henry I's Coronation Charter of 1100. Nonetheless, the intervening century was one that witnessed momentous changes both in law and in the relationship between law and politics. Through to the reign of Henry I, English law was touched only occasionally and at second hand by influences from the continent. Normandy itself had little by way of any native tradition of jurisprudence before the Norman conquest of England in 1066. The law codes and 'capitularies' of the French kings, descended at one or more removes from the laws of imperial Rome, were perhaps not entirely unknown in England but played no

Historiated initial from a manuscript of the Decretum, *1170–80.*

discernible role in the drafting of Anglo-Saxon law codes. From 1100 or so, all of this began to change. To start with, we find the records of English law themselves increasingly open to European influences. The *Leges Henrici Primi* (*c.*1115), like its Anglo-Saxon predecessors, is for the most part insular in outlook, even though it cites (inaccurately) the codification of the laws that passed under the name of the Roman Emperor Theodosius. Its most cosmopolitan authority is the Bible, quoted frequently as a source of universal legal principle. Twenty or so years later, European voices at last begin to be heard. The *Leges Edwardi Confessoris* (*c.*1140) may well have used the much earlier Bavarian Law as a general model for its account of kings of the present age recording and reissuing the laws of their ancestors. It also and undoubtedly quotes from the Life of Lebuin, an Anglo-Saxon missionary, which describes the assemblies and lawmaking activities of the Saxons of Germany. From 1139, with the recruitment of the legal expert Master Vacarius to the household of Archbishop Theobald of Canterbury, we have our first direct evidence for English knowledge of the *Corpus Iuris Civilis* and the laws of Rome as transmitted via the *Code of Justinian*. Vacarius was probably an Italian, trained first and foremost as a theologian. He was employed in England for his contacts with Italy and his skill as a pleader in the increasingly frequented courts of the Pope and Church. Even so, by teaching Roman law in England, and by composing a digest of legal knowledge, the so-called *Liber Pauperum* (or *Book for Poor Scholars*) he deserves to be commemorated as the first lawyer to have practised in England in an identifiably professional as opposed to amateur or occasional capacity. It is all the more significant that Vacarius' expertise spanned both the civilian law of the *Corpus* and the canon law of the Church, since this

was a period of transition in which the laws and legal pleadings of the Church, themselves derived from Roman imperial models, became subject to newly streamlined procedures and the codification of earlier legislation. Just as Justinian's code to a large extent consisted of the collection and reconciliation of a vast number of earlier imperial decrees, so canon law was embodied in the decisions of earlier popes reported in collections of 'decretals' (papal letters issued at any point in the millennium since Christ's ministry, judged particularly significant for their establishment or clarification of legal principles). Several such decretal collections had circulated in England from the 1070s onwards, used for example by advocates in the great jurisdictional disputes that had erupted between the archbishops of Canterbury and York. What changed in the twelfth century was the increasing standardization and professionalization of canonical expertise. At much the same time that Master Vacarius was at work on his *Liber Pauperum*, an expert canonist, whose work goes under the name of 'Gratian', set about compiling what amounted to the greatest collection of papal decretals yet made, known as the *Decretum*, arranged in such a way as to harmonize canon law within a series of categories, from the fundamental principles on which such laws were assembled to the specific laws affecting the sacraments and the definition of Christian faith. As early as the 1150s, Gratian's *Decretum* was itself beginning to penetrate the consciousness of the bishops of Normandy and England. In due course, a full-scale translation of it was to be made into the Anglo-Norman vernacular.

The international twelfth century

Thus far, the advances in Roman and canon law, as in the recording of the laws of England themselves, can be associated with wider mental impulses. In particular, the twelfth century is widely associated with the rediscovery of classical learning (the so-called Twelfth-Century Renaissance). In tandem with this we find a striving towards the distillation of knowledge into works of deliberately encyclopedic scope. We also find an increasingly international circulation of personnel, so that legal experts whose careers might previously have been confined to England were now encouraged to seek training in Paris or Bologna, itself from the 1150s emerging as an internationally renowned training academy for experts in Roman or canon law. Law itself, like other areas

Illuminated page from a late 12th-century manuscript of the Decretum, *with glosses.*

of intellectual endeavour, was increasingly professionalized. To all this there was a distinctly political dimension. The law schools of Bologna flourished in the midst of prolonged wars in northern Italy between the adherents of the Pope and those of the German kings claiming authority as Holy Roman Emperors. Italy's lawyers were obliged to take sides in an increasingly embittered political landscape in which law itself was crucial to the defence of rival political causes. Much the same dilemma faced those expert in English law, obliged in the earlier twelfth century to support either King or Church in the prolonged disputes between Henry I and archbishop Anselm of Canterbury. From 1135, when Henry I died leaving no son to succeed him, rival political parties emerged, each with its own tame legal experts, keen to support the claims either of Henry's daughter, Matilda, or his nephew,

'King' Stephen. Fearing that such legal experts might favour the cause of his rival, King Stephen is reported deliberately to have forbidden the teaching of Roman law in England, bringing an end to the teaching career of Vacarius at some point in the late 1140s.

But this did little to stem either the evolution of English law or the influx of European influence. To understand why this was so, we need now to turn from the wider evolution of English law to the particular circumstances in which Magna Carta was brought to birth. Magna Carta was in part an attempt to restate the good old laws of the English past. At the same time, it represented a treaty intended to bring peace between the English and the latest in a line of kings believed fundamentally to have perverted English law. It is to this dynasty that we must now turn.

Henric'
secund'
Rex qnt'

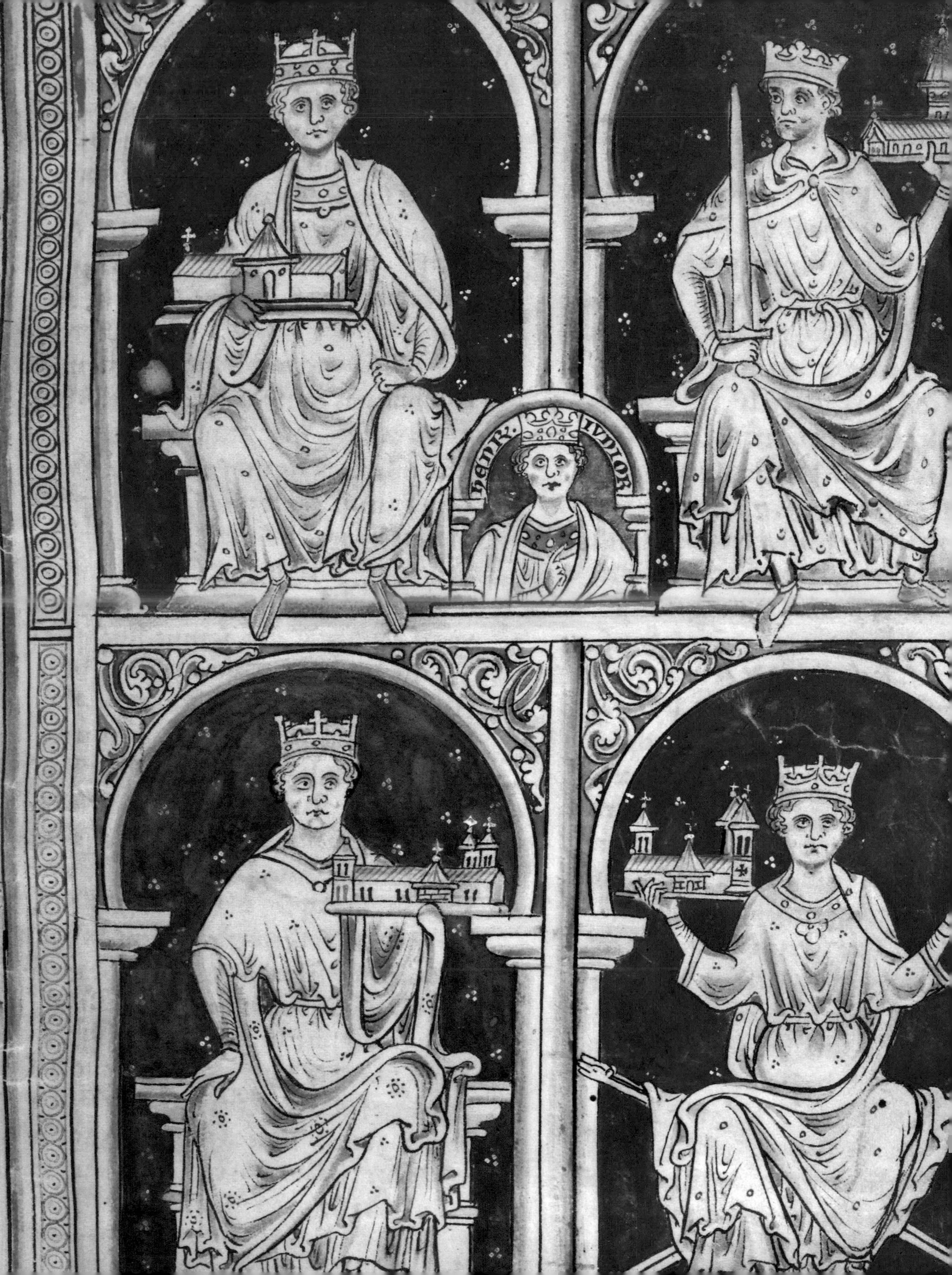

Iohañes
Rex sep
timus

Chapter Three

Plantagenet Tyranny and Lawmaking

Nicholas Vincent

> *Between a tyrant and a prince there is this single or chief difference, that the latter obeys the law and rules the people by its dictates, accounting himself as but their servant.*
>
> John of Salisbury, *Policraticus* (c.1159)

Magna Carta was issued in 1215, in an attempt to bind a particular ruler, King John, in obedience to the law. John's misrule, however, was an inherited family tradition. To understand Magna Carta, we need not only to understand the legal culture from which it was nurtured, but the family that provoked its birth.

The family that 'came from the devil'

From the accession of King John's father in 1154, through to the deposition of John's grandson's great-great-grandson, King Richard II, in 1399, the Plantagenet dynasty was destined to rule England for 250 years. The Plantagenets were of ancient stock, descended from lords who as early as the tenth century had established their authority over the city of Angers on the Loire. These 'Angevin' counts had thereafter projected their power north and south. In the process, they had made themselves hereditary enemies of the rulers both of Normandy and of France. By the time of its entry into English history, the family was extremely well connected, not least as a result of its association with the crusader kingdom of Jerusalem where, in the 1130s, King John's great-grandfather came to rule as King. This eastern connection, however, was itself the product of the family's already unsavoury reputation, having first been established in a series of pilgrimages to

The devil's dynasty: clockwise from top left, Henry II, Richard I, Henry III and John, with Henry II's eldest son (d. 1183) at the centre, in a 13th-century manuscript of Matthew Paris's Historia Anglorum.

37

Mélusine reveals herself, 15th-century woodcut from Germany.

wife of King Louis VII of France and heiress to the whole of Aquitaine, the region stretching from the Loire to the Pyrenees. By the time he crossed to England in December 1154 to be crowned as King, Henry II thus found his inheritance almost miraculously transformed. From his mother he inherited England and Normandy, from his father Anjou, from his wife the whole of south-western France. Combined, these lands represented the largest collection of estates gathered together in the hands of a single French ruler since the time of the emperor Charlemagne (d. 814), three and a half centuries earlier.

As we have seen, Henry II inherited a system of law from his grandfather, Henry I, itself descended from the laws of the pre-Conquest Anglo-Saxon kings. Almost immediately, Henry II set about transforming this system.

Jerusalem undertaken by Count Fulk 'the Black' of Anjou (d. 1040) in penance for his many sins. In legend, the family claimed descent from a mythical ancestress named Mélusine. Challenged to attend Mass, Mélusine had instead revealed herself as a she-demon, half woman, half snake. Hence the gibe pronounced by St Bernard in the 1140s, that this was a family that 'came from the devil, and to the devil will surely return': the devil's brood. Their name, the 'Plantagenets' was probably derived from the adoption of the broom plant (the *plante-de-genêt*) as a heraldic device by Geoffrey 'Plantagenet', count of Anjou from 1129 to 1151. It was via Geoffrey's marriage in 1128 to Matilda, the sole surviving child of King Henry I, that the Plantagenet family first acquired its interest in the throne of England.

For nineteen wearisome years following the death of Henry I in 1135, Matilda waged war against her cousin, Stephen of Blois, who had seized power as King. With her husband Geoffrey Plantagenet, in the 1140s Matilda conquered Normandy. With her eldest son, the future King Henry II, she launched campaigns against England. In 1153, quite suddenly and to many contemporaries with uncanny ease, her cause achieved victory. Stephen's own heir died, so it was rumoured, in punishment for plundering the lands of the Church. Rather than prolong an already exhausting war, Stephen declared his willingness to recognize Matilda's son, Henry, as his future successor. Within a year, again entirely unexpectedly, Stephen himself was dead. Henry, his nominated heir, had two years earlier married Eleanor, the divorced

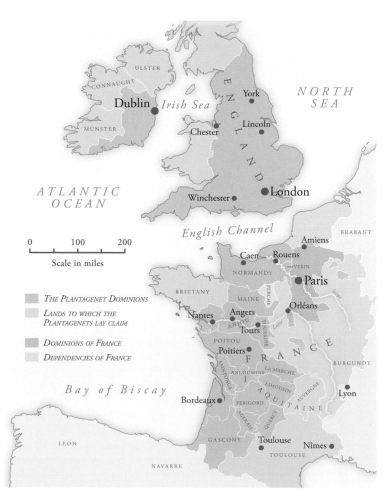

Angevin dominions in the 12th century.

Henry II's court: reputation and reality

Unlike his son King John, Henry II is today remembered as one of the 'good' kings of English history. His court was a magnificent affair, reported in a detail that deliberately rivalled the literary splendour of the court of Charlemagne, itself modelled upon the courts of the emperors of ancient Rome. Here Henry II and his courtiers devised the system of law and administration against which Magna Carta represents a long-delayed reaction. Whoever wrote the Great Charter of 1215, the political malaise that it was intended to cure was first incubated at the court of Henry II.

The court of Henry II as portrayed in the 1968 film The Lion in Winter, *with Peter O'Toole (second from left) and Katharine Hepburn (seated) as Henry and Eleanor.*

Henry II and English common law

For his legal reforms, Henry II is often described as architect of the 'common law', a system of law based, first and foremost, upon procedure and precedent rather than upon a written constitution or code. Britain still has no written constitution. Law is made by judges acting in accordance with tradition and a sense of justice to implement statutes decreed by the executive or government working through the legislature (today Parliament, in the Middle Ages the King and his counsellors). Judges and the judiciary wield one of the great instruments of state, interpreting rather than blindly obeying such statutes. All of these powers operate under the ultimate authority of the sovereign King or Queen. It is sometimes assumed that Henry II created a deliberately distinctive 'English' system, set apart from the laws either of the Church (canon law) or of imperial Rome (Roman, or 'civilian' law). Nothing could be further from the truth.

As we have seen, since the reign of Cnut in the 1020s, there had long been a general absence of written legislation in England, or at least of legislation that was officially promulgated and preserved. The Coronation Charter of Henry I, renewed by King Stephen, is virtually our only official 'statute' to survive from the century after 1066. Far from refusing to issue written laws, from the 1150s Henry II, albeit

haphazardly, began to decree 'assizes' and laws, committed to writing and broadcast to the realm. Rather than intentionally creating an eccentric English law, Henry II himself was obliged to work from within a system already of great antiquity, in which custom and correct procedure had long taken precedence over any idea of a constitution or body of written law.

At the same time, English common law has never been entirely divorced from wider European traditions. Even in its isolationist heyday, in the seventeenth and eighteenth centuries, it admitted arguments and modes of thought that had themselves first been tested in ecclesiastical or civilian (continental Roman law) courts. In the twelfth century, when this common law system is first properly reported, the lawyers who established customs or procedures and who drafted the few surviving statutes were themselves, in many cases, just as accustomed to pleading in church or civilian courts as they were to pleading in the courts of the King. Many of them were churchmen. Those who were not, like Ranulf de Glanville, Henry II's justiciar and chief law officer of the 1170s and 1180s, were surrounded by clerks expert in canon law. One of Glanville's cousins was bishop of Rochester. Glanville's nephew was a famous archbishop of Canterbury who in due course succeeded as justiciar. All these experts, laymen and clerks, knew at least something of Roman law. All of them came from

Anglo-French backgrounds that themselves guaranteed European influence. Ranulf's father, sprung from a family of Norman-French descent, had in the 1140s taken part in the crusader conquest of Lisbon. Ranulf himself was to die campaigning in Palestine on the Third Crusade. Canon law continued to operate for those cases, most notably involving marriage, wills and testaments, in which laymen found themselves drawn into Church courts. It survived even the

Protestant Reformation. Cases in the English ecclesiastical courts were still being pleaded in Latin as recently as the 1850s, and the college of experts trained in such procedures was not dissolved until 1912, with the death of its last surviving member. Meanwhile, the courts of Admiralty, only just beginning to emerge in the thirteenth century, have always followed Roman rather than common law procedures, even though administered under the wider remit of the common law.

The tombs of Eleanor of Aquitaine and Henry II, in the nave of the abbey church of Fontevraud, Anjou, France.

A stranger in his realm

As a French-speaker, raised on the Loire, familiar with the legal traditions of western France, Henry II was to a large extent an exotic stranger in England. His supporters claimed that he could understand the English language, though he never supplied proof of this by speaking it. English was for peasants and nursemaids, French the spoken tongue, and Latin the written language of the elite. Henry visited England, hunted in his great forests there, and used the wealth of England to finance his wars in France. All told, however, he passed less than half his life in England, either as boy or as King.

The great quarrel: Henry II and Thomas Becket, from an early 14th-century manuscript of Peter of Langtoft's Chronicle of England.

Henry II and Thomas Becket: the coming of Magna Carta

Besides his legal reforms, Henry II is also famous for his great quarrel with Thomas Becket, the King's friend and chancellor subsequently promoted archbishop of Canterbury. For much of the 1160s, Becket was forced into exile in a dispute that has sometimes been interpreted as a clash between two systems of law, between the canon law of the Church as championed by Becket, set against the common law of England that Henry was in the process of refining as an instrument of royal authority. Once again, this is an over-simplification. There were as many personal as ideological causes for the Becket dispute. The King recruited the support of just as many expert canon lawyers as could be claimed by Becket's party. Moreover, in the generation that followed Becket's martyrdom in 1170, not only was it Henry II's supporters who tended to gain promotion as bishops, but it was these same English bishops who did most to seek out written judgements from the Pope, to recruit canon lawyers to their households, and in general to make England a vibrant centre for the study and propagation of papal law.

In at least three ways, however, the Becket conflict had a significant impact upon the future emergence of Magna Carta. To begin with, Becket's murder, his brains spilled out on the paving stones of Canterbury Cathedral, confirmed the widely held fear that Henry II and his family were the devil's brood, the very antithesis of the pious and subservient model of kingship that the Church held up as its ideal. Second, the Becket dispute helped reinforce the idea that respect for ancient custom, and in particular for the customs

of the reign of Henry I, was the guiding principle in English law both secular and ecclesiastical. This in turn assisted in the apotheosis of Henry I's Coronation Charter, the document issued in 1100, that we considered in the previous chapter, and that in 1215 was to be taken as a foundation upon which to build the settlement known as Magna Carta.

Henry II had come to the throne in 1154 after a twenty-year civil war in which many of the greater landed estates of England had changed hands in violent or distinctly murky circumstances, disputed between adherents of Matilda or King Stephen. Henry's response to this problem was, in effect, to attempt to abolish the legal memory of Stephen's reign, restoring all land occupied since 1135 to the claimants

Thomas Becket, stained-glass window at Canterbury Cathedral, c.1220.

Becket and one of his deacons dispute with Henry II, who listens to the evil counsel of a small devil whispering in his ear, stained-glass window at Chartres, 1205–35.

as those who rule (*regere*). Isidore himself had nonetheless been conscious of the possibility of misrule. Kings who failed to rule justly were, in Isidore's definition, no longer true kings. Precisely the same formulation was to be repeated, in the years immediately preceding Magna Carta, in the London rewriting of the *Leges Edwardi*. Here we are informed that a king who does not rule well is no longer a king and that kings who fail to protect their people risk a sentence of papal deposition, as had been the fate of the pathetic eighth-century rulers of France in the years before Charlemagne and his father were declared kings. This view can be traced back to ancient concepts of just rule and tyranny. But how to define the transition from kingship to tyranny? At what point did a king forfeit his otherwise God-given right to the obedience of his people?

whose ancestors has legitimately held it at the time of Henry I's death. In 1163, having recently secured Becket's election as archbishop, Henry II attempted to go further still. He forced upon Becket and his fellow bishops a series of laws, embodied in the so-called Constitutions of Clarendon (issued at Clarendon Palace in Wiltshire). The intention here was to regulate relations between Church and King, in effect by restoring them to the situation that Henry claimed had existed in the time of Henry I, his grandfather. Once again, we find an appeal to ancient customs, and once again, a specific appeal to the customs of Henry I. We should also note the precedent set here by the writing down of what had previously been unwritten customs, accepted but never before displayed in the harsh, and far more contentious, black and white of ink and parchment. It was his refusal to adhere to the Constitutions, themselves duly condemned by the Pope, that led to Becket's exile in 1164. It was the Constitutions, now held up as a symbol of Plantagenet misgovernment, that served as a rallying cry for Becket in his claim to be defending not just his own selfish interests but the wider 'liberties' of the English Church.

And here we come to the third great impact made by the Becket dispute in the years leading to Magna Carta. Law and sovereignty have always been highly politicized affairs. The Becket dispute nonetheless supplied a political model to future generations keen to oppose what they regarded as the misrule of the Plantagenet kings. We have already encountered Isidore of Seville defining kings (*reges*)

The martyrdom of Thomas Becket, from a 15th-century manuscript of Le Miroir Historial *by Vincent de Beauvais.*

A vision of kingship: Charles V of France at
his bookwheel, illuminated page from a
manuscript of the Policraticus, c.1372.

An answer here was already supplied to the circle of clerks around
Thomas Becket, some years before Becket's great falling out with
Henry II. In the late 1150s, John of Salisbury dedicated a book entitled
the *Policraticus* to Becket, then royal chancellor. A large part of the
book concerns the distinction between tyranny and true kingship.
John cited dozens of examples, some ancient, some very recent –
including King Stephen and his henchmen – of rulers who had become
tyrants, defined here as kings who ruled by force rather than in
obedience to law. Liberty, meanwhile, John defined, again in
accordance with Roman classical authorities, as the freedom to take
decisions determined by moral judgement. Not only was liberty a spur
to virtue, but only the virtuous man could be considered truly free.
What could be done in response to tyranny? John's answer was simple:
'It is lawful to slay a tyrant.' In other words, and as in the political
thought of the classical world, a tyrant should be deposed, even by
assassination or foreign invasion if these were the only means available.
This, superficially, seems to be John's message. In fact, his prescription
was not nearly so clear cut. John was fundamentally devoted to the
idea of equity in political as in all human endeavour. The scales of
justice should be rationally balanced, so that justice is tempered with
mercy. Since subjects owed obedience to their lords, and since kings
themselves were the earthly representatives of God, it was far better to
leave God almighty to make the ultimate decision between a tyrant's
life or death. John quotes a famous Roman law tag, 'What pleases the
prince has the force of law,' that ever afterwards has served as the
licence for unrestrained royal sovereignty, or what would much later

Classical precedents

The theory of kingship presented in the *Leges Edwardi* was the legacy
of a long tradition of political rhetoric familiar to both Greece and
Rome, in which rulers who abandoned the law ceased to be kings
and instead became tyrants. The deposition of tyrants was an
obligation imposed upon all ancient societies, whether it be by the
assassins' blades that disposed of Julius Caesar, or God's vengeance
that dealt with such biblical tyrants as Nebuchadnezzar or Saul.

Silver denarius issued by Brutus in 42BC, two years after Caesar's assassination.

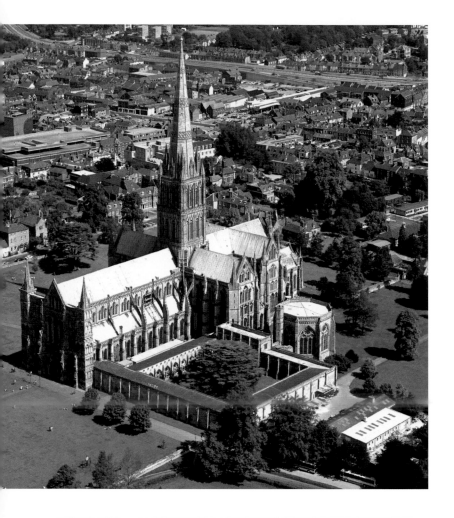

Salisbury Cathedral, a potent symbol of the English Church freed from the Babylonian captivity of the royal castle.

come to be called 'royal absolutism'. If a tyrant truly merited death, then God himself would ensure that this was the tyrant's fate. Meanwhile, princes should be reminded that God's laws trump all merely earthly statute. Kings are servants rather than masters of the law. They must be taught the meaning of God's law as transmitted via the Bible. As in the biblical book of Deuteronomy, they must set down their own laws in writing so that judgement can be seen to be truly just.

This remains a system in which the King himself is sovereign under God. Kings are appointed, and if necessary removed, by God. There is no element here of the contractual language of mutual obligation between King and subjects that informs later political thought, indeed no real sense of society as a collective entity with rights to be defended. There is little to suggest that John's book circulated beyond a narrow circle of friends and sympathizers. Nonetheless, the thoughts that it expressed were common currency. In the greater centres of learning, none greater than the schools of Paris where John and a large proportion of the English elite attended university, the dichotomy between tyranny and justice, the marriage of liberty with virtue, and the idea that good kings should have written laws, were all of them

Pipe Rolls

As early as the reign of Henry I, the Exchequer had produced written records, known as Pipe Rolls after their rolled-up drainpipe shape. From the second year of Henry II, such rolls survive in more or less unbroken sequence, from 1155 until their abolition in 1832, the year of the Great Reform Act.

The royal Pipe Roll for the year 9 Henry II (1162-3), here showing the account for the sheriff of Nottinghamshire and Derbyshire.

Sketch of the meeting of the Exchequer, taken from the lost Red Book of the Irish Exchequer.

widely shared. John's idea of liberty as the right to act in accordance with morality is surprisingly close to that still being proposed by John Locke, more than five hundred years (and several political revolutions) later, as freedom to live under government according to law.

Becket and his supporters had called for the 'liberty' of the English Church. In this they directly echoed the terms of Henry I's Coronation Charter that opened with a promise that the English Church should be 'free'. An identical formula appears at the very head of the provisions set out in Magna Carta: 'We have, in the first place, granted to God ... that the English Church is to be free and have its rights in whole and its liberties unimpaired'. What was at stake here was far more than mumbled platitude. The Becket dispute supplied definitions and arguments in favour of the liberty of the Church that, in due course, helped extend the idea of liberty to a far wider constituency of barons and the 'free men' of England. What had begun as a quarrel between two powerful egos, Henry II's and Becket's, helped define the aspirations of those many others placed under a seemingly all-powerful royal sovereignty. If Henry II was Magna Carta's demonic stepfather, then Thomas Becket, in spirit if not in person, was a prominent assistant at Magna Carta's birth.

The King's justice: reform and resistance

Henry II's great leap forwards in law and administration was accompanied by an ever more sophisticated undertow of rhetoric against Angevin tyranny. For the moment, however, there was little doubt that it was the King rather than his critics who held the advantage. Having established his dominion in England and France, Henry turned to the means by which his lands should be governed. To supervise the collection of royal finance, the Exchequer was revived as an annual, soon to be biannual meeting of royal officials named from the chequered cloth on which income and expenditure were accounted.

During the period of Becket's exile in the 1160s, spurred on by the financial and political needs of his 'empire', Henry II had begun to demand new procedures in criminal law. His so-called 'Assize' of Clarendon (1166), the first of his new statutes for which we have a surviving text, requires that juries of twelve men from every hundred, and four men from every vill, report under oath against all suspected robbers or murderers, who in turn were to be detained by the sheriffs for trial before local law officers. In counties where no gaol existed, gaols were to be built (proof, incidentally, that the King's justice remained, as late as the 1160s, a relatively limited affair). Exile and outlawry were decreed for all notorious criminals. At much the same

The courthouse at Oakham, Rutland, constructed during the reign of Henry II.

Seal of Henry II.

time, Henry began to refine the processes by which claims to land were judged in his courts. Further assizes were promulgated, intended to assist those whose property was unjustly seized to recover possession. These assizes have fanciful French names (*novel disseisin, mort d'ancestor*). We have considerable evidence for their implementation. We know far less of the precise circumstances, dates, or indeed the texts by which they were first enacted. The intention was clearly to speed procedures in the King's courts, to ensure that heirs could secure their inheritances and that those recently dispossessed obtain restoration of their property. In all of this the King could pose as the author of justice and protector of the righteous. Beyond this, he gained very practical advantages both financial and political.

By opening his courts to a flood of new litigation, the King was

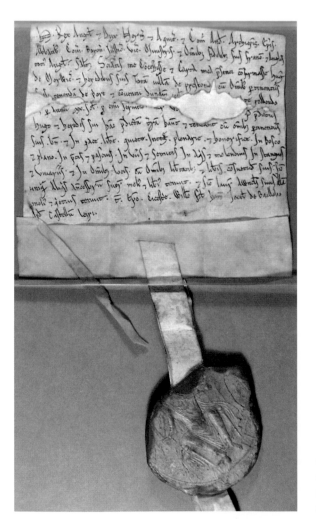

Sealed writ issued by Henry II, c.1160.

forced to bear the cost of employing judges and officials to ensure that such cases could be heard. But this was more than offset by the profits of justice. For each royal letter (or 'writ') initiating an action in law, and for every decision made in his courts, the King charged a price. Individually, this price might not be high: a few pennies for a routine writ, a few shillings in fines (or 'amercements') for an unsuccessful litigant. Taken collectively, however, and given that the richest in the land were prepared to pay handsomely in bribes or sweeteners, this was a system from which potentially limitless profits could be made. Furthermore, in political terms, the more routine business that could be attracted into the courts of the King, the fewer cases were now completed in the courts of barons, bishops or knights. Such great men, previously the jealous guardians of the right to judge their own dependants, found their courts now starved of litigants, of authority, and in the crudest terms of cash. As throughout history, the court with the most efficient procedures, and the best record of enforcement, tended to win out against its competitors. By transforming his law from a last resort into a court of first instance, Henry II not only reaped a handsome financial profit but exalted his sovereign power above all other lords.

The King's courts required not only litigants but suitors, panels of local knights, jurors in each hundred, by whom cases could be prosecuted and from whom sworn testimony could be obtained. Once again the refinement of this system promised immediate advantages to

Scotland and the north in the rebellion of 1173–4.

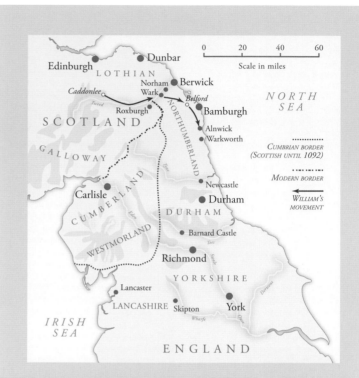

the King. Obliged to attend the King's courts on a regular basis, knights and local landowners were drawn into law enforcement. They themselves became the unpaid instruments of royal authority. At the same time, they acquired experience in doing justice and were equipped with a basic practical knowledge of the law. In the longer term, on their own initiative and in many ways against royal interest, such men were encouraged to form political societies at the level of shire or region, transcending the local rivalries that might otherwise have kept them divided and therefore politically weak. Knights began to meet ever more regularly, to discuss matters of the King's law. And as ever, law was never far from politics. Resentment against laws inequitably enforced could all the more easily boil over into political opposition, as it did in 1173, three years after Becket's martyrdom.

The King decisively defeated this rebellion. Thereafter, his law bit ever more deeply into the jurisdiction of local lords. New assizes confirmed the King's day-to-day control over both criminal and civil litigation. New written instruments were devised to record decisions reached in the King's courts. Reports of court proceedings were officially enrolled, in due course to become not only historical documents but a means by which legal expertise could be transmitted from one generation to another. The procedures of the law were themselves refined through use.

For one view of this system created by Henry II we can turn to a semi-official source, the treatise 'On the Laws and Customs of the Realm of England', composed in the 1180s by a lawyer very close to the

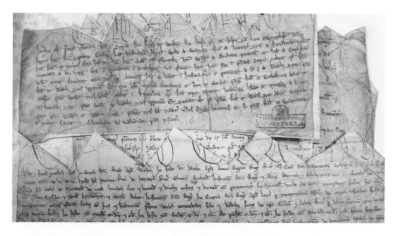

Final concord, registering the agreement of a land conveyance, an example of the new documentation employed in the King's courts in the 12th century.

The rebellion of 1173–4

A number of the greater lords of Henry's lands, both in England and France, had long wished to reassert their local independence. Hostile neighbours, including the kings of France and Scotland, and the count of Flanders, helped stir this discontent. The King's new assizes, his demand for money and men to carry out his conquest of Ireland (begun in 1171), and his role in the death of Becket for which he was internationally vilified, provided the spark for rebellion in 1173. Rebellion itself attracted the King's eldest son, himself married to a French bride. Even Henry's wife, Eleanor, joined the malcontents, angered by her husband's infidelities and his refusal to recognize her own authority in Aquitaine. In the rhetoric of rebellion, Henry was portrayed as a tyrant, murderer of a sainted archbishop. The French invaded Normandy, the Scots northern England. A Flemish army landed in East Anglia. But these attacks were repelled one by one. The King of Scots was taken prisoner, the French driven out of Normandy. The Flemings were massacred at a battle outside Bury St Edmunds. In the aftermath, not only was the King restored to authority, but that authority itself was magnified beyond all previous expectations.

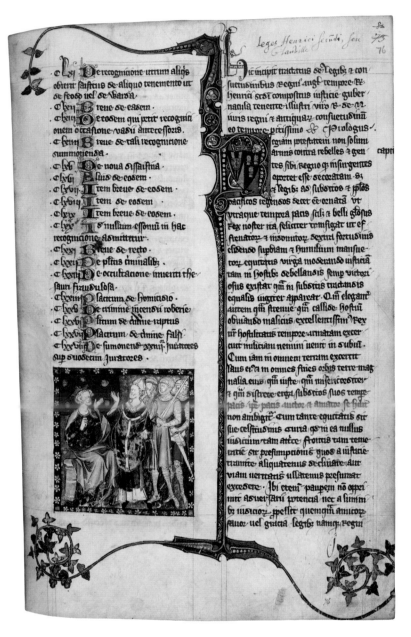

Illuminated page from Glanvill, *in an early 14th-century compilation of royal statutes and London ordinances, here showing Henry II with bishop and barons.*

prologue that sets out the author's intentions. Royal power, we are informed, must not only be supported against rebels and foreign enemies, but adorned with laws. The laws of England are unwritten. Indeed, the author declares that it would be impossible to reduce them to writing, both because of the ignorance of those who might write them down, and because of their sheer variety. What can be recorded however, are the 'uses' of the law (we would call them procedures) that will here be set out in words appropriate to those who work in courts ('curiales'). Meanwhile, 'What pleases the prince has the force of law' (a tag that we have already encountered in John of Salisbury). Henry II is a just and merciful king 'whose praise has gone out to all the world' (here quoting directly from Psalm 18). Henry is the 'author and lover of peace' (here quoting directly from the Roman Missal). This is sycophancy of a rare degree, with *Glanvill* attributing qualities to Henry II that had originally been ascribed to King David and even to Almighty God.

Manuscript of Ralph Niger's Bible commentaries, in which he was highly critical of the Plantagenet kings, preserved in the library of Lincoln Cathedral.

King's court, generally (though perhaps mythically) identified as Henry II's chief justice, Ranulf de Glanville. This book, known as *Glanvill*, supplies our first proper view of the common law as a mature and functioning system. It is the first such source to set out a definition of the common law as comprehending pleas that are either criminal or civil, each in turn divided between pleas that could be judged only before royal (later 'crown') courts and those that could be decided locally by sheriffs. For the most part, its concern lies with procedures, only incidentally with principles. It sets out a series of fifty or so common forms, 'writs', by which actions could be sued in the King's court. It describes in detail the rules by which these 'writs' were pleaded. Here the law is displayed in purely functional terms. The treatise opens, however, with something rather more abstract, a

Geoffrey of Anjou, detail of an enamelled copper plaque from his tomb.

Tales of tyranny

Henry II's father Geoffrey of Anjou, it was rumoured, having castrated a bishop, had demanded that the victim parade through the public streets carrying his severed member in a jar before him. Henry II, so it was reported, had such fits of temper that once, contradicted by a courtier, he had torn the cloak from his back and sunk to the ground, rolling around in the dust in his fury, biting the straw.

Lincoln Cathedral, Ralph Niger's final destination and home to his surviving books.

Glanvill's is, to say the least, a very unbalanced opinion of Henry II as lawmaker. For an alternative viewpoint we can turn to that generation of clerks and chroniclers brought up in the shadow of the Becket dispute. Far from presenting the Plantagenet court as a beacon of justice and enlightenment, such men proclaimed that Henry II was a tyrant, descended from a long and tyrannical line. Our most remarkable indictment of Henry comes from a chronicler and former supporter of Becket named Ralph Niger, who died some years before the issue of Magna Carta. A former servant of Eleanor of Aquitaine and of Henry II's rebellious eldest son, Ralph ended his days as a canon and schoolmaster at Lincoln Cathedral, where many of his own books are still preserved. Henry II, Ralph claims, deliberately delayed his judgements so that justice could be bought and sold. Rather than work through honest judges, he promoted serfs and common foot soldiers as his officials. A debaucher of the wives and daughters of his barons, he had transformed the monasteries of his kingdom into kennels for his hounds. An oath-breaker and corrupter of youth, he had disposed with ancient laws, each year proclaiming his own new 'assizes'. He set aside charters and overthrew the rights of towns. The law that he decreed for the forests was a scandal. He preferred the usury of the Jews to the law of Christ. He ordained barbaric punishments, commanding the cutting off of hands and feet. And so on, and on, through a catalogue of tyranny that occupies three entire pages of the modern printed edition and that might have made even Nero or Caligula blush.

Somewhere between these two extremes, between the sycophancy of *Glanvill* and the denunciations of Ralph Niger, the legacy of Henry II's reign was one of glory tarnished by extortion, of laws proclaimed yet, in their implementation, bent to the private interest of the King. England was governed by a powerful dynasty, but one that treated the realm as its own private estate, to tax or trouble as family interest dictated. This was the tradition of Angevin or Plantagenet kingship against which Magna Carta was intended to supply a remedy.

Chapter Four

The Tyranny of King John

Nicholas Vincent

King John was the greatest tyrant born of woman.

Matthew Paris, *Chronica Majora* (*c.*1240–53)

Henry II was denounced by his critics as a tyrant. He was nonetheless an effective tyrant: an empire-builder, conqueror of Ireland, the survivor of numerous scandals up to and including his involvement in the death of Thomas Becket. By contrast, his younger son, John, was to be remembered as a tyrant with no redeeming qualities. Attempts, since the sixteenth century, to present John as a great military commander, or as an administrator of genius, have all met with failure. The modern view of him remains very much that of the English monastic chronicler, Matthew Paris, writing in the 1240s: 'Hell itself is defiled by the presence of King John.'

John's early years

There were early plans for John, still only six or seven years old, to marry an Italian heiress. These came to nothing, although the attempt to endow John with a portion of his father's lands was one of the sparks that led to the great rebellion of 1173–4. At around this time, and following the arrest of his mother, John himself was handed over to be educated by the nuns of Fontevraud on the Loire. As a result, he was perhaps the most literate of the Plantagenet brood, in later years the possessor of a large library of books, many of them theological.

His father's continued success as an empire-builder transformed John's prospects. In 1171, Henry II had seized control over what had recently developed as a campaign of freelance conquest in Ireland led by Anglo-Norman knights. His success here meant that there was land with which to invest his youngest son. In 1185, aged perhaps eighteen, John crossed to Ireland to enforce his lordship. The expedition was in

King John's tomb, at Worcester Cathedral.

Illustration from a manuscript of Gerald of Wales, c.1196–1223, depicting the unruly Irish later subjugated by John.

one sense a resounding success, establishing an English military domination that was to persist for the next seven centuries. At the same time, for his deliberate humiliation of the Irish kings (he is said to have insisted on pulling their long red beards), John set Anglo-Irish relations on an uneasy and ultimately tragic course. It was this same combination of cruelty and contemptuousness that was to lead England down the road to Magna Carta.

At this stage, there was no real prospect that John himself would become King. He had two elder brothers still living. Even though Geoffrey, duke of Brittany, died in 1186, John's other surviving brother, Richard, duly succeeded to the throne of England in 1189, following the death of their father, Henry II. Richard was in the full flower of manhood, already the father of at least one illegitimate son, in due course married with full prospects of fathering legitimate heirs. Richard was a great general, hero of the Third Crusade. In his realm of England, however, his performance was less heroic. To pay for his wars, and then for the great ransom of nearly £70,000 (many billions

An inauspicious name

What was wrong with John? For a start, there was his name. He was born the youngest of Henry II and Eleanor of Aquitaine's many children, on Christmas Eve 1166 or 1167. The uncertainty here itself demonstrates quite how low John stood in the family pecking order. His four elder brothers William, Henry, Richard and Geoffrey had all been named after previous kings of England or dukes of Normandy. John was a cuckoo in this particular nest, named for no apparent reason save perhaps for the proximity of his birthday to the feast of St John the Evangelist (27 December), or as a male counterpart to his elder sister Joan, born a year or two before him.

The children of Henry II, in an early 14th-century genealogy: from left, William, Henry, Richard, Matilda, Geoffrey, Eleanor, Joan and John.

Château Gaillard in Normandy, France, constructed by Richard I 1197–8, lost by King John to Philip of France in 1204.

in today's money) that had to be raised to pay for his release from captivity in Germany returning from crusade, he treated England as a cash cow, imposing taxes and 'scutages' (payments made in lieu of personal military service) at unprecedented levels. His prolonged absence in the East led to political crisis. From this the French King Philip Augustus did his best to profit. Philip invaded Normandy. He had the explicit support of John, left behind at the time of Richard's departure for the Holy Land, and now locked in rivalry with the ministers whom Richard had appointed to govern in his absence.

Troubled succession and disastrous rule

For his alliance with Philip of France, John was branded a traitor. When Richard returned from the East, John was forced to sue for pardon. The words attributed to Richard on this occasion are highly significant. John, Richard is said to have declared, should be forgiven: 'He is a mere boy.' John was by this time nearing thirty years of age. Even so, as late as 1199, there was no certain prospect that John would

succeed his brother as King. Richard might still father an heir. Geoffrey of Brittany had left a son, christened Arthur, a name that suggests a desire that he follow in the footsteps of the mythical Arthur of Britain, reuniting the lands of Britain and Brittany. There was no certainty, either in England or France, as to who had the better claim to a family inheritance disputed between a younger brother (John) and a nephew (Arthur). In the 1180s, *Glanvill* had raised precisely this issue, but reached no firm conclusion.

As a result, when Richard died in April 1199, of a wound from a crossbow bolt shot fortuitously as he oversaw a siege in south-west France, both John and Arthur advanced more or less equal claims to Richard's throne, Arthur as the son of an elder brother, John as the last of the surviving sons of Henry II. In the event, it was his age, the speed with which he advanced on England, and the fluency with which he and his supporters argued his cause that secured victory for John. Already, he had surrounded himself with a court in waiting, with a group of administrators, knights and clerks, for the most part raised from the lower levels of royal service, who in due course were to prove

Left: John in majesty, obverse of his seal. Below: Isabella of Angoulême, in the nave of the abbey church of Fontevraud, Anjou, France.

highly efficient, but at the same time highly arrogant enforcers of his will. Within a decade or so, they were being openly described as the King's 'evil' councillors. In April 1199, John was recognised as duke of Normandy. A month later, on the feast of Christ's Ascension, he was crowned King in Westminster Abbey. The threat from Arthur seemed to have been neutralized in 1200, when John made peace with King Philip of France, his feudal overlord, agreeing to surrender the southernmost parts of Normandy in return for the withdrawal of French support for Arthur's cause.

Having begun well, John proved himself, within the next five years, one of the most catastrophic rulers in English history. Disaster followed disaster and in uncanny mirror image of his father's triumphs. John did very badly what Henry II had done only too well. Where Henry II had built a great Anglo-French empire, John proceeded to lose all but a small part of his French estate. Henry II had made free with the wives and daughters of his barons, and imprisoned his own queen rather than lose control of her estates in France. By contrast, John provoked outrage, first by repudiating his wife, Isabella of Gloucester, then by marrying again. His new bride, a

French heiress perhaps only eight or nine years old, Isabella of Angoulême, was already betrothed, although not as yet married, to Hugh de Lusignan, one of the greater landholders of south-western France. Hugh had scruples and had therefore not consummated the marriage. John had no such qualms. Hugh joined forces with Arthur of Brittany. But their rebellion failed. In August 1202, Arthur and his supporters were taken prisoner in a lightning raid that carried John, in a week, more than two hundred miles from his starting point in

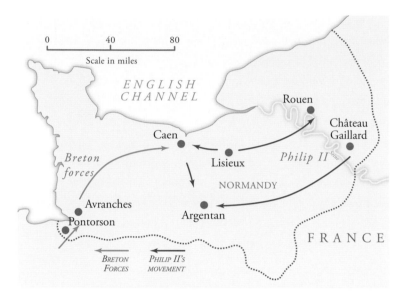

Philip's invasion of Normandy, 1203–4.

Normandy to the castle of Mirebeau in Poitou. But here John once again miscalculated.

His father, Henry II, had faced down rebellions in the past. Indeed, Henry's greatest triumphs had been achieved in direct consequence of his crushing of the rebellion of 1173–4. John by contrast, once again snatched defeat from the jaws of victory. Thrown into captivity, Arthur disappeared. Hugh de Lusignan appealed to the King of France, and, as John's feudal overlord, King Philip demanded that John produce Arthur. When no reply came, Philip sanctioned not only an invasion of Normandy but the disinheritance of John's entire French estate. In doing so, he seems to have made use of recent canon law judgements by the Pope, allowing a lord in crimes equated with treason to punish not just the guilty but their innocent heirs. For the past 150 years, Norman and Plantagenet kings had disinherited rebellious barons and earls, in a way never before attempted by the kings of France. One of the great ironies of Philip's dealings with John is that, calling canon law to his assistance, the French King turned what had previously been techniques of Plantagenet 'tyranny' against a Plantagenet king. Once again, law marched hand in hand with politics. Once again, we find a potent mixture of English, Roman and continental influences. Rather than stand and fight, in December 1203 John fled with his baggage and treasure from Barfleur to Portsmouth. Rouen fell six months later, followed by the entire Plantagenet dominion as far south as Poitiers.

The mystery of Arthur's fate

Rumours flew regarding the disappearance of Arthur of Brittany. Some claimed that he had fallen from the castle walls of Rouen attempting escape, others that he had been killed by John or John's henchmen, perhaps in a fit of drunken rage.

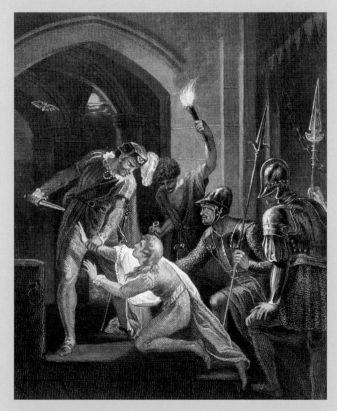

A mystery which fired the imagination: the murder of Arthur, engraving by J. Rogers from an original by W. Hamilton, 1793.

Philip declared Normandy and John's French estate confiscated not just for John's lifetime but in perpetuity, now annexed to the French Crown. Only Gascony, in the far south of France, remained under a degree of English control, and here only because English government in these southern parts had traditionally been light to the point of non-existent.

Maquette of a 19th-century bronze of Stephen Langton in the Lords Chamber, Westminster Palace.

Langton's beginnings

Born in Lincolnshire, and growing up in the aftermath of the Becket conflict, Stephen Langton had perhaps first been schooled at Lincoln, in precisely those surroundings in which Ralph Niger was busily denouncing the Plantagenets as ungodly tyrants. For at least twenty years before 1205 Langton had lived abroad, teaching at the schools of Paris, themselves under the protection of the French King Philip Augustus. It was in Paris that he came to the attention of a young Italian student, named Lothario di Segni, in 1198 elected Pope Innocent III. Innocent III was himself a lawyer, with an uncompromising idea of the obligation imposed upon the Church by God to advise and if necessary to discipline Christian kings.

Any medieval king who sustained losses on this scale proclaimed himself fallen from God's grace. The Normans, it was supposed, had triumphed at Hastings because God was on their side. By the same calculation, John's loss of Normandy in 1204 declared him a tyrant justly deprived of rule. Worse was to follow. Henry II, however rapacious his administration, had been an absentee from England for more than half of his reign. Exiled from France, John was now confined to England. His English barons, previously spared too close a familiarity with the Plantagenet court, now found themselves confronted by a King never more than a few days' march away, likely at any moment to turn up to inspect their resources, and in the worst cases to do rather more than inspect their wives and daughters.

Stephen Langton: Becket's successor

Henry II had withstood denunciations from the Church, even after his quarrel with Archbishop Becket; even after Becket himself lay dead, his blood soaking into the political consciousness of England. John had been crowned King by his own more pliable archbishop of Canterbury, Hubert Walter, Glanville's nephew and previously one of the great presiding figures in English law. Shortly after the loss of Normandy, Hubert died.

From 1205, there was a succession crisis in the English Church. John sought to have his own candidate elected. The monks of Canterbury, and the Pope, refused. Instead, in June 1207, the Pope insisted on consecrating an Englishman as archbishop. His name was Stephen Langton.

Langton shared the Pope's uncompromising theological understanding of human history. Kings, he taught, had been sent by God not as a reward to the people of Israel but as a punishment for Israel's sins. Kings who taxed their peoples beyond absolute necessity were tyrants. So were kings who ignored the teachings of the Church or who promoted as bishops their own cronies from the Exchequer. So were kings who refused their people a written law, a Deuteronomy. Langton denounced such kings as tyrants just as John of Salisbury, or Thomas Becket, or Ralph Niger, had denounced tyranny in the past. Langton was anathema to King John, tainted not only by his teaching but by his long residence amongst John's enemies in France. His first action after consecration as archbishop was to have a seal made for

*Innocent III,
13th-century mosaic
from Rome.*

joining Langton in France. The dead were denied burial in consecrated ground. Mass and the other sacraments were refused to the faithful. The King seized what he could from the Church. Indeed, John grew rich on the profits of expropriation. Without the mediating influence of the Church, the barons of England were themselves bled dry by the King's extortions. John assembled a vast war chest to pay for reconquest in France. Beneath the surface, however, deeper treasons began to bubble. There were rumours that the Pope intended deposing King John and placing Philip of France, or Philip's eldest son, on the English throne. A French invasion fleet was assembled. In 1212, a conspiracy was unmasked in which at least two leading barons, Robert fitz Walter and Eustace de Vescy, were alleged to have plotted the King's death. Both men fled to France. There they joined the group of exiles around Langton. A common front emerged, uniting John's enemies both baronial and ecclesiastical, French and English.

John himself was on the verge of a great campaign of reconquest. Rather than remain at odds with the Church, he sought compromise. Once again, there was a woeful contrast here with the record of his father, Henry II. Following Becket's death in 1170, Henry had been forced into compromise with the Church, but a compromise in which

*The refighting of
Becket's wars: Langton's
counterseal, depicting
his predecessor's
martyrdom.*

himself displaying the martyrdom of Becket, a red rag to any Plantagenet bull. From Rome he travelled north to Burgundy, taking up residence in precisely those places where Becket had passed his exile of the 1160s. Langton was clearly determined to refight Becket's wars. John would not allow him into England. The result was a stand-off.

Like Becket before him, Langton now appealed to the Pope. Unlike Pope Alexander III who had been powerless to oppose King Henry II, the new Pope, Innocent III, was determined to make a stand. It was Innocent who had forced the election at Canterbury. When King John refused to accept Langton, it was Innocent who placed England and the royal court under a sentence of Interdict and excommunication. For six years after 1208, the services of the English Church were suspended. Monks and bishops were forced into exile, many of them

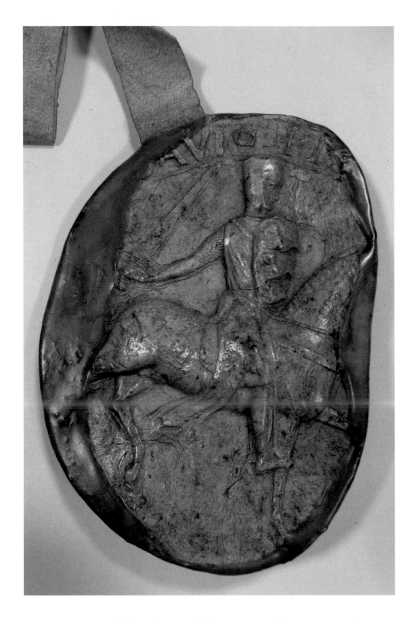

*King John on horseback,
reverse of his seal.*

Henry maintained his rights and claims more or less unimpaired. Few
if any bishops or churchmen had dared openly support the baronial
rebellion of 1173–4. As a result, opposition to Henry II had remained
divided and easily crushed. For the last fifteen years of his reign,
Henry had not only re-established control over his bishops but posed
as a most improbable devotee of Becket's newly established cult. John,
by contrast, was humiliated. His clerical and baronial opponents now
made common cause. In the spring of 1213, faced by the prospect of a
French invasion, John surrendered England and Ireland to the Pope as
a papal fief, promising a perpetual annual rent from England to Rome
of 1,000 marks (£666 – today, something approaching £1 million).
There was cunning here, and there were precedents set elsewhere in
Europe, not least by the kings of Aragon and Sicily. By declaring
himself a papal vassal, John could hope to call upon the Pope's

protection against the French. But to many in England this appeared a
humiliation. In particular, in the greater English monasteries it was
feared that the realm's surrender would lead to direct interference by
the Pope in what had previously been carefully guarded monastic
independence. This perception was important, since it was in the
monasteries that history was written, by monastic chroniclers serving
as the chief news gatherers and spin doctors of their day. The surrender
of 1213 was thus added to the chroniclers' already long list of King
John's 'crimes'.

In the aftermath of John's surrender, Langton was at last permitted
to cross to England. It was expected that he would now lift the
sentence of Interdict imposed since 1208. But he did no such thing.
On the contrary, he preached against the vices of England and the
court. The services of the Church, he declared, would only be restored
when full compensation was paid for John's seizures of Church
property. In 1214, according to the chroniclers, it was Langton who
was the first to rediscover the Coronation Charter of Henry I,
henceforth proclaimed as a model of good law to which King John
should be bound. Although no more trusted by the barons than by the
King, it was Langton, as we shall see, who now brought his distinctly
European intelligence to bear upon England's political dilemmas.

Politics and justice under John

What, meanwhile, of John's own understanding of politics and
English law? We know a great deal more about John than we do
about most previous kings in English history, thanks to the survival,
from 1199 onwards, of the earliest of the so-called 'chancery rolls'.
There is much in these rolls that speaks not just of routine but of
the King's personality.

Take, for example, a notoriously gnomic letter sent by John, only a
few days after Easter 1203, the festival at which he allegedly
commanded the slaying of Arthur of Brittany. Writing to his mother
and others of his friends in Gascony, John declared that he had
dispatched a messenger with news. What that news was, his letters fail
to specify. But his correspondents were asked to believe that 'the grace
of God stands better with us' than his messenger could possibly tell.
Was this a coded reference to Arthur's murder, ridding the King of a
hated rival, or was it an entirely innocent expression of piety? There are

many more such ambiguities. In 1200, the wife of the King's chief forester, Hugh de Neville, offered the King two hundred chickens 'so that she may lie one night with her husband'. Does this hint that, as some have suggested, she was the King's mistress seeking temporary respite from duties? Or was she, as seems more likely, chiding the King for keeping her husband too hard at work? In either case, the fact that such drollery was officially recorded tells us much about the humour of the court. Peter de Maulay, one of the King's foreign henchmen, in later legend reputed the executioner of Arthur of Brittany, stood very close to the darker secrets of the reign. In May 1212, no fewer than twenty-five fellow courtiers, including two bishops and five earls, offered guarantees for Peter's future good conduct. One of them, Henry fitz Count, the King's cousin, undertook to be whipped. Was this a genuine transaction, suggesting that Peter had temporarily fallen out with the King, or was it an elaborate joke? In either case, it does little to dispel our impression of a court gripped by intrigue, in which even the King's closest friends and relations had constantly to watch their own backs.

Just as we learn much from the chancery rolls about John's

The chancery rolls

Carefully preserved in the National Archives, the chancery rolls represent virtually day-by-day copies of a vast number of the King's outgoing letters. Quite why they begin in 1199 remains uncertain. Perhaps because of a new European-wide tendency to demand not just memory but written records of the past. Perhaps because the surviving rolls are merely the latest in a more ancient series, the earlier parts of which were somehow lost. More likely, the rolls testify to the particular pressures of the 1190s, to the need to maximize royal income and maintain communications between the King and his scattered Anglo-French estate. Perhaps, too, they were intended to satisfy John's curiosity (or paranoia) that his instructions be enforced.

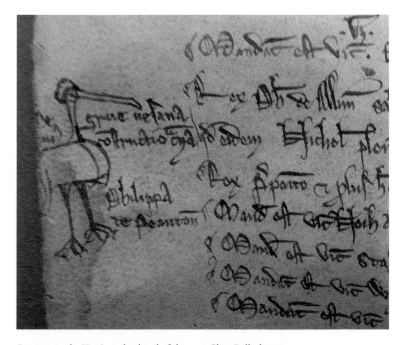

Intrigue in the King's circle: detail of the 1216 Close Roll, depicting Philippa of Paulton, a humble petitioner at John's court, as a 'mad crane'. Such 'jokes' speak volumes of the cruelty of John's regime.

Justice under John: a mercenary inflicts punishment on four men, from the Chronica Majora *of Matthew Paris, 1250s. Note the relative sizes, as portrayed here, of persecutor and persecuted.*

personality and politics, so from the records of his law courts we know a great deal about his enforcement of justice. By the 1190s, indeed as early as the 1170s, a system of professional courts had emerged in which the judges sitting at Westminster, originally at the Exchequer and subsequently in Westminster Hall at a recognised 'bench' (literally a row of seats), conducted regular tours of England, known as 'eyres'. Royal justice was thereby brought to the shires and localities. Some judges accompanied the King himself as he toured his lands, dispensing justice in an assembly that was to develop into the court 'before the King' (*coram rege*). Herein lay the origins of that great division between the courts of King's Bench (*coram rege*) and Common Pleas ('the bench') which continued to characterize English justice for the next six hundred years. There was considerable overlap between the personnel of these courts. Most judges performed a variety of duties as royal administrators, not yet as dedicated officers of the law, certainly not as figures in any way independent of royal control. From the 1180s, we have access to the earliest surviving law reports kept by justices' clerks, and to the 'final concords' by which parties to disputes had their settlements set down officially in writing.

What emerges here is the already sophisticated nature of routine. Attorneys were already a feature of these courts, semi-professionals appointed (and paid) to plead on behalf of litigants. Decisions are frequently marked 'to be discussed with the King'. King John himself insisted that judicial duels be transferred from the Bench to his own court, so that he might himself see the fight. We find these courts expected to act virtuously, as when King John sent a writ insisting that his justiciar 'do nothing contrary to the custom of our realm'. A point of procedure was decided in 1205 'by common counsel', precisely the same phrase that was to occur ten years later in clauses 12 and 14 of Magna Carta as a prerequisite for the levying of royal taxation.

At the same time, there is no doubt of the influence, indeed intimidation, that the King continued to exercise over judicial process. Many cases went ahead only after painful delays, themselves the result of endless procedural complications or the sheer difficulty of access to royal judges either at Westminster or in the localities. Justice itself could still be bought. The Fine Rolls, recording the offers of money made to the King, set out innumerable instances of payments to speed or influence judgement, and the chroniclers delight in stories of corrupt judges brought at last to death and the fires of hell. As in the chancery rolls, there was an element of subversive humour at work in John's law courts, as when the clerk of the rolls insists upon referring to one particular attorney as 'Sighing and Weeping' or 'Grief and Sighing'.

The King himself was keen to emphasize his God-given role in the delivery of justice. A royal charter to the bishop of Lisieux, issued within the first few months of John's reign, opens with a long and solemn declaration that kings and princes are obliged to preserve justice and especially to support the Church. Hoping to end the Interdict, in 1213 John issued letters declaring his intention to quash all measures taken against 'the custom of the realm or ecclesiastical liberty'. This pre-empts the phrasing of Magna Carta by a full two years. As early as 1204, 'the customs of England' were referred to in royal letters forbidding that any under-age ward be summoned to supply evidence of his landholding. This pre-empts aspects of Magna Carta clauses 4–5 by a full decade. Not just barons and bishops, but towns, cities and entire communities received charters from the King and such charters bristle with reminders of individual or corporate liberties. In 1204, for example, the men of Devon offered 5,000 marks (roughly £3,300 – today, perhaps £10 million) for a royal charter that declared that only Dartmoor and Exmoor were to remain under the jurisdiction of the King's foresters. The King's sheriffs were to hold no more than one 'tourn' (or obligatory assembly), and this itself was to be used only for the prosecution of crown pleas, not to enrich the

The tyrant King John hunting a stag with hounds, in a 14th-century illumination.

sheriff. The sheriff must allow the county to go bail for the release of prisoners from the county gaol so that no one be detained merely out of the sheriff's spite or hatred. If the sheriff should unjustly offend the men of Devon, he was to be punished and another sheriff appointed to 'carry out his duties well and lawfully'. The men of Cornwall offered 2,200 marks (roughly half the Devon fine) for similar privileges, but with an added clause stating that the county's sheriff was to be chosen by the King from amongst an elected group of men themselves chosen by the county. In these two charters alone there are elements that pre-empt half a dozen clauses of Magna Carta. Law, legality and respect for local custom were already central to the concerns of political society, long before the issue of Magna Carta. The problem here lay not in the rhetoric but the execution of royal justice.

We see this most clearly in the notorious case of William de Braose.

Remains of the 12th-century castle at Corfe, where William de Braose's wife and eldest son were imprisoned and allegedly starved to death by John.

The persecution of the de Braoses

William de Braose had risen as one of John's favourites to control vast estates in Wales and Ireland. He was present at court at the time of Arthur's disappearance. Indeed, some of the stories that emerged about Arthur's death may have leaked out via William de Braose and his wife Matilda, a woman with a loose tongue. We know about Matilda's chatter thanks to an extraordinary report circulated by the King in the summer of 1210. By this time, John had turned against William's entire family. He had invaded William's lands, seized his castles, and imprisoned William's wife and eldest son. Wife and son, so it was alleged, were deliberately starved to death in the dungeon of Corfe Castle. This was one of half a dozen atrocities for which John has ever afterwards been branded a tyrant. Yet the King's letters of 1210 employ the language of justice to explain away his treatment of the de Braoses. The King, they proclaim, had acted 'according to the custom of our realm and by the law of our Exchequer'.

The story they tell runs as follows. William owed 5,000 marks (in today's money, perhaps £10 million) to the King for lands in Ireland. The money had not been paid. The Exchequer demanded the seizure of William's assets, but William had responded with rebellion. His wife, taken prisoner attempting to flee from Ireland, offered the King 40,000 marks (today, more than £1 billion) so that her husband might be restored to favour. Three days later, she changed her mind and withdrew the offer. Having been removed from Ireland to England, she changed her mind again. She now promised not just 40,000 marks but a further 10,000 marks in punishment for her indecision. When time came for repayment, she could produce no more than fifteen ounces of gold and just over £17 in coin. As a result William and his family had been duly and properly outlawed. So, at least, the King's letters reported. In reality, the 50,000 marks (more than £33,000 – today, well in excess of £1 billion) offered by William's wife was a sum that contemporaries would have recognized as absurd. The average baron at this time could boast an annual income of £1,000, the King perhaps £30,000. The entire realm of England had struggled to produce £66,000 as a ransom for King Richard I. Although dressed up in the language of justice and law, the King's action was both brutal and extortionate. His letter was not so much a justification as a threat. What had been done to the de Braoses, it suggested, might very easily be done to others.

The King's abuses

John's atrocities were indeed grave. He regularly demanded hostages from his barons, whose reluctance to deliver up their sons and nephews can only have been strengthened by the rumours that circulated over the fate of Arthur of Brittany, or the starvation of the de Braose heir. He was accused of lecherous assaults upon his barons' wives and daughters, up to and including the wife of his own bastard half-brother, the earl of Salisbury. A clerical servant of the court, accused of plotting against the King, is said to have been crushed to death under a leaden cope. Like many such stories, this was no doubt exaggerated. So was the accusation that John had considered converting to Islam. So was the charge that his Queen was a sorceress and adulteress, whose lovers the King condemned to strangulation in her bed. What is significant here is that such stories, however warped in the retelling, were widely circulated and just as widely believed. John was the sort of man whom contemporaries believed capable of atrocity. In politics, perception is every bit as significant as performance.

How could John's criminal capacities be curbed? Not by law alone. Far from preventing his excesses, law existed to serve the King. John's manipulation of law was nothing new. The 'feudal' structures of landholding introduced into England after 1066 were themselves constructed so as to favour the great over their inferiors, King over barons. When one of the King's tenants died without heirs, or with successors who were under the age of legal majority; when a husband died leaving a widow or daughters, there were rich profits to be made. Wardships, widows, and escheats (lands left vacant for a lack of heirs) could be sold to the highest bidder. Henry I had done this. So had Henry II. John merely followed their well-trodden path.

Again a few examples must suffice. In 1200, John had put aside his first wife, Isabella of Gloucester, to marry Isabella of Angoulême. So that the King could continue to control her estates, Isabella of Gloucester was nonetheless kept at court, as part of what at times amounted almost to a royal harem. In 1214, with the King hard-pressed for money, she was at last sold off to Geoffrey de Mandeville, himself heir to the earldom of Essex. Geoffrey offered 20,000 marks (today, tens of millions of pounds) for his bride. This was a vast sum, all the more remarkable because it was made regardless of the port of Bristol, the richest of Isabella's properties, withheld on behalf of the

King. Isabella herself was by this time well beyond the age of child-bearing. Indeed, it had been her failure to produce children, as early as 1200, that had first persuaded John to divorce her. In effect, therefore, Geoffrey was persuaded to offer a vast sum for life interest in only part of a barren wife's estate. The absurdities ran deeper still. At precisely the time that he was negotiating for Isabella, Geoffrey de Mandeville found his own estate the object of a speculative bid from another baron, Geoffrey de Say, who in 1214 offered the King 15,000 marks to be recognized as true heir to the Mandeville lands. In the meantime, the Mandeville claims both to hereditary custody of the Tower of London and to the title 'earl of Essex' went deliberately unrecognized by the King. Each stage of these arrangements was accompanied by a

The White Tower of the Tower of London, built in the late 11th century: claimed for the Mandeville estate but deliberately denied to Geoffrey de Mandeville by King John.

Silver penny bearing a portrait of Henry II, minted in Winchester, 1205, in the reign of King John: the fees charged by the King's mints to recoin old money were an unsuccessful attempt to raise funds.

which John's father, Henry II, had raised resources in the 1160s or 70s. Kingship itself was becoming more costly, and as a result a great deal more difficult.

John's exploitation of feudal custom, his manipulation of the law and his confiscation of the lands of the Church, resolved his financial difficulties. By 1214, thanks to a decade of plunder, John was at least as rich as his father had been, perhaps a great deal richer. Henry II had used his wealth for conquests both in France and Ireland. John poured his treasure into armies and alliances intended to encircle his chief rival, the King of France. John crossed to Poitou, to attack Philip from the south. His allies campaigned in Flanders, threatening Paris from the north. There, at Bouvines outside Lille, on Sunday 27 July 1214, disaster struck. In a single day of battle, John's northern alliance was annihilated.

combination of bribery and extortion so entangled that, when rebellion against the King eventually broke out, both Geoffrey de Mandeville and Geoffrey de Say joined the rebels.

There could be few justifications for such dealings save for John's urgent need of money. Here, whatever his personal debauchery, John perhaps fell victim to economic forces beyond his control. His plans to reconquer his lost estates in France coincided with a period of rampant monetary inflation across northern Europe. The causes are still uncertain. Some would argue a glut of newly mined German silver, others the pressure on resources at a time of rapid population growth. Whatever the cause, the effects fell with particular severity upon those, such as John, whose income derived from fixed rents paid in return for land. Such rents failed to keep pace with inflation. Any attempt to raise them was bound to excite political tension. The high levels of taxes levied by King John, his efforts to tax trade through an early experiment in customs duties, and the general rapacity of his financial administration, were all attempts to combat this underlying economic reality. They stand in unhappy contrast to the ease with

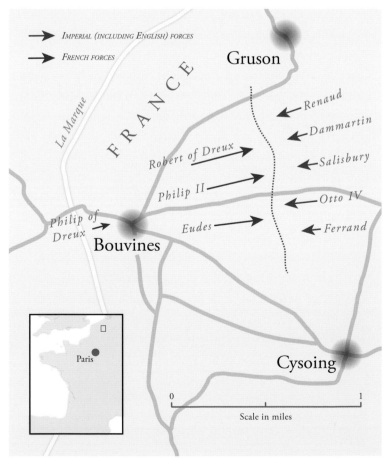

The Battle of Bouvines.

Resistance gathers

From Bouvines, the road to Runnymede was both direct and speedy. Deprived of his northern alliance and with his treasure now exhausted, John once again fled defeated from France. In England, tensions had already begun to build against him. Baronial and ecclesiastical malcontents made common casuse. For the past few years, in an attempt to fend off the threat of foreign invasion, John had regularly commanded the seizure of French and other foreign ships in English ports. This had led to reciprocal seizures by the King of France and had been bitterly resented by the men of London whose fortunes were dependent upon foreign trade. London itself now joined the growing list of malcontents persuaded of John's unfitness to rule. In 1214, even before Bouvines, many great men had refused either to send knights or to pay scutage for the King's campaigns in France. Instead, they rehearsed arguments first raised by the Church, as long ago as the 1190s, that the English baronage was not liable for service outside England or Normandy. There were many in 1214 who harboured even more ancient grievances against John and his dynasty, stretching back to the seizure of estates by Henry II. Memories of the great rebellion of 1173–4 began to stir.

By the autumn of 1214, perhaps thanks to Archbishop Langton, perhaps by other less dramatic means, the text of Henry I's Coronation Charter had begun to circulate, rallying demands that King John himself reform his rule. The King was persuaded to issue a charter of liberties for the English Church, promising that henceforth bishops and abbots would be elected by their own communities, rather than being imposed by royal command. Chroniclers began to take notice of meetings of barons and churchmen, at Bury St Edmunds and London, at St Albans and no doubt elsewhere, as the tide of protest against John's administration began to mount. A group of barons emerged, known collectively as the 'Northerners'. Within a year of Bouvines, they and their fellow contrariants had forced the King into the settlement we know as Magna Carta.

England's first political party

Many of the 'Northerners' were more closely associated with East Anglia and the home counties than with the far north. They nonetheless served as yet another rallying point for those aggrieved with the King. Their leader, Robert fitz Walter, adopted the title 'Marshal of the Army of God': evidence that these men believed not only that they had the support of the English Church but they were fighting, almost as crusaders, in a holy cause. Their collective name, the 'Northerners', qualifies them as the first identifiable political 'party' in English history.

Seal-die of Robert fitz Walter.

circumuallando roborare. Et rusūpto spū
uiuidiore reliquos omes. hinc iñ ad modū
nauis uelificantis requora uelocit sulcantr
impetuosissime diuisit. ense tribilit fulmi
nante. z hostiu cruore sepius inebriato. dōn suc
omis acies ad ipm illese z indempnes tñsmeare.
Quo cū puenirent sui comilitones: congre

tempe z
suspensa
nam. ho
respirar
z exatir
tulit ost
z defessi

imnif dcctatū eſt. ⁊ utrobiq;
nia. Tandem p̄ multoy run
tati pedem retulerunt ut
uſaret p̄ eōflictū. Similɩ ⁊
Quod tū moleſte nimis
anguiſ ın ulcōe eſtuabat
gnatoz ceſſare erubeſcebat.

The ultimate means of coercing the King: battle between King and rebels, from an early 14th-century manuscript of Matthew Paris's Vitae Offarum.

Chapter Five

Magna Carta: Defeat into Victory

Nicholas Vincent

They all exulted in the belief that God had compassionately touched the King's heart, had taken away his heart of stone and given him one of flesh, and that a change for the best was made in him by the hand of the Almighty; and all and every one hoped that England, being by the grace of God freed in their time from, as it were, the Egyptian bondage, by which it had been for a long time previously oppressed, would enjoy peace and liberty, not only by the protection of the Roman Church ... but also on account of the wished-for humiliation of the King, who they hoped was happily inclined to all gentleness and peace.

Roger of Wendover, *Flores Historiarum* (c.1228–35)

The year 1215 was by no means the first in English history when a king had been forced into negotiations with his subjects. King Stephen in the 1140s, King Henry I in 1100, and any number of Anglo-Saxon kings before them, had been obliged to promise concessions in return for continued possession of the throne. There was no easy means to restrain an incompetent or tyrannical king other than to make war against him, threatening to deprive him of rule and ultimately of life. Since 1066, no King of England had died in battle or been deposed. The threat of deposition or death was nonetheless the ultimate means by which his subjects could persuade a king to reform. Magna Carta was forced upon King John in June 1215 after a year of threatened rebellion. As the campaigning season approached, a series of meetings took place between King, Church and malcontents throughout the winter months of 1214–15. Now or never was the time for the barons to make their move.

67

Desperate measures

On Ash Wednesday, 4 March 1215, in the hope of placing himself under an added degree of papal protection, the King took vows as a crusader. By this stage, negotiations were perhaps already being committed to writing. A document known as the 'Unknown Charter' (in reality one of the better-known documents in English history, see page 33), rediscovered in the French national archives in the 1890s, takes the form of a copy of Henry I's Coronation Charter of 1100, followed by a series of a dozen or so clauses beginning with the statement 'King John concedes that he will arrest no man without judgement nor accept any payment for justice nor commit any unjust act.' In embryo, this supplies the first hint of what was to emerge as clauses 39 and 40, in many ways the most famous clauses of Magna Carta. In all likelihood it dates from the spring of 1215. As early as

July 1213, John is said to have been persuaded to swear an oath that he would uphold the (largely mythical) *Leges Edwardi Confessoris*. History was itself now conspiring against the King, with the barons drawing precedents from the reign of the Confessor and Henry I in an attempt to use custom to bind their sovereign.

Throughout these months, John did his best to postpone the inevitable. To bishops and barons he granted a flurry of new privileges. Large tracts of royal forest were officially abolished, including whatever remained of the hated forest laws in the county of Cornwall. On Easter Sunday, 19 April 1215, the King granted privileges to the men of Bayonne, within sight of the Pyrenees in the far south of what remained of his French empire, conceding them the right to self-government as a 'commune'. Bayonne had to be pacified if Gascony were to remain under English control. Without Gascony, the supply of foreign mercenaries that the King was now drawing into England

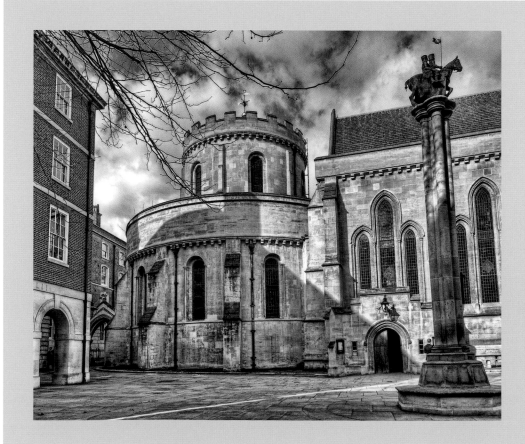

The mayoralty: John's concession to London

Londoners had long craved self-government. In the 1190s, the city had rebelled in the name of a 'commune', rapidly and violently suppressed. On 9 May 1215, on the same day that he himself departed the city, the King granted London's citizens the right to elect their own mayor. This concession came too late, however. On the same day that he issued his charter, John departed, first for Windsor, then south-west towards Southampton to meet his newly arrived French mercenaries.

The Temple Church, London. As John's position became increasingly desperate, he established himself at the New Temple, where he granted privileges to the city of London.

*The Articles of the
Barons, a draft version
of Magna Carta.*

might itself run dry. On 9 May, himself now established at the New
Temple in London, the King granted similar privileges to the men of
London. That same evening, having fled westwards to Windsor, he
issued letters agreeing that four royalist barons and four representatives
of the 'barons who are against us' should arbitrate disputes, under the
ultimate authority of the Pope. The following day, he promised the
malcontents that, until arbitration was completed, he would not 'go
against' them 'by force or by arms save by the law of our realm or by
judgement of their peers', words that directly foreshadow Magna Carta
clause 39. The negotiations that were to reach fulfilment at
Runnymede were now officially under way.

By 12 May, news had reached court that the malcontents had
gathered at Brackley, a favoured tournament ground in
Northamptonshire. There, on 5 May, they had publicly repudiated
their oaths of homage to the King. Five days later, on Sunday 17 May,
whilst London's chief citizens were at Mass, a group of lesser men
seized the city on behalf of the rebel barons. Not only was John
deprived of his capital and chief treasury, but there was now a threat
that the rebels would league with the King of France. Westminster
Abbey, since 1066 the traditional coronation church of England, was
now at the rebels' disposal. What was there to prevent the French
making good on the disinheritance pronounced against John since
1203, and seeking not only to depose John as King but to plant a
French prince on his throne? The rebels, meanwhile, had placed
themselves in a difficult situation. Offered arbitration both by the
King and the Pope, they had instead preferred to repudiate their
homages and to place themselves openly at war with John.

The creation and essence of the Charter

It was against this background that the terms of Magna Carta were
hammered out. The precise circumstances of their drafting elude us,
even though we have a remarkable collection of written relics that
played a part in negotiations. These include a dossier, today preserved
in the British Library, of Latin and French versions of the coronation
charters of kings Henry I, Stephen and Henry II (see page 32), that
was perhaps carried to Runnymede in the summer of 1215. Better
known, the so-called Articles of the Barons survives as a draft, very
close to the final form of Magna Carta, sealed by the King as proof of

his agreement to the details. This was almost certainly carried away
from Runnymede by Archbishop Langton, which would explain why it
was later preserved in the archiepiscopal archive at Lambeth. From
there it was stolen at the time of the impeachment of Archbishop Laud
in the 1640s, on the eve of a later English Civil War. Today, this too
resides in the British Library.

View of Runnymede and Windsor Castle, by Robert Gallon, late 19th century.

Runnymede: neutral ground

It is some indication of the location's neutrality that Magna Carta is the first document in which the place name 'Runnymede' is recorded. A contemporary, translating Magna Carta into Anglo-Norman French, was so bemused by the name that he wrote it in the wholly unintelligible form 'Roueninkmede'.

As Langton's involvement makes plain, the negotiation of Magna Carta was a sophisticated and multi-faceted affair. This was no mere exchange of boasts and insults but a desperate bid to preserve the peace. As we have seen, peace, and its maintenance, was a priority enjoined on kings and churchmen since the very beginnings of Christian kingship. If England were to be spared the horrors of civil war, then it was essential both that the potential combatants receive satisfaction and that the King be publicly brought to compromise. Hence the need for a location for debate that was neither too close to the rebel stronghold in London nor too overshadowed by the King's great castle at Windsor. Runnymede, the meadow lying on the shifting course of the Thames between Windsor and Staines, was an appropriately liminal space in which tents could be pitched and justice be seen to be done.

The first thing to be said about the text that was agreed on 15 June 1215, and that was thereafter issued to the realm as a final record of peace, is that it is exceptionally long. Kings of the past had issued lengthy charters. A charter granted by Henry II to the monks of Caen in Normandy runs to more than seven thousand words, written in two columns on a piece of parchment more than two feet square. Magna Carta, at roughly half this length, and about two thirds of its surface area, is nonetheless an impressive achievement. Each of its 3,500 words had to be laboriously drafted, negotiated and just as laboriously copied out for distribution to the realm. As yet, it was referred to merely as 'the charter of liberties'. The title 'Magna Carta' came later, from 1218 onwards, to distinguish 'the big' ('Magna') charter from the smaller charter of liberties (the 'Forest Charter') issued to cover those parts of England under the law of the forest.

Many of the elements in its drafting derived from English legal procedures, from the precedents supplied by the 'laws' of Edward the Confessor, and the Coronation Charter of Henry I. Others were more exotic. Magna Carta names at least thirty-six individuals besides the King. These include an Irish archbishop, the King of Scotland and his constable, a cardinal of the Roman church, an Italian clerk, and at least ten men of French birth, including the Breton Philip d'Aubigné and no fewer than eight of the relatives and friends of Girard d'Athée, the King's trusted henchmen from the region of Tours on the river Loire. No wonder, then, that there are elements to Magna Carta that carry us well beyond England. There were continental precedents. We have already found King John imitating the kings of Aragon and Sicily in swearing feudal homage to the Pope. Like the King of Aragon, he had sought protection for himself as a crusader. The same King of Aragon, Pedro II, had in 1205 drafted (but apparently not issued) a charter of liberties for his subjects, promising an end to new or excessive taxes, the appointment only of local men as royal officials to administer 'common justice' according to the right and custom of the land, to be appointed 'with the counsel of magnates and the wise men of that land', the whole of this arrangement being secured under oath by the King.

North of the Pyrenees but still within the same jurisprudential orbit, in December 1212, Simon de Montfort, leader of the Pope's crusade against the heretics of southern France, had issued laws known as the 'Statute of Pamiers'. Approaching the scale of the 1215 English Magna Carta, this document amongst other things outlaws the sale of justice, legislates on the disposition of heirs and widows, and forbids the rulers of the new crusading state of Toulouse from demanding service save by grace and at the ruler's pay. Ten of the eleven opening clauses of the Statute of Pamiers guarantee freedoms

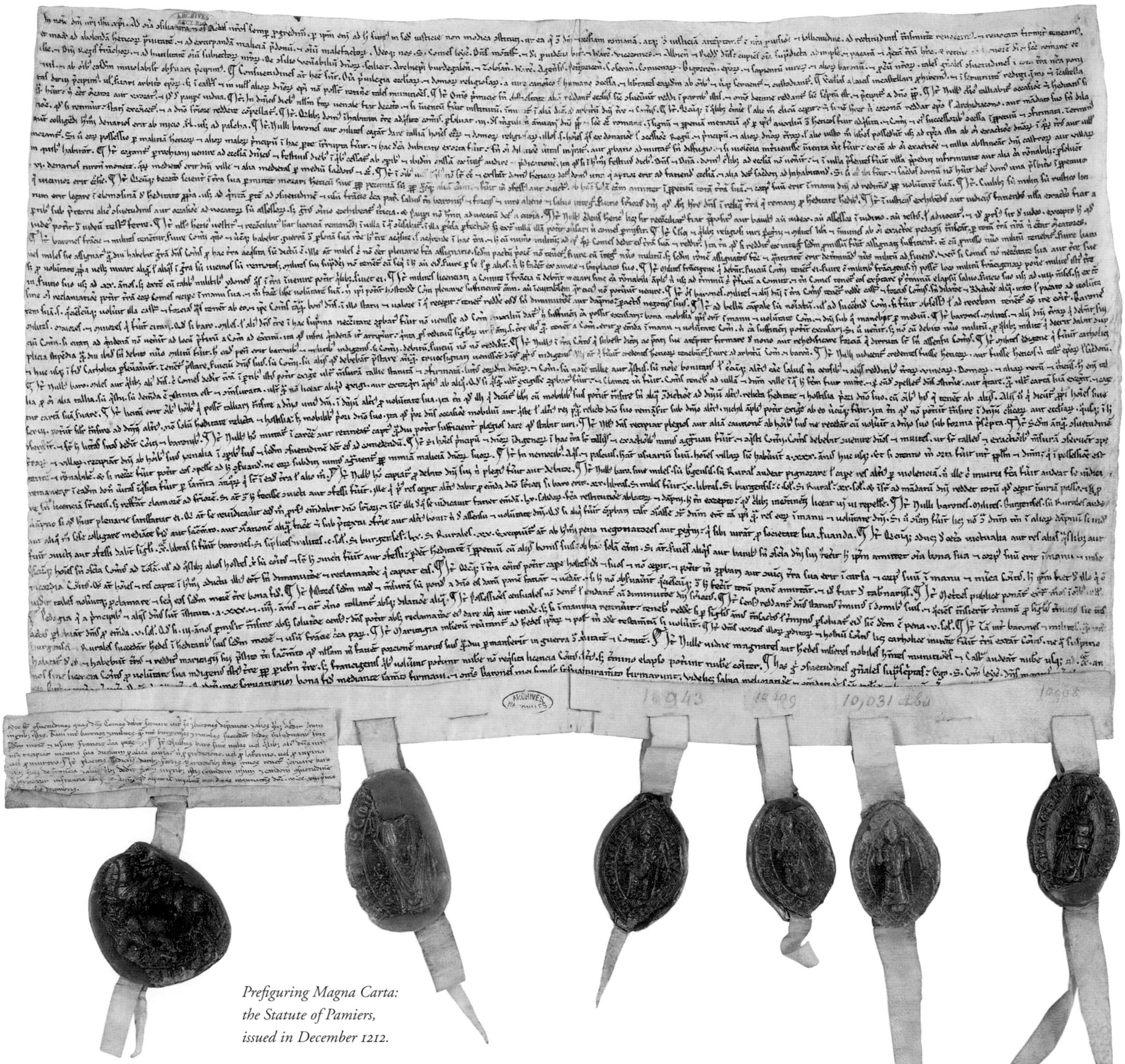

*Prefiguring Magna Carta:
the Statute of Pamiers,
issued in December 1212.*

to the Church. Much of this forestalls the terms of Magna Carta. The Statute of Pamiers could certainly have been known to those who gathered at Runnymede. Stephen Langton's brother was himself a member of Simon de Montfort's army in southern France. When the English barons, in 1212, had plotted against the life of King John it was to Simon de Montfort that they are said to have turned as a potential alternative.

The mention of Stephen Langton here carries us on to those clauses of Magna Carta that may reflect Langton's very particular conception of the obligations of King and people. The sanctions clause (c.61) of Magna Carta, for example, that appoints a group of twenty-five barons to oversee enforcement, may owe something to St Augustine's commentary on the Gospel of St John, a text that Langton had undoubtedly read, and that defines twenty-five as a number peculiarly appropriate to the 'Law'. Twenty-five, St Augustine had declared, was the square of the number five and hence of the five books of law making up the Old Testament Pentateuch. Clause 40 of Magna Carta, forbidding the sale of justice, rehearses a principle already to be found in English ecclesiastical legislation from the 1180s onwards, reiterated both in Simon de Montfort's Statute of Pamiers and in decrees that Langton had issued, as recently as 1214, for his own diocese of Canterbury. Perhaps Langton took a direct hand in drafting Magna Carta clause 60, with its attempts to extend liberty not just to the direct dependants of the King but to those placed under baronial or other lordly power. Certainly there are echoes here of a notion that occurs in Langton's theological writings, of a 'congregation of all the faithful', lay and ecclesiastical alike, placed under the leadership of the Church.

Certainly there can be little doubt that Langton took an interest in the drafting of the very opening clause of Magna Carta, promising 'liberty' for the English Church. But here he may have acted with intent more partisan than universally benevolent. Read carefully, the clause on Church freedom is not only the most solemn of the Charter's sixty or so clauses, granted not to man but to God, but the clause with greatest lawyerly subtlety. The rest of the Charter offers a settlement clearly dictated by the circumstances of 1215 and the imminent threat of civil war. Clause 1, by contrast, is careful to distinguish the liberties of the Church, already conceded by King John by the winter of 1214–15, from anything agreed subsequently, after 'the dispute that arose between us and our barons'. In other words, whilst the King might later attempt to wriggle out of those clauses granted under compulsion and the threat of civil war, the clause for the Church was guaranteed regardless of war or peace.

Immediately after clause 1, and here closely modelled upon the terms of Henry I's 1100 Coronation Charter, there follow concessions to barons and other men intended to regulate the financial profits that could be extracted from feudal rights such as wardships, widows and escheats (cc.2–8). Here too, Magna Carta went further than any previous concession wrung from an English king, not only in the detail with which custom and good practice were defined, but because its terms were extended to a far wider community than just the barons

and great men addressed in earlier coronation charters. Magna Carta was offered by the King to 'all the free men of our realm' (c.1), a constituency that would have included not just barons and knights but many landowners and town-dwellers – at an extremely rough estimate, ten to twenty per cent of the population, in legal terms (themselves only now achieving definition) distinguished from peasants owing servile obligations to their lords.

More than this, Magna Carta is one of the earliest concessions made by an English king to conceive of the realm as a corporate entity capable of self-expression. Clauses 12 and 14, for example, not only require that taxation command the 'common counsel of the realm', but lay down strict terms by which all those holding land from the King – barons, bishops and others – would be properly summoned, with at least forty days' notice, to supply such 'common counsel'. Clause 13 guarantees the 'ancient liberties and free customs' not just of London but of all cities, boroughs, towns and ports. Again at a very rough estimate, this perhaps involved one hundred corporate communities across England. Clause 21 decrees that earls and barons would not be arbitrarily fined by the King, but only with the consent of their peers and according to the gravity of their offence.

The concept of 'peers' reoccurs most famously in clause 39, protecting all 'free men' against seizure or imprisonment 'save by the lawful judgement of (their) peers and/or by the law of the land'. Most remarkably of all, clause 60 demands that all the King's subjects, both laymen and clerks, observe the same 'customs and liberties' towards their own men as the Charter guaranteed to those who held directly from the King. In other words, this was not merely a series of concessions forced by selfish barons upon a reluctant king. It represents a much more general settlement intended to ensure good lordship for great and small, for the dependants of barons as much as for the barons themselves. This same sense of communal responsibility extends to the so-called 'sanctions clause', clause 61. This announces the formation of a rump of twenty-five barons, appointed to ensure the Charter's enforcement, if necessary by warning or compelling the King to obey the terms of his own award. Should the King still refuse, the twenty-five barons were authorized to seize the King's castles and lands, acting together with an entity referred to as 'the commune of all the land' (in Latin *communia totius terre*). Here the earlier communal privileges granted to towns and cities such as Bayonne or London find expression in an entirely new concept, what would later be called 'the community of the realm'.

The King, in this reading, was no longer the sole motivating power within the body politic, but bound by contractual obligation to the community of his subjects. Here, Magna Carta offers a truly revolutionary interpretation of royal sovereignty as something subject not just to God but to popular consent. We are a long way here from 'democracy'. We are, nonetheless, in a new world, so far as the Plantagenet kings were concerned, in which the King, previously the supreme earthly judge of right and wrong, found himself liable to be judged by his people. Clauses 12 and 14, subjecting royal taxation to the 'common counsel of the realm', can be thought of as forerunners to the idea of 'no taxation without representation'. They certainly established precedents for summoning the King's subjects to council meetings increasingly, from the 1230s onwards, known as 'parliaments' (in French 'speaking togethers'). Thus did Magna Carta attempt to place the King under the rule of law.

There is much more to the Charter than this. Besides the financial and 'feudal' clauses, there are clauses intended to protect the King's subjects from the rapaciousness of sheriffs, foresters and other local officials (cc.9, 16, 20, 23–6, 28–33, 38, 44–5, 47–8). There are long sections on law and legal procedure (cc.17–19, 24, 34, 36, 38, 45). These were intended to guarantee regular, inexpensive and open access to the King's justices. Some of these clauses, such as clause 34, on the writ praecipe, may appear dry technicalities. In fact clause 34 represents a politically highly significant attempt to protect the jurisdiction of baronial courts against arbitrary incursions by the King. Other clauses govern trade and merchants, establishing fixed national measures for wine, corn and cloth (c.35), and a degree of protection for international trade both in peace and wartime (c.41). Others were intended to reinforce the distinction between the King's henchmen and the officers of the law. Bailiffs, sheriffs and constables were not to sit as judges in the more significant pleas (c.24), and all that sat as judges should know the law of the land and intend to implement it (c.45). This too represents a significant step on the road towards an impartial judiciary recruited from a distinct legal 'profession'. There are clauses (cc.9–11, 26) intended to limit the King's manipulation of debt, especially debt to Jews. Widows and heiresses were protected, but women in general were treated as under the authority of men, forbidden, save in the case

of a husband's death, from giving testimony in court that might lead to arrest or imprisonment (c.54).

Some clauses are definitive, clause 40 for example ('To no one shall we sell, to no one shall we deny or delay right or justice'). Others were merely negotiating points pending further discussion, most notably those that concern the royal forests (especially cc.47–8, 53), and the peace to be made with the Welsh and the Scots (cc.56–9). Some clauses are universal (c.51, 'Immediately after restoring peace, we shall remove from the realm all alien knights, crossbowmen, sergeants and mercenaries who have come with horses and arms to the injury of the realm'). Others were determined by the specific circumstances of the summer of 1215, in particular clause 50 (that names a series of the King's alien constables, all of whom were to be dismissed from office but with no firm timescale), and clause 61 that forbade the King from seeking the annulment of the Charter from any higher authority, here tacitly ruling out the possibility of an appeal by the King to the Pope.

And here we come to the greatest of the difficulties in which the makers of Magna Carta found themselves entangled. No manner of written guarantee could disguise the fact that the King himself remained sovereign under God. Like all earlier royal charters, Magna Carta was an act of the King's grace, issued in the King's name, opening with John's resounding titles as 'King of England, lord of Ireland, duke of Normandy and Aquitaine, count of Anjou'. As the Charter itself declares, this was a settlement issued 'at the prompting of God and for the salvation of our soul and the souls of all our ancestors and heirs, for the honour of God and for the exaltation of holy Church and the repair of our realm'. What if the King should decide, within a matter of weeks, months or years, that the terms of Magna Carta were no longer appropriate? What was to prevent the authority that had granted the Charter from in due course rescinding it? God himself exercised the power both to reward and to chastize. If God could alter his purposes, why not the King? The sanctions clause, clause 61, establishing a baronial committee of twenty-five as the Charter's guardians, bound by oaths to the wider community of the realm, was a makeshift vainly devised to prevent an inevitability. Kings of the past had made promises. Some such promises, including the Coronation Charter of Henry I, had been committed to writing. Few if any of these promises had been kept.

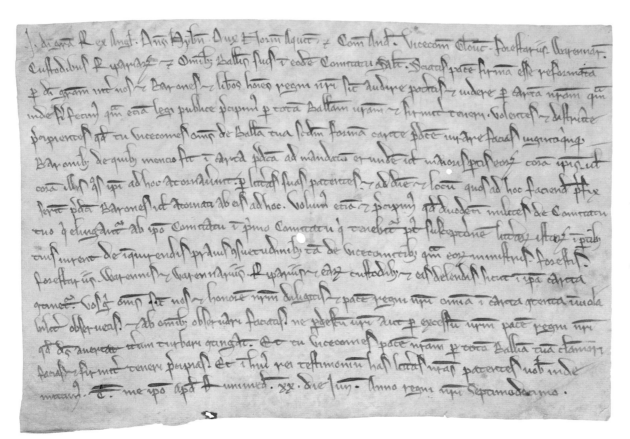

The Hereford Cathedral letters patent, issued at Runnymede on 20 June, five days after Magna Carta, intended to re-establish peace between King John and the barons.

After Runnymede: annulment and civil war

On 19 June, four days after the King's acceptance of Magna Carta, a 'firm peace' was made between King and barons in which John reaccepted homage from the rebels and declared an end to hostilities. There followed an uneasy period of two months during which King and barons waited for one another to make good on promises that neither side believed would be honoured.

Magna Carta was itself distributed to the country at large. Quite how many copies were sent out remains unknown, although the expectation was that it was to be read out loud in each of the thirty or more county or greater liberty courts of England, probably in both Latin and French, perhaps too in English. To judge from the King's instructions, preserved in the chancery rolls, sealed versions of Magna Carta were still being copied and dispatched as late as 22 July. Langton and the English bishops seem to have played a leading role in the Charter's distribution. A more conventional charter would have been publicized via the King's sheriffs. But in this instance it was against the misdeeds of the sheriffs themselves that various of the Charter's clauses were directed. Certainly three of the four surviving 'originals' come from ecclesiastical archives (including one of those now in the British Library, once wrongly supposed to have come from Dover Castle). It is worth noting that Magna Carta itself was not recorded in the official chancery roll of royal charters issued in the summer of 1215. Perhaps this was a result of oversight, or the document's peculiar status.

Perhaps it suggests a more sinister reluctance to preserve a text whose lifespan was not expected to be long. Besides the 'official' text to which the King put his seal, the intense negotiations of May and June 1215 ensured that particular clauses were sometimes communicated to the country at large not from the 'official' version sealed by the King but from drafts or unofficial copies. Many such variants are still being discovered. The most significant occurs in clause 2, setting the 'relief' or money payable by an heir to inherit an earldom or barony at £100. In negotiations, this had originally been set as £100 for a earldom but only 100 marks (£66 – today, perhaps £60,000) for a barony. Unofficial copies of Magna Carta, made ultimately from drafts carried away from Runnymede, retained the distinction between £100 for an earldom, 100 marks for a barony.

As this implies, Magna Carta remains in many ways not only an impressive but an enigmatic text. Despite several centuries of scholarly enquiry, by no means all of its secrets have been revealed. It is nonetheless important to bear in mind quite how short-lived it proved to be. Agreed to on 15 June, and distributed in the six weeks thereafter, it was by the second week of September 1215 practically redundant: a record of peace negotiations that had failed. All told, King John's Magna Carta enjoyed legal validity for less than twelve weeks. Why was this so?

Despite repeated requests from the King, the barons refused to surrender London. Whatever the terms of Magna Carta clauses 50 and 51, the King would not dismiss his constables. Despite clause 61,

Pope Innocent III,
13th-century fresco from
Subiaco, Italy.

forbidding appeal to a higher authority, the King sent envoys to Rome. They went ostensibly to complain against Archbishop Langton's failure to enforce an earlier sentence of papal excommunication against the rebels. They took with them a copy of Magna Carta. No Pope, reading clause 61 of the Charter, could be in any doubt that this was an unlawful settlement. It was an axiom of canon law that no contract imposed under threat of violence could claim the force of law, be it a marriage or a constitutional instrument. John was not only the Pope's vassal but had taken vows as a crusader. He was doubly under papal protection. Clause 61 authorized the baronial twenty-five to use violence to compel the King's obedience. No medieval sovereign claiming divine sanction could countenance a settlement that, more or less at sword-point, intruded a committee of guardians between God and King.

In England, the crisis came at the end of August, after the harvest, and at the latest possible moment when either side could still hope for appropriate weather in which to conduct a military campaign. In part the crisis erupted over Langton's position and his custody of Rochester Castle. Guarding access to Dover and the coast, and hence to any French invasion force, Rochester was a strategically vital fortress. Since the reign of Henry I, it had been given into the custody of the archbishops of Canterbury. Langton had retained custody throughout the negotiations of 1215, albeit under careful watch from the King. The King now wrote to demand the castle's surrender in letters that pleaded royal 'necessity'. Langton replied that no surrender could be made 'without judgement'. Both of these concepts, 'necessity' and 'judgement', had been crucial to the thinking behind Magna Carta.

The Fourth Lateran Council, 1215, illustration from
Matthew Paris's Chronica Majora, *1250s.*

Despite the prolonged delay in communication between England and Rome, the Pope continued to react to events. On 18 June 1215, only now informed of the baronial renunciation of homage, he had demanded that the archbishop and bishops condemn the rebels and place their lands under Interdict. On 7 July, informed by the King of the Church's lukewarm support but apparently not as yet of the Runnymede negotiations, the Pope sent more inflammatory letters appointing three commissioners – Peter des Roches, bishop of Winchester, the abbot of Reading and Master Pandulf, an Italian long resident in England – to ensure obedience to the King. All three men were courtiers. They published the Pope's letters at Dover on 5 September 1215. In the process, they declared not only that the rebels were excommunicate but that for his failure to implement the papal sentences of June and July Langton would be suspended from office as archbishop. The rebels, so the King's commissioners declared, 'nullify the approved customs of the realm and establish new laws ... despoiling the King of his royal dignity'. Although Magna Carta was not specifically named here, there could be no doubt that it fell within the ban now placed upon 'all constitutions and assizes' made by those described in the commissioners' letters as engaged in 'conspiracies against the King'. The Pope himself, informed of the Charter's terms,

The 'original' Magna Carta

Today, four 'originals' of the 1215 Magna Carta survive – two in the British Library, one at Salisbury, one at Lincoln. The 'original original', the text to which John agreed and put his seal at Runnymede, has long since disappeared. The closest we come to it is a copy issued under the seals of Langton and other bishops, testifying to the accuracy of this particular version, itself known only from a copy made twenty or more years later.

The British Library, London

BL MS Cotton Augustus II. 106, said to have been rescued
by the antiquarian and MP Sir Robert Cotton (1571–1631) from
his tailor just as it was about to be cut up into suit patterns.

*BL MS Cotton Charter XIII. 31a. This is the
only extant 1215 Magna Carta to have retained
its seal. The manuscript was damaged in a fire
of 1731 which destroyed part of the collection of
Sir Robert Cotton, and is now almost illegible.*

Lincoln Cathedral

*Lincoln Cathedral's is the most travelled of the surviving copies
of the 1215 charter, having been displayed at two World Fairs
(New York in 1939 and Brisbane in 1988). Its protracted stay in
the United States during wartime is recounted on pages 159–62.*

Salisbury Cathedral

*The Salisbury 1215 Magna Carta was housed at Old Sarum
Cathedral and then moved to the archives of the present Salisbury
Cathedral. It was mislaid in the mid-17th century during repairs
to the Cathedral library but rediscovered in the 19th century.*

Papal bull issued by Innocent III on 24 August 1215, annulling Magna Carta.

had issued his own letters annulling Magna Carta. These letters, known from their opening Latin words as *Etsi karissimus* ('Although most dear'), dated 24 August, arrived in England towards the end of September 1215. As early as the commissioners' letters of 5 September, however, Magna Carta was officially dead and done for. Attention now shifted to the priorities of war. Throwing off all pretence that it was still in the neutral hands of the archbishop, the rebels now occupied Rochester Castle. On 17 September, the King issued the first of many instructions for the seizure of rebel lands.

In any civil war, natural advantage always lay on the side of the King. Short of killing a king, it was almost impossible to bind him to any permanent compromise. Law itself was founded upon the concept of royal sovereignty. From 1066 onwards, English kings were immensely wealthier than even the wealthiest of their subjects. The royal court was attended by a large body of household knights, a standing army in embryo. Even in time of civil disturbance, in those parts of England still under royal control, the traditional royal tax-gathering machinery not only outweighed whatever baronial resources could be mustered but helped finance the recruitment of mercenaries, in 1215 from both Ireland and Gascony. The King's court had traditionally attracted those with greatest administrative talents, both secular and ecclesiastical. Such men tended to invest the Crown

The tomb effigy of William Marshal, earl of Pembroke, in the Temple Church, London.

with intellectual and administrative resources well beyond those of the baronage and at least equal to those of the Church. Talented courtiers of this sort were to play a significant role in the events of 1215. Hubert de Burgh, a Norfolk knight, previously steward to John's household, was now entrusted with custody of Dover Castle. Peter des Roches, the French-born bishop of Winchester, had remained loyal to John throughout the Interdict. He now brought to the King the vast resources of his bishopric (the richest in Europe, barring only Milan and Rome). William Marshal, earl of Pembroke, had risen through service at the courts of both Henry II and Richard I, to enjoy a close though by no means unclouded career at the court of King John. There were many other royalists of almost equal talent, most of whom now remained faithful to John. Set against them, Langton was now an exile suspended from office. With only one exception, the English bishops were reluctant openly to oppose the King. The exception, Giles de Braose bishop of Hereford, was a son of the King's disgraced minister William de Braose, but of little practical assistance to the rebels. The rebel barons were therefore placed at an immediate disadvantage. It was they who had first provoked war by their refusal of arbitration and their renunciation of homage. They now found themselves outnumbered and out-resourced in both material and intellectual terms. In the autumn of 1215 they did what rebellious barons of the past had always been forced to do. They turned to assistance from beyond the realm of England.

The coronation of Henry III, from Matthew Paris's Chronica Majora, *1250s.*

Henry III and his successors: the victory of Magna Carta

Two weeks later, at Bristol, on 12 November 1216, Magna Carta was reissued, not now as an assault upon royal privilege but as a manifesto of the King's future good government. The boy king, Henry III, was without a seal. Magna Carta was therefore authenticated with the seals of its new sponsors, the King's guardians and chief ministers, William Marshal and the papal legate Guala. Since the legate acted in the name of the Pope, this was in effect not only to bring Magna Carta back from the dead but to grant it explicit papal approval.

The barons already had the support of the Scots and the native Welsh. They now sent envoys to King Philip Augustus of France inviting a French invasion of England. Philip in turn appointed his eldest son, Louis, to command this French army. Since 1200, Louis had been married to a Spanish princess, Blanche of Castile, herself a granddaughter of Henry II of England. Via Blanche, Louis now claimed to be King of England not only by baronial election but by right of blood. His claim here was founded upon the controversial French sentence of 1203, in which John had in theory been condemned to disinheritance for the murder of Arthur of Brittany. What had begun as a domestic dispute between King and barons, was transformed in the autumn of 1215 into an international campaign of warfare and propaganda. There was considerable irony here. English barons who had first opposed King John citing the costs of his foreign adventures and the obnoxiousness of his foreign friends, now found themselves leagued with Louis of France, Llewelyn of Wales and Alexander of Scotland, against a crowned and anointed English King.

There followed two years of civil war. John retook Rochester and imprisoned its garrison, demanding vast ransoms for their release. He harried the north. Louis of France occupied south-east England save for Dover and the Weald of Kent. The circumstances of Stephen's reign seemed about to be repeated, with a potentially irresoluble stand-off between an Angevin party confined to the south-west and north, and a French claimant ruling from London. But here, events intervened. Campaigning in Lincolnshire, in October 1216, John fell ill and died. His body was carried to Worcester for burial. His crown passed to his eldest son, Henry, in 1216 a boy only nine years of age. On his deathbed, John placed Henry under the protection of the Pope and the papal legate then operating in England, Guala Bicchieri, a native of Vercelli in northern Italy. Henry was crowned by the legate at Gloucester Abbey on 28 October 1216. Without papal sanction, and with no English bishops to conduct the ceremony, Louis dared not seek coronation as King in rebel-held Westminster.

Magna Carta of 1217 from the Bodleian Library, Oxford, bearing the seals of William Marshal (right) and the legate Guala.

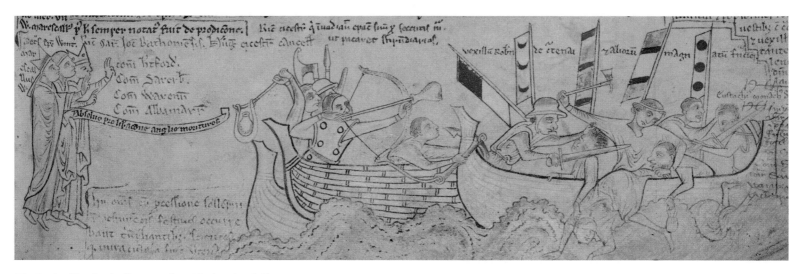

The Battle of Sandwich, illustration from Matthew Paris's Chronica Majora, *1250s.*

Over the next twelve months, the royalist regime inflicted defeats upon Louis and the rebels, most notably in a great battle at Lincoln in May 1217, followed by a naval engagement fought off the coast of Sandwich in Kent. Louis was forced to leave England and the rebels sued for peace. In token of royal magnanimity, in November 1217, Magna Carta was once again reissued. In both 1216 and 1217, considerable modifications were made to the text of the Charter. In particular, those clauses of 1215 that had most threatened royal sovereignty were tacitly removed, above all the sanctions clause that had effectively licensed the barons to make war on the King should the King not implement the barons' wishes.

In 1217, and in accordance with the clauses of 1215 that had required future reform of the forests, the King issued a distinct charter of liberties intended to regulate the royal administration of those parts of England placed under forest law. In 1225, desperate to trade off a reissue of Magna Carta in return for a grant of taxation from his subjects, Henry III once again confirmed both Magna Carta and the Forest Charter, sending exemplifications into each of the counties of England. Archbishop Langton, now restored to favour, played a central role in this process. It was this fourth, 1225 issue of Magna Carta that was to become standard thereafter. A failed peace settlement was thus transformed into a permanent legislative instrument, jealously protected by those whose rights it was believed to guarantee.

Pressure from the county communities, from the knights of the shire and from those whose careers were passed largely outside the confines of the royal court led to yet further reissues throughout the next seventy years. In 1234, for example, after a period in which Peter des Roches sought to restore royal government to many of the arbitrary devices of King John, Henry III guaranteed to uphold Magna Carta as a means of signalling his breach with the controversial policies of his

Initial resistance

Not all of King Henry III's courtiers were enthusiastic supporters of Magna Carta. The French-born bishop of Winchester, Peter des Roches, who had acted as papal commissioner in 1215 to suspend Archbishop Langton, and who after 1216 acted as Henry III's personal tutor, spent much of the next twenty years attempting to restore royal government to the arbitrary authority that it had boasted under King John. Nevertheless, in the country at large, Magna Carta had already begun to acquire totemic status, guaranteeing the King's free subjects against the revival of royal tyranny.

The tomb effigy of Peter des Roches,
in Winchester Cathedral.

Above: 1225 issue of Magna Carta, originally housed at Lacock Abbey, Wiltshire. Above right: Forest Charter of the same year.

minister. Three years later, in 1237, the King made similar promises, this time distributed in the form of a supplement to Magna Carta, county by county. All told, between 1225 and Henry III's death in 1272, the King promised on nearly a dozen occasions to uphold the terms of both Magna Carta and the Forest Charter. In 1253, this was accompanied by a solemn sentence of excommunication, sanctioned by the Pope. The year 1253 was the first in which we can be certain that Magna Carta was proclaimed to the realm at large not only in Latin and French but in the English language of the 'common' people. The role of the clergy here further embedded the idea that Magna Carta was not just a secular instrument but something central to the constitution of the English Church. Henceforth, 'the charters of liberties' were preserved not only in the books of statutes compiled by common lawyers, but in the more important of English canon law collections.

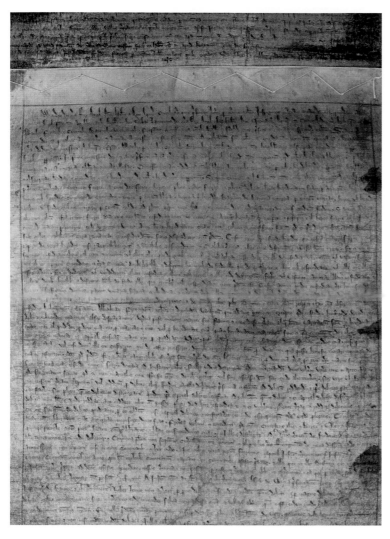

Statute Roll of 1297, containing the first enrolment of Magna Carta.

Only in 1225 and again in 1265, when the 1225 charter was reissued at the height of the regime of Simon de Montfort, effectively with the King under close baronial arrest, do we have certain evidence that the text of Magna Carta itself was sent into the counties under the King's own seal. For the most part, the King's commitment to uphold Magna Carta involved not the physical distribution of full texts, but the issue of letters promising renewal and respect for the Charter's terms. Nonetheless, by the 1260s, so many such promises had been extorted from the King that it was virtually inconceivable that Henry III or his successors could in any way seek to annul Magna Carta. Visitors to Magna Carta today are often perplexed by the fact that so many

'original' Magna Cartas are reported to survive. They can be viewed not just in London, but in Hereford, Lincoln, Durham, Oxford, in the borough archives of the small Kentish town of Faversham, and even, thanks to sales in modern times, in Washington and Canberra. Only four of these documents come from the Magna Carta of 1215 issued by King John. Most come from subsequent issues: a single example from 1216 (now in Durham), four from 1217, four from 1225, four from 1297, and five (or possibly six) from 1300. Set against the four 'original' Magna Cartas issued in the name of King John, far more were issued by Henry III (nine exemplars) or Edward I (nine or ten).

The last two issues, of 1297 and 1300, were intended to buy support for Edward I, King John's grandson, in the midst of expenditure on foreign warfare that had provoked baronial and popular outcry. They are nonetheless significant since it was the 1297 issue that was the first to be copied onto the chancery's official 'Statute Roll'. In the process, it became the text thereafter treated as definitive under English law. The 1297 Magna Carta purported merely to recite the text of 1225, but did so from a defective copy in which the distinction between the 'reliefs' payable by earls or barons (£100 versus 100 marks), elided at Runnymede, was once again reasserted. In this way, an editorial 'mistake' entered English law. The 1297 charter was issued by the King's ministers governing England during Edward I's absence in Flanders. It was therefore authenticated with a royal seal of absence. To repair this anomaly, the Charter was reissued, in identical terms, in 1300, this time under Edward's great seal. This would appear to be the last occasion that Magna Carta was distributed as a fully fledged charter under the King's seal. From 1300, kings were content merely to confirm their general adherence to the Charter, without reciting its clauses in full.

Political debate, meanwhile, had moved on. In the 1230s, particular significance attached to the right of the King to annul his own charters, a problem only ineffectively addressed in Magna Carta clause 61. By the 1250s, it was the right of the King to control his own expenditure and patronage that was of principal concern, problems only partially addressed by Magna Carta's already archaic terminology. In 1297, the reissue of Magna Carta had been accompanied by a pledge of future reform, the so-called 'Confirmation of the Charters', written in French, specifically conceding that there should be no taxation granted without communal assent: no taxation without representation,

The 1297 Magna Carta now housed in Canberra, Australia (see pages 164–6).

a rallying cry not just in 1297 but for generations as yet unborn.

All of these later disputes touched upon subjects inherent to Magna Carta but in circumstances that demanded new remedies. Magna Carta meanwhile had been transformed from failed peace, to law, and thence into legend. It is to the legend that we must now turn. So far, we have attempted to supply a context and a narrative for Magna Carta's emergence. We must now place ourselves in the hands of other experts to explain why Magna Carta continued to matter into the later middle ages, to Britain's Stuart and Hanoverian kings, to the Victorians, to America and other English-speaking nations, and ultimately to all today concerned with liberty and the rule of law.

Chapter Six

Magna Carta in the Later Middle Ages

Anthony Musson

Know ye that we to the honour of God and of holy Church, and to the profit of all our realm, have granted for us and our heirs, that the Great Charter of Liberties and the Charter of the Forest, which were made by common assent of all the realm, in the time of King Henry our father, shall be kept in every point without breach.

Edward I's Confirmation of Charters (1297)

Magna Carta retained significance for contemporaries during the later Middle Ages. Whilst the immediate historical context, actors and circumstances altered over time, the situation in which monarchs repeatedly found themselves – in need of money – did not. Their relationship with various communities, financially and judicially, became flashpoints for both constitutional/parliamentary action and 'popular' upheaval. Indeed, the way royal revenues were obtained, the uses to which they were allegedly put (rewards and bribes) and their ultimate purpose (seemingly in furtherance of dynastic ambitions in Scotland and France) left questions as to how such policies amounted to (in the jargon of the time) 'the common profit of our people'. The root of dissatisfaction lay in the King's discretion, his favouring of certain individuals and his arbitrary treatment of others. Moreover, the strategies and policies adopted by individual monarchs translated into broader issues concerning due process in the law, including renewed sensitivities to judgements of treason and the treatment of property rights. Such controversies brought justice centre stage in politics with national implications. Magna Carta was continually looked to symbolically for guarantees as to royal conduct. According to the anonymous Worcester Annalist the consensus amongst the leading

Presentation of the Statutes of England *to Richard II, from a late 14th-century manuscript of the work.*

barons gathered in Parliament in 1300 was that 'when we have secure possession of our forests and of our liberties, often promised to us, then we will willingly give a twentieth, so that the folly of the Scots may be dealt with'. Magna Carta's legal status, though, however borderline or ambiguous technically, was regarded by contemporaries as akin to legislation and even referred to in the late fifteenth century as the 'laudable statute of Magna Carta'.

The Great Charter as authority

For lawyers, it was from the late thirteenth and early fourteenth century that Magna Carta took on the mantle of the pre-eminent statute of the realm. Symbolically placed at the head of their bespoke volumes of statutes (which usually included other legal material such as treatises and/or registers of writs), it provided an initial reference point preceding the great legislative canon promulgated by Edward I. Although the 1215 original or the 1225 version might have been expected to head up these collections, as the legislative line-up proceeds chronologically and normally includes the Provisions of Merton (1235) and the Statute of Marlborough (1267), it is in fact the text of Edward I's 1297 confirmation that was habitually copied in preference to earlier versions. Magna Carta was equally included by late thirteenth- and early fourteenth-century copyists in manuscript collections of earlier legal texts, intending it either as the apotheosis of a tradition of early English laws (that included the Anglo-Saxon *Institutio Cnuti* and the *Leges Edwardi* as well as the late twelfth-century treatise *Glanvill*) or as an extension of that tradition.

Not surprisingly, Magna Carta played an important part in legal education. Surviving moot questions, problems drawn from particular statutes, indicate that disputation on areas of law espoused by the Great Charter was a theme favoured by lawyers, probably members of the emergent Inns of Court, as early as the 1340s. Although surviving examples do not focus on the 'due process' clauses (c.39, c.40), they query and offer solutions to a number of technical issues. These include problems presumably of contemporary legal interest such as whether a lord, who does not obtain the wardship of an infant who is under age at his ancestor's death, may distrain and avow for relief when the heir comes of age (c.3), the construction of c.31 and the extent of a woman's entitlement to an appeal of felony in particular circumstances

Chaucer's Sergeant of the Law, from the Ellesmere manuscript of the Canterbury Tales, *a famous representation of a 14th-century lawyer.*

(c.34). Readings or lectures on individual clauses of Magna Carta by benchers (senior members) of the Inns of Court and Chancery became common during the fifteenth century and beyond, and although precise dates and topics for readings are sparse, records from Henry VI's reign onwards show that all clauses were covered by readers at least once over the intervening years. The notes or texts of some of these survive, including one on tourns and franchises given in about 1475 by William Catesby, a legal adviser to Richard III, who was executed in the change of regime ushered in after the Battle of Bosworth in 1485.

Dissemination and discussion of Magna Carta's provisions was not restricted to the legal profession; public proclamation enabled it to reach a broader audience. In 1404, the bishop of Rochester produced a copy of Magna Carta and read it during a parliamentary debate on what he considered were unlawful royal plans for clerical taxation.

Emphasis on its (envisaged) accessibility, if not applicability to all, was facilitated by transcripts sent to sheriffs to be read out 'before the people four times a year' (at Michaelmas, Christmas, Easter and Midsummer). Regular recitation of Magna Carta in the county court, the shire's prime meeting point, combined with recitation of the Statute of Winchester of 1285 (measures for local policing), afforded attendees in the localities a firm basis of the key tenets in the English judicial system. Following parliamentary assent new legislation, some of it citing or endorsing Magna Carta, was also proclaimed in towns and cities, at fairs and markets, and in the countryside at important crossroads. The language of proclamation equally assisted its absorption. We know from chronicles and the instructions sent out to sheriffs that Magna Carta and other statutes were not read out solely in Latin (or necessarily in French), they were translated by the crier himself and proclaimed (in the local dialect) for the benefit of people for whom English was their native (*patria lingua*) or mother tongue (*materna lingua*). This offered a broader range for its reception and comprehension.

The raising of legal consciousness at all levels through these methods can be observed in the citation of Magna Carta in litigation. Indeed, the Great Charter had immediate significance for anyone involved in legal actions for whom its clauses were either perceived as a source of law or at least cited rhetorically as compelling justification for remedy. One early fourteenth-century petitioner, Thomas de Fynmer, for instance, though lacking precise reference to Magna Carta, accorded it a legislative basis when he stated that it was '*ordained by statute* that no man be ousted from his free tenement'. Another, Robert de Thorp of Suffolk, desiring remedy 'according to law and according to points of the Great Charter' pleaded several distinct 'points' of the Charter during the course of his lengthy petition. Entitlements to wardships and marriages 'according to the form of the Great Charter' were requested too, while supplications to the King citing it directly were made by those who had been deprived of their free tenement, who had erroneously been charged puture, whose lands held in wardship had suffered waste, and by a number of widows, like Joan de Siggston, anxious to secure the customary and reasonable share of her husband's goods. Like Domesday Book, copies or extracts of which were often called into court by judges for consultation, Magna Carta needed to be correctly interpreted. In responding to a petition of 1307

Henry III on a canopied throne beneath the title 'Magna Carta', from a late 14th-century manuscript of the Statutes of England.

addressed to the King and council by the widowed Joan de Besilles (concerning inheritance of a manor that had been held in chief of the King by her late husband by petty serjeanty, that was required for maintenance of her child but was now in the King's hand), it was specified that the Great Charter itself was to be consulted – literally 'viewed' – by the earls, barons and chancery clerks before a decision could be made.

The name Magna Carta characterizes its length as a document, not just its importance, and sight of the Great Charter through the public display of copies (in churches, for example) as well as hearing it being

The death of
Wat Tyler at
Smithfield, London,
during the Peasants'
Revolt of 1381,
from Chroniques
de France et
d'Angleterre,
c.1460–80.

read out underlined its physical nature and a sense of its authority. Hearing it, albeit at regular intervals, rather than reading it personally at leisure, brought the possibility of inaccuracies and misunderstandings. For some the capacity to digest it fully may have been limited to certain memorable clauses or the gist of what was presented. The enigmatic demand by the rebels of 1381, for 'no law but the law of Winchester', may exemplify this. Even though the rebel peasants never mentioned Magna Carta itself, in 'the law of Winchester' they certainly invoked a particular paradigm of values

accorded special status in their eyes and analogous to Magna Carta, which if read in conjunction with the rest of Wat Tyler's demands included the abolition of outlawry and serfdom so that 'all should be free and of one status'.

Whether understood precisely or not, individuals and communities alike based their claims for legal remedy from the King on the 'purport' or 'tenor' of the Great Charter and the rhetoric of 'law and reason'. The city of London's 'franchises and ancient customs' were enshrined in Magna Carta, a fact explicitly mentioned by its citizens

Domesday Book, a possible icon of freedom for the rebels of 1381.

The 'law of Winchester'

The source of 'the law of Winchester' can only be speculated. The rebels of 1381 may have been referring obliquely to the Statute of Winchester, but it is just possible they meant Cnut's *Winchester Code*, laws decreed at Winchester in the eleventh century that like their thirteenth-century counterpart contain many provisions of fundamental importance to the local community and the operation of justice, and significantly for their apparent ideals it begins: 'I will that just laws be established and every unjust law carefully suppressed and that every injustice be weeded out and rooted up with all possible diligence from this country. And let God's justice be exalted; and henceforth let everyman, both poor and rich, be esteemed worthy of folk-right and let just dooms be doomed to him.' Whether Wat Tyler and his associates were aware of this ancient code, incidents in Bury St Edmunds and St Albans

during the revolt involving demands for the most ancient charters (reputedly of Cnut and Offa respectively) demonstrate that the rebel leaders had a reverence for documents evidencing ancient customs and privileges.

Another alternative is that they were referring to Domesday Book, also known as the 'roll of Winchester' or 'book of Winchester' because it originally resided in the royal treasury there. Domesday Book, the result of William the Conqueror's attempt to provide a written record of property-holding rights, was regarded (erroneously) by many as a statute and was at least quasi-law in the minds of the many litigants who cited it as source of proof in property disputes as

well as villeins who used it to assert that their manor had the privileges of 'ancient desmesne' status. Requests for exemplification of entries in Domesday crescendoed during the fourteenth century and climaxed in 1377 when peasants from at least forty villages attempted to use it to obtain their freedom. In the context of the Peasants' Revolt four years later, Domesday Book may have been viewed as an iconic 'law' legitimating claims to freedom. In many ways, however, the precise source does not matter: they were invoking a symbolic body of law associated with the old royal capital, albeit of unspecified date or provisions, popularly perceived to be a framework of fundamental principles.

('as it is in the Great Charter') in complaints made both individually and communally to the Crown, but were also employed by the men of Yarmouth, anxious to be able to proclaim their usages, and the tinners of Cornwall, who argued the benefits of Magna Carta should apply to the whole realm. Indeed, reason and history were used by numerous communities to justify their continued enjoyment of freedoms and privileges. In a case in the King's Bench in 1384, for example, the reeve and burgesses of Padstow sought to uphold their privilege to hear contracts relating to maritime matters on grounds that since the Great

Charter of the liberties of England acknowledged that the barons of the Cinque Ports and all other seaports are allowed all their ancient liberties and free customs, so too should Padstow, an ancient Cornish town and a port where their ancestors from time immemorial had used and enjoyed certain franchises (including the right to hear all pleas pertaining to maritime law). Even peasants and villeins appear to have grasped the significance. In the early fourteenth century, the customary tenants of the manor of Bocking in Essex articulated their complaints against a new bailiff in terms of breach of customary

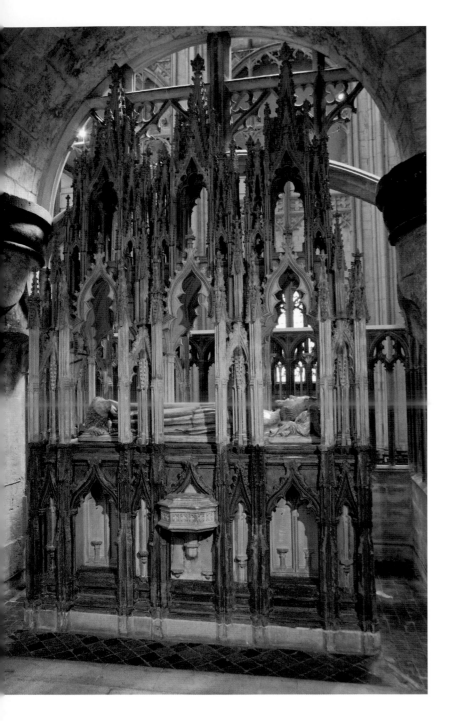

Edward II's tomb, in Gloucester Cathedral.

there have been no people of so free a condition as they were in the time of the Princes and all say thus'.

Concern for upholding Magna Carta was reflected in the phraseology of those petitioning the King for redress of grievances either personally or as part of a broader group and wider agenda. The archbishop of York, William Melton, for instance, complained in 1330 that 'duresses' caused by the conduct of the royal bailiff in Hull were 'against the law of the land and the Great Charter which the King is bound to maintain and keep'. Similarly, employing this rhetoric in asserting claims to privileges and franchises, the city of York prefaced a series of petitions concerning obstructions on the rivers Ouse and Ure (1315–22) with statements that the Great Charter of franchises of England in all its points should be firmly maintained and kept. The burgesses of Oxford in 1328, too, felt that grants made to the University were 'contrary to their liberties, the law of the land, and the Great Charter' as well as prejudicial to the Crown. This rhetorical device or formula was now arguably an integral, if not essential feature of the discourse of complaint.

The rolls of Parliament and various statutes, ordinances and treaties of the period similarly demonstrate that Magna Carta was enshrined in the lexicon of political/constitutional debate between the King and his subjects. During Edward II's reign accusations of infringement of the Great Charter and the corresponding need for its observance

practice, the unreasonableness of new demands and framed assessment of their liability for amercement as being 'by their peers according to the extent of their trespass'. While the phraseology and language of the petition to their manorial lord suggests they may have obtained legal assistance, they clearly regarded Magna Carta as applicable to them as they claimed the steward's behaviour was 'against all reason and the Great Charter'. In Wales a group of unfree tenants who petitioned for the restoration of a mill and confirmation of usages enjoyed before the conquest of Wales (1282–3) felt justified in doing so since 'in all Wales

The Guildhall and river Ouse, York.

Below: The execution of Hugh Despenser the Younger.
Right: The coronation of Edward III. Illuminations from
a manuscript of Jean Froissart's Chronicles, *1470s.*

(along with his coronation oath) were continually levelled. Indeed, invocation became not only a mantra, a phrase repeatedly used by those seeking to restrain the King's actions, but was symbolically utilized at times by the King himself. The final clause of the Ordinances of 1311 (restraining Edward II), for example, required Magna Carta to be upheld in all its points. Yet the King, in objecting to the Ordinances, contended they were contrary to Magna Carta and his coronation oath. Edward II also took a stand against the barons' demand for banishment of the younger Despenser in 1321 on the basis of a whole raft of legal principle: Magna Carta, the common law, his coronation oath and (even) the Ordinances. At his trial in 1326 Despenser's traitorous behaviour was admonished using the same rhetorical phrases.

Confirmation of Magna Carta became a marked point of principle in a series of parliamentary petitions submitted by the commons to Edward III from the 1330s to the 1360s, which formed the basis of the so-called 'six statutes' identified in the sixteenth and seventeenth centuries as important glosses on Magna Carta. Certain key points of significance to the rights of the King's subjects, those providing due process under the law, notably c.39, 'No free man will be taken or imprisoned or disseised or outlawed or exiled or in any way ruined … save by the lawful judgement of his peers and/or by the law of the land,' and c.40, 'To no one shall we sell, to no one shall we deny or delay right or justice,' were emphasized partly in response to certain relevant high-profile cases involving treasonous behaviour, and partly a reflection of judicial concerns about procedural matters regarding the drawing up of indictments and the trial of prisoners in gaols. Although villeins were not included in the remit of the original wording ('no free man'), by the mid-fourteenth century this had somehow subtly altered to 'no man'. Whether or not it had always been implicit, it was not until 1442 that the omission of women from the scope of c.39 was broached. As a result of the case of Lady Eleanor Cobham, who was

Westminster becomes the seat of justice

Over the course of the thirteenth century clause 17 (prohibiting common pleas following the King) had been glossed to signify that suits should ordinarily be heard in a fixed place, in other words, in Westminster Hall, and thereby established the permanent venue of the central courts. Although for short periods during the fourteenth century, the Exchequer and common bench needed to be closer to the royal household and so were removed to the headquarters of operations against the Scots in York (as had occurred during the campaign against the Welsh in 1277), complaints relating to c.17 were comparatively rare. Richard II's rebuilding of the Great Hall in Westminster Palace in the 1390s provided the symbolic confirmation that Westminster was the preferred and permanent location for English justice.

The hammerbeam roof of Westminster Hall introduced under Richard II, illustration from The Microcosm of London, *1808.*

accused of treason, but had never been brought to trial in a secular court, the lacuna was remedied by extending to 'ladies of great estate' the right of trial before the judges and lords.

Against this backdrop should be set a judicial system that in the fourteenth and fifteenth centuries was evolving to meet royal requirements in dispelling problems of public order and enforcing penalties against criminal behaviour as well as meeting the needs of growing numbers of private suits brought by a litigious population at the encouragement of a burgeoning legal profession. Magna Carta played a crucial role both in facilitating and regulating the changes that occurred in central and local justice. In levying fines on local communities during the inquests of the 1340s, for instance, the royal justices were warned of the dangers of breaching Magna Carta.

A shift in the balance of judicial power towards the local communities also occurred during the fourteenth century with the rise of the justices of the peace. This crystallized an enduring ideal of local justice that was already enshrined in Magna Carta (and restated in the Statute of Westminster II of 1285) in the association of knights of the shire with the itinerant justices in hearing assizes in the shires. Under the *Articuli super Cartas* the keepers of the peace (forerunners of the JPs) were accorded the power to try offences against the charters, while local enforcement of the Crown's responsibility under Magna Carta for weights and measures was also achieved through the inclusion of jurisdiction in the commissions to justices of labourers in 1357 and then the 1361 peace commissions. A century later, concern that sheriffs and their underlings were arresting and imprisoning innocent people led to the statute of 1461, which ensured that indictments taken at tourns were sent to the JPs, substantially eroding the sheriff's jurisdiction over criminal matters and effectively transferring it to JPs. While the balance offered by a local magistracy gave communities a degree of autonomy in their dealings with the Crown, the Great Charter nevertheless was held up as a frame of reference for the frequency of judicial proceedings, especially with regard to the meeting of the county courts and the sheriff's tourns. The optimistic stipulation in 1215 that assizes should be held on a quarterly basis, though never fully realized (following the reorganization of the circuits in 1328–30 the recommended frequency, confirming Westminster II, was three times a year) was nevertheless adopted as the model for the timing of peace sessions.

Magna Carta illuminated

Scenes in miniature contained within the illuminated initial letter of texts of Magna Carta in manuscript books of statutes dating from the fourteenth and fifteenth centuries provide an opportunity to examine perceptions of the Charter through a different lens. Each scene, a cocktail of the artist's (and commissioning patron's) imagination, perceptions, historical sensitivity, factual knowledge, aspirations and ideals, offers an interpretation or contextualization of contemporary constitutional discourse in visual format. Owners of these books ranged from lawyers and administrators to ecclesiastical and lay landowners, civic corporations and merchants. Most of the Magna Carta miniatures simply portray the sole figure of a king enclosed within the initial letter. Medieval people were familiar with royal images and understood their associated symbolism both in an ecclesiastical context (symbolizing God or biblical monarchs) or in the secular world (serving as an icon of royal government). The King should be viewed in conjunction with the written text, however, to which he is normally looking or pointing (either with a raised index finger or a sword). His gesture not only serves as a directional device for the reader, but can be regarded as underlining the text's importance and endorsing its authority.

The Great Charter itself is depicted in some of the scenes, either as a parchment document affixed with a green seal or in the form of a book with a green cover. The symbolism associated with its physical appearance is significant. First, the colour is probably not immaterial, for green, notably the green wax of Exchequer bureaucracy, has connotations of the exercise of royal authority. Indeed, a number of clauses in Magna Carta deal with matters of finance and judicial procedure. Secondly, as was common in medieval art, representation of the sealed document provides visual shorthand for its recitation or proclamation (which usually accompanied presentation of charters and, as mentioned above, had its basis in historical reality as by royal decree Magna Carta was regularly proclaimed in the shires). Furthermore, the seal itself symbolizes the solemnity of the grant and corresponds too with the seal that was physically attached to the Charter, the wax impression being an overt (and continuing) reminder of the King's will and consent to its provisions. Finally, in some scenes the Charter is demonstrably being presented to (or handed over by) the

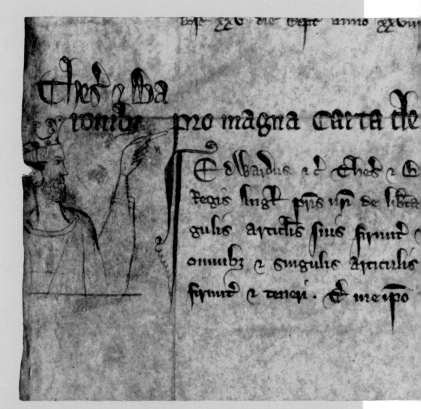

Authority in miniature

An Exchequer memoranda roll of 1300 has the marginal figure of a bearded and crowned Edward I pointing to a request that the barons of the Exchequer should observe the clauses of Magna Carta. The formal iconic qualities and rigidity of the kingly figure in the margin of the roll here and in the miniatures of initials offer gravitas to the portrayal. The picture is emblematic of royal judicial authority. It conveys the notion that it is *his* law (royal law) that is enshrined in the words of the text and given effect through *his* person (and likewise the apparatus of justice he controls). In this there are clear parallels with royal charters issued to individuals and institutions, the scene in the opening initial and overall design of which were intended to convey in visual terms their charter's authority and legal effect.

niã nouis supueniëtib' causis nouis ë remedijs succurrë
ccirco ego bartholomeˀ brixiëfis côfidës de magnificëtia
toris apparatū decretoʒ duxi i meliˀ reformādū: nõ de
endo alicui nec attribuendo mihi glofas quas nõ feci:
fectū folūmodo:ubi correctio necessaria videbaf: uˀ ppˀ

de ap.significauit i fi. ʒ extra de pben. cū iã dudū: ʒ exˀ
in primis ʒ.ff.de ꝑdi. ʒ de.falfa ʒ.ff.de fta.ho.fūma.
Difcrepant.non tamen fūt côtrarie.nã transire p ag
humana phibet.sed phibitio ʒ pmiffio non funt contra
ifidelem dimitti:apoftolus phibet:ut.xxviij.q.i.iam nu

Jn noie fancte et idiuidue trinitatis
Jncipit côcordia difcordantiū cano
num: ac primū de iure pftitutionis

pant : quoniam alie aliis gentibus
placët.§as lex diuina eft: ius lex hu
mana . Tranfire per agrum alienū

Miniature from a 15th-century manuscript of the Decretum of Gratian, showing the presentation of the work to the Pope.

King or raised aloft by an archbishop in ceremonial fashion, with judges, lords and other courtiers in attendance. Visual and aural elements thus combine with the written text to accord significance and legitimacy to it as well as bearing witness to the presentation event through a pseudo-historical re-enactment scenario. The images, therefore, underline the Charter (and the statute book in which it is contained) both as a physical entity and as having a continuing psychological and legal impact.

The format of this opening initial would have resonances in a wider context for those who possessed other genres of illuminated manuscript, for in some ways the scene is an iconographical construct: it is reminiscent of (or a variation on) the presentation, a common motif at the preface to volumes commissioned by or dedicated to a royal or lordly patron. The seated patron is shown being handed and

graciously accepting the book in question, whether it is a chronicle, romance or treatise. There is a more constitutional precedent for this presentational scene in volumes of canon and Roman civil law: the introductory miniature to the *Decretales* shows the text's compiler presenting it to Pope Gregory IX, while the *Codex*, the product of Roman jurists' codification, is received by the Emperor Justinian. In these scenes there is an implication that Pope and Emperor, respectively, by accepting the volume of laws are approving and certifying the authenticity of its texts. This motif has its precedents in books of English statutes, too, for example in one late fourteenth-century volume a kneeling cleric is presenting a book to an enthroned Richard II. In another volume the King even appears (from his pointing gesture and the scribbling scribe) to be dictating the law. The observer may query, however, whether the book represents something

Thomas Hoccleve presents his Regement of Princes *to the Prince of Wales, the future Henry V, c.1411–13.*

Comment le roy richard
reʃigna la couronne z ʃon
romulme angleterre en
et nouuelles
vindrentau
duc de lancaʃ
tre q le roy
richaut le demandoit et

la main au conte derby
duc de lancaʃtre
Chupittre lxxvi
moult doulcement et ʃe
humilia treʃgrandemēt
enuers lui comme cellui
qui ʃe veoit et ʃentoit en
grant danngier et lui

The deposition of Richard II,
1399, illumination from
Jean Froissart's Chroniques
de France et d'Angleterre,
c.1460–80.

The politics of illumination

In the case of late thirteenth- or early fourteenth-century volumes the constitutional crisis leading to the reissue of Magna Carta in 1297 and 1300 was then still, for some, within living memory, as too, were the events leading to Edward II's deposition. This gave the images contemporary political resonance and, because of the provenance of at least one particular book, the opportunity to influence future constitutional affairs. The book in question (now MS 12 in the Harvard Law Library) is believed to have been a present from Philippa of Hainault to Prince Edward on the occasion of their betrothal in 1326. The initial 'E' of Edward I's confirmation of Magna Carta in this volume comprises a double scene (one above the middle bar of the letter and one below it): the upper picture, a king seated on a throne, holding a book in his left hand, supported by archbishops and laymen, may represent the original issuing of Magna Carta under John; the lower picture is similar

in composition, but presumably depicts its reissue under Edward I, itself the outcome of another bout of constitutional debate. The image cannot have been formulated without regard to recent political events and was given greater clarity of meaning by Edward II's deposition in 1327. It would, therefore, have held particular significance not just for contemporaries who had lived through the constitutional upheaval, but for the new King himself, whose very position as monarch lay in the hands of the archbishops, magnates and judges portrayed alongside the King. For viewers of Magna Carta initials in the late fifteenth-century statute books the two centuries immediately following 1297 were not without constitutional upheaval too and must be read in light of the deposition of Richard II in 1399, couched in terms of his disregard for Magna Carta and use of the royal prerogative to flout the rule of law, and in turn that of Henry VI in 1461 who, in complete contrast to Richard II, failed in his duties of kingship because he exercised no political will at all.

promulgated by the English King as just lawgiver (supported by the great men deployed alongside him), or in fact signifies royal concessions and a guarantee of royal behaviour won by the people (represented by those who are pictured holding it or gathered near it). Royal confirmation of the laws of the realm was expected of a monarch at his coronation. Yet, a straightforward transference of the concept of the King as benevolent lawgiver, certifying the authenticity of texts, as in the Justinian and papal models, does not sit well with the historical context of Magna Carta as coincident with, and a product of, acute constitutional crisis.

The monarch's constitutional position and his royal obligations are highlighted in a number of miniatures. Contemporary responses to the representations may have varied according to how Magna Carta was understood by different sections of medieval society and how it came to be reinterpreted over time. While Magna Carta itself is not explicit about grounds for 'deposition', a coronation scene (depicted in an image accompanying the Charter) focuses attention on the King's oath, taken during the ceremony, to uphold the laws and customs of the realm. The image of a king being crowned by two archbishops and apparently receiving Magna Carta from them could thus be interpreted as representing a compact between the King and his people and a potent reminder that the King was not above the law.

The pictures employed in Magna Carta texts on one level are simply illustrating aspects of kingship, law and justice, but in their juxtaposition of different representational elements in fact insinuate a range of possible meanings thereby manipulating the reader's response to the image. One fourteenth-century volume of statutes, for example, contains solely images of religious icons in the illuminated initials. Magna Carta is represented by the Madonna and Child, perhaps linking the symbolism of 'the Word of God made flesh' and the Charter's concern with 'reason' (via twin meanings of 'logos'). It is perhaps surprising, however, to find that some of the fourteenth- and fifteenth-century law books adopt an apparently antithetical stance to the King and the law. In the illuminated manuscript tradition, the margins, which were populated with images of hybrid animals and birds and other grotesques, were regarded as inhabiting the informal space of the page (the space framing the text, an efflorescence of both the conscious and the subconscious mind). In the case of law books, the appearance of potentially subversive or anti-authoritarian elements

The King's oath to uphold the laws and customs of the realm, symbolized by the sealed parchment (Magna Carta) handed to him at his coronation, from a mid-14th-century manuscript of statutes.

may represent the disorder of the imagination vying with the ordered world not just of the written word, but the legal text itself. Their inclusion suggests that the patron/illuminator wanted the viewer to engage in a more sophisticated manner, perhaps within an alternative discourse on the nature of authority through images implying criticism of the monarch, the prevailing political regime or the judicial system.

An interloper, for example, constituting a deliberate intrusion into the space occupied by the King, appears in several Magna Carta initials. The image disturbs and challenges the viewer's response to the traditional regal scene. In one, a head, looking upwards at the King, pokes into the initial from the decorated border. Elsewhere in the same collection a man dressed in blue with a blue feather in his cap inhabits the left-hand corner of the miniature and is pointing at the King with his index finger. Is he mimicking the King's actions (and thereby

A threat to the rule of law? Figure brandishing a cudgel and looking towards the King, from an early 14th-century manuscript of statutes.

Effrontery and symbolism: a figure baring his bottom below the text of Magna Carta, from an early 14th-century manuscript of statutes.

endorsing them) or is he poking fun at the King (a pun on *iudex/index*) and judging *him* in effect? In another, a figure with a red hood in the left-hand margin grasps the bottom rung of the 'E'. He too is looking up towards the King, but this individual is brandishing a cudgel. He may represent opposition to (or a threat to) the rule of law that the King is seeking to impose through his statutes. This may even be a pictorial reference to the so-called 'baston' or club-wielding gangs made up of outlaws and returned soldiers (also pictured in certain chronicles) that the notorious 'trailbaston' commissions of the early fourteenth century were issued to combat.

The most outrageous or shocking for our twenty-first-century sensibility for its effrontery (though medieval readers would not have baulked quite so much at the obscenity) is the scene below the text of Magna Carta in one early fourteenth-century statute book in which a figure has pulled down his breeches and is baring his bottom. On the one hand this could be taken simply as a comical, if somewhat inappropriate vignette, in which the King and by implication, the constitutional importance of Magna Carta, are mocked profanely. However, there is a deeper symbolism here, which goes beyond this particular illustration and links it with other iconographic and literary contexts, notably the contest of wits known as *The Dialogue of Solomon and Marcolf*. The paradigm of wisdom and equity, King Solomon, is pitted against a foolish but cunning peasant, Marcolf. *The Dialogue*, which appears in iconography in England from at least the early fourteenth century and survives in verse form in manuscripts from the early fifteenth century, has its origin in scholastic disputation and initially takes the form of a 'discourse of opposites', a dialectic in which different sources of authority are set against each other. They move on to a series of riddles set by Solomon, which Marcolf proves empirically, rather than using logic. Finally, Marcolf sets Solomon some proverbs, which he is unable to fathom, possibly because of their absurdity. In the course of their encounter, Marcolf makes a number of retorts or repudiations with relevant legal or jurisdictional connotations that could relate to the figure in the statute book, among them: 'A naked ars no man kan robbe or dispoyle' and 'An opyn arse hath no lord'.

The 'laudable statute of Magna Carta' was many things to a great variety of people during the later Middle Ages. It operated on political, legal, linguistic and visual levels. As Sir James Holt observed, the Great

King or fool?

A link with the *Dialogue* could also explain another unusual illustration of Magna Carta, a version executed for sergeant-at-law Thomas Pygot (d. 1519) in the mid-fifteenth century. The King is wholly absent from the miniature and has been replaced by someone who from his familiar dress resembles a jester or court fool. The fool figure has a bird on his arm and his legs are either side of the bar of the initial letter as if riding it, mirroring depictions of Marcolf riding a goat with an owl or hawk on his arm, the complex answer to one of the proverbs he sets Solomon. Marcolf's challenges make the wise King seem foolish and the fool wise (a trope we are more familiar with from Shakespeare). Indeed, Marcolf himself states: 'He is holden wise that reputeth himself a fool.' The prevalence of this conceit makes it likely that the inherent irrationality highlighted by the image may thus be read as a clever visual pun that in turn signals the deeply held notion that the King ought to rule in accord with reason. This is further underlined by the damning retort from Marcolf: 'There is no King where no law is,' issued when Solomon refuses to honour his promise of reward (to make him rich and have a name above all others in the realm). In this initial there is no King, only a fool. This in turn has contemporary resonances with Henry VI's failure of kingship and manifest lack of authority.

Charter's significance lies both in its status as a constitutional document and its existence as an argument. The former is on the one hand tangible parchment venerated in the churches and museums in which it resides, yet characterized by 'repeated interpretation' by historical actors in the context of a particular age; the latter is intangible, but sustained, given substance and in turn revitalized as a result of the 'continuous element of political thinking' that underlies it. Texts invoking or referencing Magna Carta (chronicles, statutes, the Parliament rolls, private petitions, readings and moots of the Inns of Court together with the records of cases appearing in the law courts) provide a significant insight into the Charter's political and legal influence and evidence of its practical application during the later Middle Ages. Those who used it did so as part of the language of complaint, adopting a rhetorical tone that mixed deference with expectation of remedy. They are invaluable sources for its reception by a range of persons within medieval society and the applicability of its clauses to (or extension of their original meaning to include) a variety of circumstances. Its essence and importance, however, were not solely the province of the written word: Magna Carta's significance was underpinned by its communication both aurally and visually. The construction of images in the statute books reveals the complexity of contemporary political thought and the significance of the visual as a means of conveying it. The subversive images are the product of a dialectic about political and judicial authority. Arguably, wisdom/reason is found to be incomplete without its antithesis. In turn, while the images provide a positive underscoring of royal authority, they also underline the overriding importance to contemporaries of good governance and the qualities required of a just king.

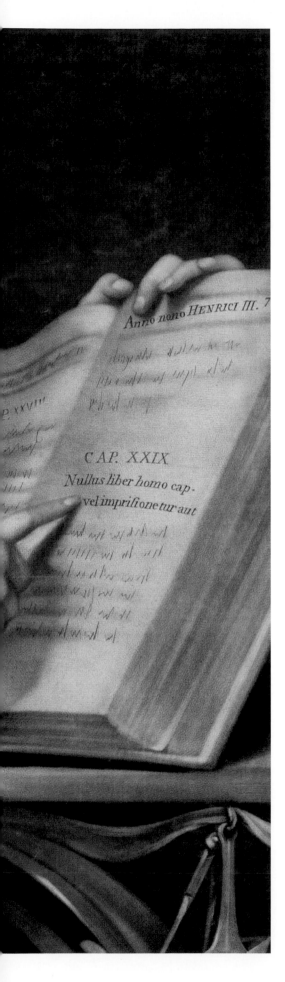

Arthur Beardmore teaching the principles of Magna Carta to his son, engraving by Robert Edge Pine, 1763–4.

From *Liber Homo* to 'Free-born Englishman': How Magna Carta Became a 'Liberty Document', 1508–1760s

Justin Champion

> *Magna Charta is such a fellow, that he will have no Sovereign.*
>
> Edward Coke, 17 May 1628

Bishop Stubbs, in his profoundly influential *Constitutional History of England* (1875–8), claimed that 'the whole of the constitutional history of England is little more than a commentary on Magna Carta'. If one were forced to identify a historical period when the modern veneration for the document and an appreciation of its significance for conceptions of political and individual freedom and liberty began in earnest, then the seventeenth-century rediscovery of the historical artefact and the powerful elevation of its status to national prominence was a turning point in the reception of the text. In 1500, invoking the authority of Magna Carta might not have meant much to men outside the legal profession; doing so after 1700 would have been appreciated by a public audience that included politicians, pamphleteers and princes.

Over the decades, roughly from the times of Sir Edward Coke (1552–1634) to the turbulence of the 'Wilkes and Liberty' controversies in the 1760s, the fierce contest concerning the reputation and iconic authority of Magna Carta moved from being first embroiled in the battles between kings and parliaments over the nature of law, and then

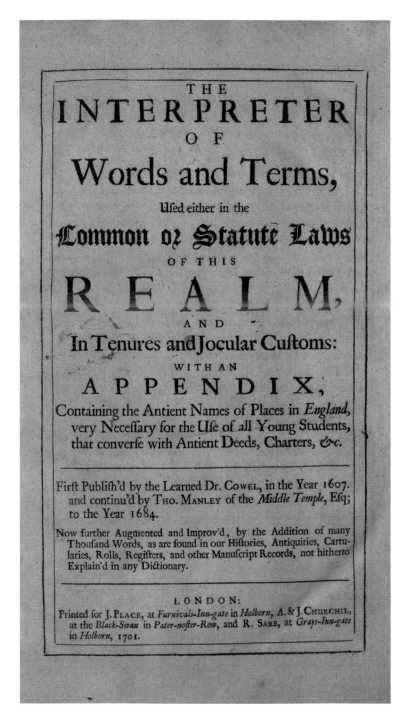

THE
INTERPRETER
OF
Words and Terms,

Uſed either in the

Common oʒ Statute Laws

OF THIS
R E A L M,
AND
In Tenures and Jocular Cuſtoms:

WITH AN
A P P E N D I X,
Containing the Antient Names of Places in *England*,
very Neceſſary for the Uſe of all Young Students,
that converſe with Antient Deeds, Charters, &c.

First Publiſh'd by the Learned Dr. COWEL, in the Year 1607.
and continu'd by THO. MANLEY of the *Middle Temple*, Eſq;
to the Year 1684.

Now further Augmented and Improv'd, by the Addition of many
Thouſand Words, as are found in our Hiſtories, Antiquities, Cartu-
laries, Rolls, Regiſters, and other Manuſcript Records, not hitherto
Explain'd in any Dictionary.

LONDON:
Printed for J. PLACE, at *Furnivals-Inn-gate* in *Holborn*, A. & J. CHURCHIL,
at the *Black-Swan* in *Pater-noſter-Row*, and R. SARE, at *Grays-Inn-gate*
in *Holborn*, 1701.

Title-page of the sixth edition
of Cowell's The Interpreter.

the prerogatives of sovereignty and individual property, through to a set of conflicts between the 'people' and any who claimed the power of government. After the Glorious Revolution of 1688 Magna Carta embodied the core principles of the 'ancient constitution', and was regarded as evidence of the legitimate contractual relationship between government and people. A free British polity, such as that secured in the successful Hanoverian accession after 1714, was built upon the values of personal freedom and property rights derived from Magna Carta, instantiated in the Statutes of the Realm, and reaffirmed in the Bill of Rights (1689) and the Act of Succession (1701). At different times then, different men clothed their claims for political and personal freedom in the universal authority of Magna Carta. The events of 1215 became not simply a legal and historical precedent, but an enduring and almost unchallengeable constitutional symbol or myth.

Sir Edward Coke and the reinterpretation of Magna Carta

Writing in 1607, the civil lawyer John Cowell (1554–1611), in his provocative work *The Interpreter* (a dictionary of English legal definitions), described Magna Carta as 'a charter containing a number of laws ordained the ninth year of *Henry* the third, and confirmed by *Edward* the first'. He continued, 'I reade in Holinshed that King John, to appease his Barons, yielded to laws or articles of government much like to this Great Charter, but we nowe have no auncienter written lawe than this'. Cowell was unusual for his day in that he defended the authority of the monarch and civil law above that of the ancient constitution and common law. Kings had absolute power, even above the law. Parliament served simply to offer counsel to the monarchy. Cowell was not unusual, however, in his belief that Henry III had granted the Charter; the history of the barons extracting constitutional concessions from a tyrannical King John was obscured in this commonplace narrative. The standard chronicles avoided any explicit account of John's troubles in Runnymede meadow, in favour of presenting him as suffering from the predatory and illegitimate attentions of the Papacy. King John was a victim, rather than the butt of constitutional animus. Within a decade or so, the constitutional significance of Magna Carta was prominent in the turbulent contestations between King and Parliament over the rights and liberties

William Hogarth's caricature of John Wilkes, champion of the 'genuine spirit of the Magna Carta', 1763.

Magna Carta propaganda

From the mid-seventeenth century into the nineteenth, the use of representations of Magna Carta in many popular political prints and caricatures was profound – whether being trampled upon by tyrants, or acting as means of support for freedom, or simply identifying the 'good' agents in a scene (with Magna Carta in their pockets, hatbands or hands) the image and words became a public meme of significance. The iconography of Magna Carta invoked, for the various and extensive audiences that consumed such propaganda, a clear set of political principles associated with 'British' liberty, and freedom and resistance to corruption in all forms. In these protean ways, Magna Carta not only became a symbol of the enduring constitutional freedoms of liberty, but also a powerful invocation of the moral right of protest by individuals.

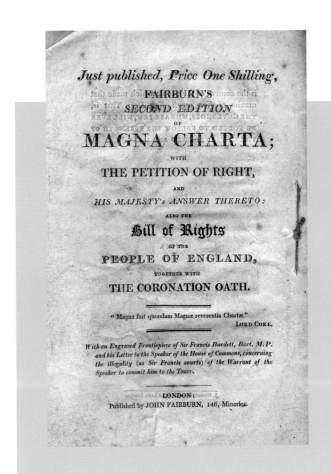

Just published, Price One Shilling,

FAIRBURN'S
SECOND EDITION
OF
MAGNA CHARTA;
WITH
THE PETITION OF RIGHT,
AND
HIS MAJESTY'S ANSWER THERETO:
ALSO THE
Bill of Rights
OF THE
PEOPLE OF ENGLAND,
TOGETHER WITH
THE CORONATION OATH.

"Magna fuit quondam Magnæ reverentia Chartæ."
LORD COKE.

With an Engraved Frontispiece of Sir Francis Burdett, Bart. M.P.
and his Letter to the Speaker of the House of Commons, concerning
the illegality (as Sir Francis asserts) of the Warrant of the
Speaker to commit him to the Tower.

LONDON:
Published by JOHN FAIRBURN, 146, Minories.

Coke and the Stuarts

James I of England (r. 1603–25) complained of Coke's 'exorbitant and extravagant opinions', confiscating his papers and confining him to the Tower of London in 1621. A decade later, after the constitutional crisis which resulted in a reaffirmation of the principles of the Great Charter in the *Petition of Right* (1628), it was rumoured that Coke was preparing 'a book concerning Magna Carta'. Charles I (r. 1625–49), embittered by his treatment in Parliament, forbade the publication, anxious that it 'somewhat may be in prejudice of his prerogative, for Sir Edward is held too great an oracle amongst the people'. In 1634, as Coke expired on his deathbed, his study was searched and some fifty or so manuscripts were confiscated. It was much of this material which was published in 1642 in three substantial volumes. These commentaries became the standard textbooks on English common law for subsequent generations.

'There was once great reverence for Magna Carta': Coke quoted on the title-page of an 1810 edition of the Charter, with the Petition of Right.

of the *liber homo*. One man, Sir Edward Coke, building upon a lifetime of legal research, and the growing national historical consciousness of an 'ancient constitution' was almost single-handedly responsible for this transformation. As he commented in his *Fifth Report*, 'The auntient and excellent Lawes of England are the birth-right and the most auntient and best inheritance that the subjects of this Realm have, for by them he injoyeth only his inheritance and goods in peace and quietnes, but his life and his most deare Countrey in safety.'

On 12 May 1641, the very day Lord Strafford, one of Charles I's 'evil' counsellors, was condemned to death on the scaffold, the House of Commons commanded the publication of the writings of Coke, who had been dead for nearly a decade. The reported instruction insisted that 'This House doth desire, and hold it fit, that the Heir of Sir Edward Cooke do publish in Print his Commentary upon Magna Carta, The Pleas of the Crown, and The Jurisdiction of Courts, according to the Intention of the said Sir Edward Cooke'. The second volume of Coke's *Institutes* was eventually published in 1642 by the combined efforts of six London publishers, consisting of some seven

hundred-plus pages of commentary, commencing with eighty pages praising the enduring significance of Magna Carta. The House of Commons had ordered the publication because the Crown had suppressed it for over a decade. As we will see below, from the early 1620s, Coke had resisted what he regarded as the illegal expansion of Royal Prerogative and the civil law into the jurisdiction of the common law, and consequently over the rights and liberties of the community.

Coke's commentary in the second part of the *Institutes* is the first comprehensive account contextualising Magna Carta with a variety of relevant historical and legal materials. Although modern historians might charge Coke with anachronism in his integration of seventeenth-century ambitions into the medieval document, his work was the starting point for regarding the Charter as laying the foundations of fundamental law (and for establishing how the judiciary and Parliament had adapted its principles to circumstances). Those 'Golden passages in the Great Charter of England', specifically clause 39 ('no free man …'), were still being reprinted in the aid of American liberty in 1776.

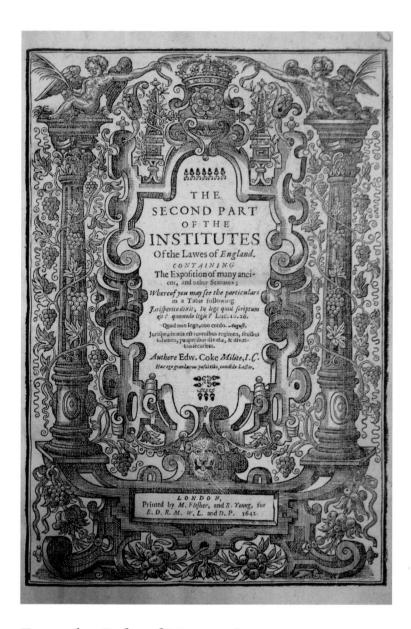

*Title-page of the
second volume of Coke's*
Institutes, *1642.*

tuition and teaching had been driven by the circulation of, and oral interaction with, manuscript works derived from speeches, addresses and lectures, after 1500, printed volumes of statutes, abridgements and collections become dominant.

The most prominent and innovative genre – which became the dominant way in which lawyers and gentlemen encountered Magna Carta – were the collections of *Antiqua Statuta*. These volumes recorded the historical evidence of legislation, and indeed were primarily focused on providing the details of those laws still in force. Their first item was Magna Carta.

Frenchman Richard Pynson (*c.*1449–1529/30), who eventually became a naturalized Englishman, was one of the first official printers to the Crown, gaining the privilege to publish statutes and proclamations. In this capacity as publisher of a range of law books, he produced in 1508, a Latin work called *Magna Charta* which, alongside a wealth of other legal documents, reproduced the thirty-seven clauses of the 1297 Magna Carta. This edition set the textual standard for nearly every subsequent reproduction into the eighteenth century when William Blackstone published the first scholarly edition in 1759 (drawn from one of the Cottonian originals of 1215). The form of this first publication is significant to the centrality of Magna Carta to the

From the *Boke of Magna Carta* to the *Statutes at Large*

The groundwork for Coke's invocation of the powerful political authority and iconic culture of Magna Carta was laid in the sixteenth century. As the growth of litigation took hold of English society so too did the need for trained, well-informed and articulate lawyers. That growing cohort of men was educated in the London Inns of Court (rather than receiving the more traditional degrees at the Universities of Oxford and Cambridge). Legal training in these 'third universities' was predominantly practical rather than conceptual: as a consequence there was a demand for textbooks and commentaries. This expansion of legal practice coincided with the newly available printing industry developing in London. Whereas before the turn of the century much

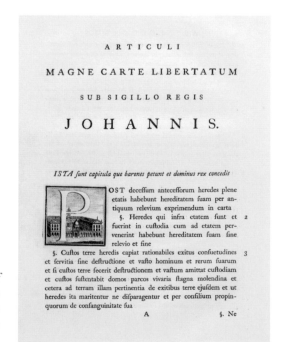

*Opening page of
Blackstone's 1759 edition
of* Magna Charta, *here
displaying the Articles
of the Barons.*

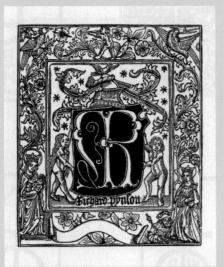

Richard Pynson's monogram, as used in his printed books during the early 16th century.

Statutes: a brief publishing history

The first manifestations of the statute genre were printed by Richard Pynson and Robert Redman (in Latin) between 1508 and 1527, followed by translations into English (first in 1534, importantly described as 'Necessarye for all yong studiers of the Lawe'), and then the multiple editions of *A collection of all the Statutes* (of which, between 1557 and 1621, there were nineteen different editions) produced by printers Richard Tottell, Christopher Barker and Thomas Wight. Such statute collections were produced 'cum privilegio' by the Crown's printers, and as the decades moved on, the books became more sophisticated, introducing indices, alphabetical orders, and useful ancillary materials to enable the reader to find what he needed, whether he was a lawyer or a Justice of the Peace. By the end of the seventeenth century the title had, under the management of Edward Wingate, become *An exact abridgement of all statutes in force and use* (1659–1741, seventeen editions). The genre is still with us in the form of the Statutes at Large, first published under that title in 1676 and then the dominant work between 1762 and 1807. In each and every one of these volumes Magna Carta held the primary place, so whether one was consulting the record as a professional lawyer, an acting magistrate, an interested party, or a politician, the Great Charter was the foundation stone for the rule of law in the country.

practices of English law, and consequently to the rise of the authority of interpretations of its content in the following two centuries. Commencing with the Great Charter, and supplementing it with a variety of other legal material – statutes, articles, ordinances and examples of writs – the work was a reference book which also included the chronologies of the monarchs and a description of the counties of England, as well as helpful indices to the contents which would allow the reader to access material efficiently. This book, and the many subsequent versions published over the next two hundred years, supplied the basic instrument of legal education and training in the Inns of Court throughout the period.

Modelled on the already copious manuscript copies of collections of statutes, which were designed for the practical use of lawyers, and provided collections of new and old laws, alongside various abridgements and commentaries, these printed titles were to become ubiquitous (and indeed a profitable business). Such handbooks laid the foundation for the everyday encounter with Magna Carta and its tradition. Much of this knowledge of the Great Charter was practical in the sense that it not only printed the text, but also provided commentary and integrated its significance with subsequent legislation. Such books were more interested in the afterlife and outcome of the Great Charter than in any constitutional discussion of how it happened. This printed tradition was a powerful element of vernacular legal humanism in England which aimed to embed the Charter in a native historical narrative. The point of such handbooks was to explain the foundations and content of current legal authority, not to enter into any debate about legitimate sources of legal jurisdiction. George Ferrers (*c*.1510–79), responsible for the first English translation between 1534 and 1542, *The Great Charter Called in latyn Magna Carta*, aimed to clarify French and Latin terms and establish what was the oldest practice, to bring students to 'a perfect judgement' of the 'pryncipples and olde groundys of the lawes'. Importantly, given the lack of interest in the crises and conflicts of John's reign as reported in the chronicles of the time, the Charter most commonly reproduced was that of 9 Henry III.

The context, then, for the impact of Coke's refashioning of Magna Carta in the seventeenth century was the ubiquity of its record in the legal textbooks of the period. Given that the recovery of the meaning and significance of Magna Carta in the sixteenth century was so

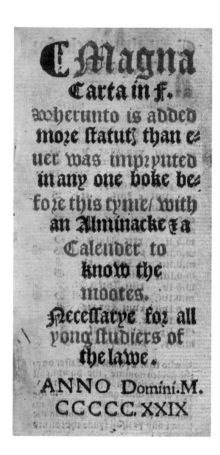

Title-page from the first English translation of Magna Carta, by George Ferrers.

closely bound up with the rise of the printing press, it was also connected to the cultural consequences of the English Reformation. As printed editions of the vernacular Bible were a powerful means for the dissemination of Protestantism throughout the realm, so the print production, from as early as 1508, of English translations of the medieval charter laid the foundation for the rejuvenation of interest in, and ultimately for the political and legal authority of the document. At the turn of the sixteenth century, the printing press was very much an agent both of authority and cultural change. Combined with the Renaissance humanist interest in the recovery of the cultures of Antiquity and the attention *ad fontes*, to the sources, of national historical traditions, it was exploited by monarchs, churchmen and lawyers with equal enthusiasm.

The development of a specific legal ideology in England was distinctive from the traditions of continental Renaissance jurisprudence which focused on canon and civil law. The practical conditions of a lawyer's career in England involved engagement with a canon of textbooks, speeches and lectures in the Inns of Court rather than the formal jurisprudential training in universities which was more common abroad. A central element of this education stressed the role of human law as a powerful bulwark of civilization and good government. The rule of law was a means for preserving both the authority of princes and the liberties of subjects. The legal tradition was good at avoiding the tough constitutional issues, but carefully defended divine right monarchy while pointing out the dangers of

tyranny, insisting upon the duties of obligation while applauding the principle of the common good.

This dominant account of the historical lineage of the law was not a simple promotion of the prescriptive authority of an unchanging custom. By invoking the importance of equity and reason which underpinned the idea of common law, Magna Carta was understood not simply as a collection of customary freedoms, but as a public statute, the first in the book, and one with a still persisting authority in the early modern period.

The Norman Yoke and the ancient constitution

For this period, however, history was politics. The various historical enquiries about the passage and origins of legal tradition enabled men to extract political principles from the evidence of the historical past. Such historical investigations, made more profound later in the sixteenth century by the foundation of the Society of Antiquaries, a group of scholar lawyers, eventually prompted challenges to the political commonplaces of the times, although the rhetoric of such enquiry was never innovation, but the restoration of an original constitution – as is embodied in the recovery and circulation of medieval works like *Mirror of Justices* by Andrew Horne (*c.*1275–1328) and the *Modus Tenendi Parliamentum* which argued for the origins of law in the reign of King Arthur, and suggested Parliament had existed in pre-Conquest times. This evolving sense of the historical past focused on a set of connected issues which became controversial as the various implications for the current polity became clear. The meaning of Magna Carta became bound up with debates about the longevity and origins of Parliament independent from the Crown, and also the impact of the Norman Conquest. The dominant account argued that Magna Carta was a recapitulation of original rights achieved in a more distant past – commonly derived from the *Leges Edwardi Confessoris* (1140) attributed to Edward the Confessor (r. 1042–66). In this respect, most men in the early modern period were unaware that the Charter was a feudal document describing liberties within the precise context of aristocratic feudal tenures. That feudal context was only to be discovered by Henry Spelman and Robert Brady later in the seventeenth century when it was put

John Selden, by John Faber Jr, early 18th century.

IOANNES SELDENUS.
ex Tabella in Bibl: Bodlejana. Oxon.
Printed & Sold by Tim: Iordan & Tho: Bakewell at ý Golden Lion in Fleetstreet

to good use in defence of the Royalist cause after the Restoration.

The alternative to the ancient constitutionalism of pre-Conquest origins was the articulation of an increasingly strident defence of the divine right of the monarchy. James I can be regarded as the innovator of a more radical account of the Crown in works such as the *Trew law of free monarchies* and *Basilikon Doron* (both 1603), wherein he defended regal authority over law and Parliament, with claims like *rex est judex, lex loquens* ('The King is judge, his word is law'), and 'kings are called Gods'. As we will see, when James claimed he had the prerogative rights to impose taxes and charges on merchants and citizens without restraint he would be challenged in the courts.

Supporters of the Crown used the fact of the Norman Conquest of 1066 as an argument to reinforce the supremacy of regal authority and jurisdiction. The contrary opinion argued that there was a pre-existing ancient constitution which preserved the legitimacy of Saxon laws and institutions. The so-called Norman Yoke then rested lightly on English institutions. Men like John Selden and Sir Edward Coke did not represent William I as an innovator, and by exploring English history up to the times of Henry II, argued for the continual persistence of a 'mixed' monarchy. Coke argued in his *Reports* (1611) that William I had indeed codified the different elements of English legal and

constitutional practice, the 'summe of which, composed by him into a Magna Carta (the groundwork of all those that after followed)'. English history established a process of serial confirmation – the Great Charter of John was simply one significant example of this process. As Coke was to point out, it had been subsequently confirmed by thirty Parliaments since Henry III. The authority of Magna Carta was then intimately bound up with a broader commitment to the idea of the existence of an ancient constitution, which might be traced back to time immemorial (before memory and written records). This in theory bound the Crown to the rule of law, to the common good and hence to the preservation of liberties.

Sir Edward Coke and the ancient constitution

Sir Edward Coke (d. 1634) was perhaps one of the least likely figures in English history to have achieved such a long-lasting impact on the history of Magna Carta. His motto was *Lex est tutissima cassis* ('Law is the surest protection'). An exceptionally wealthy lawyer who had (by the start of King James I's reign) forged a distinguished and powerful reputation built upon his erudition and forensic abilities in the application of case law, Coke made many powerful political connections building on networks in Norfolk, and despite being associated with the Puritan cause, was elected MP in 1592. His intimacies with men at court, in particular the Cecil interest, meant he was successively made attorney-general (1594) and then knighted by James I. He made his name not only in protecting the traditions of common law from challenge, but also by his furious prosecutions of Catholic enemies (such as the plotters Roderigo Lopez and Edward Squire, and Jesuits like John Gerard) as well as political rivals like Francis Bacon and Sir Walter Ralegh. His advancement to national prominence was not simply a mark of his talents, but an attempt by a frustrated monarch to restrain Coke's conduct by office. When Coke was promoted as Chief Justice of the King's Bench in October 1613, James had hoped he might become more amenable.

The spine of Coke's position in the various legal disputes he engaged with before elevation to the post of Chief Justice had been the defence of the jurisdiction and authority of the common law and its courts from challenges, in particular from institutions like the Court of High Commission or Chancery. Even though churchmen had been

Coke's aetiology

Following the insights of other lawyers in France and Germany, who traced the origins of their national legal traditions back into Antiquity, Coke suggested that an unbroken but unwritten law of England had existed since the ancient Britain of the Druids. The first King of England, Brutus of Troy, had compiled a book of laws, indeed there had been seven pre-Conquest collections made by early English monarchs. Just as the Church of England turned to its historical archives to establish a non-papal primitive Christianity, so did men like Coke reconstruct an indigenous tradition of customary law – a key element in an 'ancient constitution' – which was the foundation of English liberties. Coke's powerful point was that law was immemorial, drawing from God's reason, rather than the will of a monarchical legislator. As he put it, 'the laws have been by the wisdom of the most excellent men, in many successions of ages, by long and continual experience, (the trial of light and truth) fined and refined'.

Edward Coke, by Marcus Gheeraerts the Younger, c.1593.

empowered by the King with legal authority in the High Commission, Coke upheld the rights of common law against what he regarded as the improper exercise of prerogative.

The key to Coke's legal principles was the idea of historical custom, manifest in the exercise of the wisdom and reason of successions of judges. This was fundamentally opposed to the dominant continental tradition of civil law, which generally claimed the sovereignty of the Crown as the source of statute law. For Coke the source and authority of law drew from its connection with the past, and its slow incremental adjustment by the revisions of independent judges.

The cast of Coke's mind was historical and his native habitat the manuscript archive. Connected to the great antiquarians and collectors of his age, he also drew from the works of the early Society of Antiquaries. These historical researches into English history took him back past 1066 and the Norman Conquest, and deep into a prescriptive past. Such researches led Coke and many contemporaries to have opinions about the origins and authority of key institutions – the most controversial being that of Parliament, which they traced to pre-Conquest times. The common law of his time had authority because it connected to immemorial custom – what was called *jus non scriptum* (unwritten law). Subsequent statutes and court judgements had simply declared that ancient custom of the realm of England: as both James I and Charles I realized, this ancient constitution constrained Royal prerogative and sovereignty. That monarchs governed only under the rule of law, rather than by divine authority from above, was for Coke evident from the history of England. It would be this disposition towards the history of the law which enabled Coke to reimagine Magna Carta, not as a product of post-Conquest feudal law, but as a reconfirmation of pre-existing common law traditions.

The touch-paper for the political combustion which saw Magna Carta elevated into profound contemporary significance was the so-called Five Knights Case of 1627. Charles I, ever impecunious, had sought, as his father had done, non-parliamentary and prerogative means to raise revenue for the increasingly inflated costs of his domestic and foreign policy. In the summer of 1626 he moved to impose a Forced Loan inviting his subjects 'lovingly, freely, and voluntarily' to contribute. Although many paid – fearful of disobeying the King and indeed of being punished by the billeting of royal troops, many refused and were imprisoned. Five of these knights issued legal

writs of habeas corpus to seek bail. In November 1627 their case was heard at the court of King's Bench. Despite the respected lawyer John Selden invoking clause 29 of the 1225 revision of the Great Charter (consolidated from clauses 39 and 40 of the original 1215 issue), 'no free man …', the judges of the King's Bench confirmed that the monarch had discretionary power to imprison. In this episode what was initially a defence of the Crown's prerogative rights of taxation became an even more sensitive question of discretionary imprisonment. The attorneys for the defence, including Selden, insisted that the Crown must follow the due process of law, or by default such discretion would infringe and jeopardize the ancient liberties of free-born Englishmen. When Sir Edward Hampden was not freed on bail after the submission of habeas corpus, the affair became a matter of constitutional significance in which Sir Edward Coke took the lead.

Coke's efforts which resulted in the *Petition of Right* (1628), conceived as a recapitulation of 1215, transformed the baronial charter of privileges into a declaration of the rights of free-born Englishmen. Coke had used a forensic vigilance in the previous decade to preserve ancient birth-rights from the depradations of James and his son: he had also ensured that his reports and views were available in the vernacular. All who could read would comprehend that the phrase *nullius liber homo* ('no free man …') was the guarantee of freedom from arbitrary imprisonment. The new Parliament called in the late spring of 1628 condemned Charles' policies – illegal taxation, imprisonment without cause, martial billeting. Speaking in Parliament on 17 May 1628, Coke made it clear that there were limits on regal power in the famous phrase that 'Magna Charta is such a fellow, that he will have no Sovereign'. Charles I, despite some attempt to avoid having to, confirmed the petition in June 1628. Magna Carta was then a live and powerful resource, which meant much to the many lawyers in the House of Commons. Its application to the opposition to Charles I was not simply rhetoric, but a very effective means of bringing the monarchy to heel. The stakes for many in the country, as Sir John Eliot put it, were high, 'Upon this dispute not alone our lands and goods are engaged, but all that we call ours. These rights, these privileges, which made our fathers freemen, are in question.' Coke's dominance of the parliamentary debates, and his authoritative application of the Charter, gave it a powerful institutional voice. Transformed into the constitutional forms of the rule of law and the

John Lilburne reading from Coke's Institutes *at his trial, from*
Clement Walker, The Compleat History of Independency, *1649.*

The making of a radical

John Lilburne had experienced tyrannical and brutal
imprisonment under the prerogative Court of Star
Chamber in the 1630s (he was whipped), but also found
himself repeatedly imprisoned by Parliament in the 1640s
for his political opposition to the King's interests and
supporters. Between 1646 and 1649 he published some forty
works defending the rights of the free-born Englishman
– often focused on protecting his own circumstances and
demanding, for example, the resurrection of trial by a jury
of his peers.

Coke's legacy: parliamentarians and Levellers

The power of Coke's promotion of the tradition of liberty embodied in
Magna Carta became a resource for wider public use and political
audiences after its publication in 1642. While Crown and Parliament
took their differences over which institution was the legitimate
defender of the nation's liberty and property to the battlefield,
pamphleteers and politicians in Westminster and the provinces sought
to present their ideological arguments in terms of preserving the
traditions of the Charter of Liberties. Once again the printing press
became the means by which contested interpretations of Magna Carta
were broadcast to wide and popular audiences. Abridgements of Coke's
commentary, and other short works like *Briefe Collections out of Magna
Charta: or the Knowne good old Lawes of England* (1643), promoted an
account of government which insisted that the King and the nation
were subjected to the rule of law, and that this itself was derived from
the 'ancient Maximes and Customes' of the land. The law was 'the full
and perfect conclusions of reason' tried often and by long usage. A
consequence of this was pithily put: 'A King's Grant which is either
preputnant to Law, Custome, or Statute, is not good nor pleadable in
the Law.' Central to this position was clause 29 of the 1225 Magna
Carta (clauses 39–40 of 1215) 'No free man will be taken …' The defeat
of Charles I reinforced the triumph of the Cokean account of Magna
Carta. Yet that was not the end of the significance and possibilities of
the tradition, which were released by the turbulent conditions of first
civil war, and then revolution in the 1640s.

Soldiers fighting in the New Model Army against the divinely
appointed monarch believed they were preserving the ancient
constitution in the name of Magna Carta. Out of the turmoil and
conflict of the military war, and the complicated political manoeuvres
at Westminster, grew other, more radical, aspirations which drew from
the same stream of historical authority. Where politicians like John
Pym and Henry Vane used Magna Carta to defend the civic and
representative institutions of a properted elite (modern barons) against
the threats of arbitrary prerogative, others invoked it to empower all
free-born Englishmen with liberty. The most dramatic manifestation
of this aspiration was the eruption of democratic discussion prompted
by a combination of radical 'agitators' in the New Model Army, and
the party of civilian pamphleteers known as the Levellers, at Putney

power of Parliament, Magna Carta was mobilized to the defence of the
property and liberty of free-born Englishmen. Charles I moved against
both Parliament and Coke. He governed without calling a new
Parliament for a decade, and when opportunity presented itself he
impounded Coke's papers, thus avoiding any further publicity
regarding Magna Carta and English liberties.

Church in November 1647. Here in a unique moment in English history, the voices of the untutored foot-soldier engaged in fierce discussion with the 'Grandees' of the army, informed and provoked by a popular pamphlet literature under the title of the *Agreement of the People* (1647). Parliament, dominated by the propertied was regarded as an agent of the Norman Yoke: the army would set the people free. Where Grandees like Henry Ireton argued that property was the foundation for the exercise of birthright, other men at Putney insisted the freedom Magna Carta confirmed was a natural right extended to all men irrespective of their wealth or poverty. Works like Richard Overton's *Vox plebis, or, the peoples outcry against oppression, injustice, and tyranny. Wherein the liberty of the subject is asserted, Magna Charta briefly but pithily expounded* (1647) promoted an account of the tradition that extended liberty as a birth-right to all: 'This *Charter* of our Liberties, or Freemans *Birth-right*, that cost so much blood of our Ancestors … is that brazen wall, and impregnable Bulwark that defends the Common liberty of *England* from all illegall & destructive *Arbitrary Power* whatsoever, be it either by *Prince* or *State* endeavoured'. Explicitly drawing from Coke's commentaries (especially on clause 29 of 1225, clauses 39–40 of 1215), such popular works were bold in arguing that 'In these few words lies … the liberty of the whole *English Nation*. This word, *liber Homo*, or free Man, extends to all manner of *English* people'. Such liberty from slavery was due, not just to elites, but to the common man too.

The most vocal and significant of radical figures was John Lilburne (1615– 57), who, exploiting (once again) Coke's interpretation of Magna Carta, turned the critical arguments of the tradition against the tyranny of Parliament, not just kings. For Lilburne the medieval language of the *liber homo* was translated into a more capacious category, the 'free-born Englishman', who was not a subject but a citizen. The privileges identified in Magna Carta were the egalitarian 'Birth-right and inheritance' of all the commons of England. The long list of Lilburne's various pamphlets reinforces the centrality of freedom and liberty: *The free-mans freedom vindicated* (1646), *Foundations of freedom; or An agreement of the people* (1648), *Liberty vindicated against slavery* (1646), *The legal fundamental liberties of the people of England, revived, asserted and vindicated* (1649) and *England's birthright justified* (1645). While Lilburne developed a sophisticated political theory drawing from natural law and conceptual arguments, this embellished

a powerful element built on the historical authority of Magna Carta. In works like *The peoples prerogative and priviledges, asserted and vindicated, (against all tyranny whatsoever.) By law and reason. Being a collection of the marrow and soule of Magna Charta* (1648), he reinforced the claim that the law itself was the fount of English freedoms. Like other Levellers, Lilburne believed that Magna Carta had reconfirmed the force of earlier laws, most notably the pre-Conquest laws of Edward the Confessor. The Great Charter then declared pre-existing laws which had been corrupted by William I: those excellent laws were intended to include the common man in the activities of self-government. In his more ambitious moments, Lilburne understood Magna Carta to enfranchise all adult men in active citizenship exercising their rights as citizens, holding political office, and legitimating politics by consent. It was, he argued, the constitutional right of free-men to petition, vote and choose their parliamentary representation.

Although powerfully made, and receiving mass support in the crowds of London, Lilburne's vision was ultimately unsuccessful – he spent much of the 1640s and 1650s in prison or in exile, pleading for his own liberty. His defence of individual freedom, of the liberty of the press and, significantly for his own personal circumstances, the integrity of trial by jury became a powerful model for later eighteenth-century Whig radicals – a copy of a pamphlet recording his 1649 trial was presented to John Wilkes in 1763, as he experienced prosecution for defending English liberties.

The Charter's power broadens

With the publication of Coke's Institutes in 1642, and the radical pamphleteering of the Levellers in the mid- to late 1640s, the iconic power of an appeal to the tradition and principles of Magna Carta became ever more commonplace. The claim that Magna Carta legitimated English freedom also had a significant resonance in the context of religious liberty. From the mid-sixteenth century, the new-born Church of England had invoked the opening clauses of the Charter to defend Protestant liberties against the Papacy. During the 1580s, Puritans like James Morice and Robert Beale turned arguments from Magna Carta for the liberty of religion against the use of illegal *ex officio* oaths by prerogative courts of High Commission. By the

Interior of a London coffee-shop, late 17th-century drawing.

Rewriting Magna Carta

Such was the dominance of veneration for the tradition that unsurprisingly some moved to rewrite the terms of the Charter itself. One anonymous man, 'J.C.', published a single-sheet broadside, designed to be pasted on the walls of alehouses and coffee-shops, *Magna charta containing that which is very much the sense and agreement of the good people of these nations, notwithstanding their differences relating to worship* (1659), which outlined a nineteen-point utopian description of the modern liberties of persons, religion and politics.

1640s the 'teeming freedom' of religious sectarianism described by John Milton also claimed the privileges of the liberty of conscience and worship under the same banner. The pamphlets of prophetic figures like Thomas Tany (1608–59) and John Brayne (d. 1654) extrapolated from arguments about civil freedoms to religious liberty, often in the turbulent conditions of the Civil wars and after, in a millenarian mode. For example, Augustine Wingfield, Member of Parliament for the 1653 Nominated Assembly, published a controversial work, *Tithes totally Routed by Magna Charta* (1653), which argued against the 'oppression and lordly tyranny' of the 'pompous priests', that Church tithes were illegal unless voluntary. Other more lowly men like Ralph Wallis (d. 1669), 'Cobbler of Gloucester', used the religious liberties of Magna Carta against the claims of the entire 'pityful stinking priesthood' to exercise any pastoral jurisdiction.

Quaker authors, especially after the Restoration of the Church of

England in 1660, repeatedly sought refuge in the legal liberties originating in Magna Carta as a means to protect themselves from the persecutory attentions of the established religion. Men like Richard Farnworth (c.1630–66), in legally informed works like *The Liberty of the Subject by Magna Charta* (1664), cited the Cokean account of Magna Carta to argue in defence of the legality of Quaker meetings and their rights as citizens. As late as 1688, William Penn claimed to have designed a 'New Magna Charta for liberty of Conscience' which aimed to ensure that all religious minorities would be allowed their full civil rights. Penn organized the first publication of Magna Carta on North American soil in 1688.

After 1660, with the restoration of monarchical rule, the tradition of the Charter, and its foundational role in recovering the ancient constitution and the authority of the rule of law, became a persistent element of political discourse into the late eighteenth century. Royalist theorists relentlessly promoted divine right theories of kingship, exploiting the powerful memory of the martyred Charles I as a platform for refuting constitutional alternatives which placed the Crown under the jurisdiction of Parliament and the law. The rise to prominence of a Whig party, first in the so-called Exclusion Crisis of 1678–83, and then the Glorious Revolution of 1688–9, which opposed the potential tyranny of a Popish monarchy, promoted Magna Carta and the *Petition of Right* as core components of a constitution which preserved liberty. Political thinkers like John Locke and James Tyrrell founded their defence of the lives, liberties and estates of the Protestant free-born Englishman on the dominant conception of Magna Carta as a reconfirmation of both the historical and natural rights of the community.

Just as significant as these set pieces of political argument, composed to defend resistance against late Stuart tyranny and arbitrary government in the 1680s and 1690s, was the less abstract work of men like Henry Care (1646–88), whose *English Liberties: Or, the Free-Born Subject's Inheritance* (1680) achieved more than ten editions in England and North America over the next century. This work was a practical handbook of civil liberties, detailing all of the appropriate legal instruments, statutes, principles and institutions which could preserve freedom in a free state. As such it was used by religious dissenters against persecuting churchmen, by Whig politicians against Jacobean tyranny, and by free-born Americans against George III. Reinforcing the authority of juries, and the letter of the law, Care's book provided self-help guidance on how the tradition of Magna Carta could be employed to protect the individual from civil tyranny or clerical persecution. English liberties established that each free man had 'a fixed Fundamental Right born with him, as to Freedom of his Person, and Property in his estate'. The exercise of the act of consent in choosing representatives in Parliament, and the judicial role played by ordinary men as jurymen, were the two pillars of freedom 'whereby we have been, and are preserv'd more free and happy than any other people in the world, and (we trust) shall ever continue so'. The reproduction of Magna Carta, complete with commentary derived from Coke, reinforced the claim that it 'makes and preserves the people free'. The words of clause 29 deserved to be 'written in Letters of Gold' in every public courthouse and town hall.

The eighteenth century: Magna Carta in protest

The shift from the seventeenth century to the eighteenth saw the development of the Charter from a resource which underpinned the fundamental elements of constitutional liberty, to one which legitimated protest and resistance against invasions of personal liberty. In 1642, in 1688 and arguably in 1776, the invocation of Magna Carta framed legitimate constitutional resistance against tyrannous regimes, authorising parliamentary defence of historic, but universal, principles of freedom. The ideology of the ancient constitution had been ratified by the series of legislative statements and revolutionary acts, but it was compatible with the institution of monarchy. Although divine right theories of government and society were still powerful, the need to preserve Protestantism from continental absolutism meant that *Anglia libera* was built upon an informal constitution which insisted Magna Carta was a foundational document. The claims to 'English liberties' and the rights of 'free-born Englishmen' were mainstream – even Tory political ideology underscored a fundamental patriotism derived from this historical tradition, turning the foundational claims of liberty against the Whig ministry. The 'freedoms' of 'lives liberties and estates' were claimed by Englishmen in Britain and in the American colonies. As the dominance of the Whig ascendency under the long-lived Walpolean (1720–39) regime saw the growth of state power manifested, in particular, in the imposition of fiscal demands like the Stamp Act, the expansion of revenue from excise duties and the development of political corruption and patronage, so the constitutional authority of Magna Carta empowered oppositional interests which regarded the illegal attentions of the government as a burgeoning tyranny.

This pattern of protest is best exemplified in the political career of John Wilkes (1725–97) and his less well-known friend, radical Whig lawyer, and London Common councilman, Arthur Beardmore (d. 1771). Both used the tradition of liberty embodied in Magna Carta to defend their campaigns against press censorship and arbitrary arrest. One of the most famous incidents of the eighteenth century is emblematic of this and involved Beardmore staging his arrest for publishing radical criticisms of the royal family and government ministers in November 1762.

Pine's powerful portraits

As portrayed in a best-selling engraving, Arthur Beardmore's arrest occurred while he was seen to be teaching his young son the principles of Magna Carta, pointing out to the young boy the relevant passages – *Cap XXIX Anno nono Henrici III … Nullus liber homo*. The artist, Robert Edge Pine (1730–88), son of the engraver who had made the beautiful copy of the Charter in the Cottonian Library (1733), was also responsible for an equally successful portrait of Beardmore's associate John Wilkes (1764), depicted sitting at a desk surrounded by icons of his political views, including prominently a rolled copy of Magna Carta.

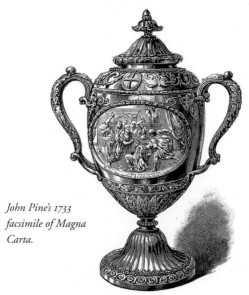

John Pine's 1733 facsimile of Magna Carta.

Engraving of a Loving Cup presented to John Wilkes in 1772. The cup depicts the assassination of Julius Caesar.

Wilkes's invocation of Magna Carta with the popular slogan 'Wilkes and Liberty' in defence of the liberty of the press and freedom from illegal detention successfully mobilized turbulent popular support for protests in the 1760s. Writing while imprisoned, Wilkes described the 'genuine spirit of the Magna Carta' as 'the distinguishing characteristic of all Englishmen': it allowed and legitimated popular resistance against all tyranny. Wilkes, drawing from the evident power of print propaganda in the example of Beardmore's portrait, mustered London crowds to his cause by the production of an extensive range of media – prints, engravings, buttons, medals, cockades and even porcelain figurines, tea pots and mugs – connecting his defence of liberty, whether it be the freedom of the press or the rights of the electorate to choose their representatives, with the historical tradition of Magna Carta. Alongside the very popular portraits, he produced more sophisticated material like the broadsheet *English Liberty established or a Mirrour for Posterity* (1768), addressed to all 'sons of

Liberty', which combined the authority of Magna Carta with the Whig transmission of that tradition and the defence of popular protest, noting that 'the People delight to honour him'.

By the end of the eighteenth century Magna Carta had become a powerful myth and ideograph capable of evoking both a defence of the national constitution and the freedoms of individual protest against tyranny. Despite its ideological role in legitimating the American Revolution, Magna Carta was still regarded as a cornerstone of authority and freedom, as opposed to the dangers of anarchy and violence which became embodied in the chaos and violence of the French Revolution. After 1789, the extent of the veneration for, and significant cultural investment in, Magna Carta is perhaps best illustrated in two examples from the turn of the eighteenth into the nineteenth century. In 1794 John Carey, hoping for a commission from the Society for the Improvement of Arts, intended to produce a copy of the Charter in gold on a satin page (which could be purple, green, black or white depending on the subscribers' desire). For five guineas, the edition, 'with an elegant, ornamented title' would be of 'the most scrupulous exactness', drawn from Blackstone's copy. The work could either be bound as a book or produced in detached pages fit for framing and glazing. Carey's proposal attracted attention amongst London booksellers. But 'the most magnificent of all editions of Magna Carta' was printed on vellum in London in 1816 by John Whittaker, under the title *Magna carta regis Johannis, XV die Junii MCCXV Anno regni xvii*, for Earl Spencer. With its richly embellished title-page and illustrations, the iconic value of the edition fulfilled Edward Coke's aspiration that the Charter would be reproduced in gold letters. By the early nineteenth century, then, Magna Carta was a symbol of British liberties venerated by both the common man and the aristocratic elite – it underwrote the constitutional freedoms of the state. As one late nineteenth-century commentator, Thomas Taskell-Langmead, noted (1875), 'To have produced it, to have preserved it, to have matured it, constitute the immortal claim of England upon the esteem of mankind.'

Title-page of 'the most magnificent of all editions of Magna Carta', 1816.

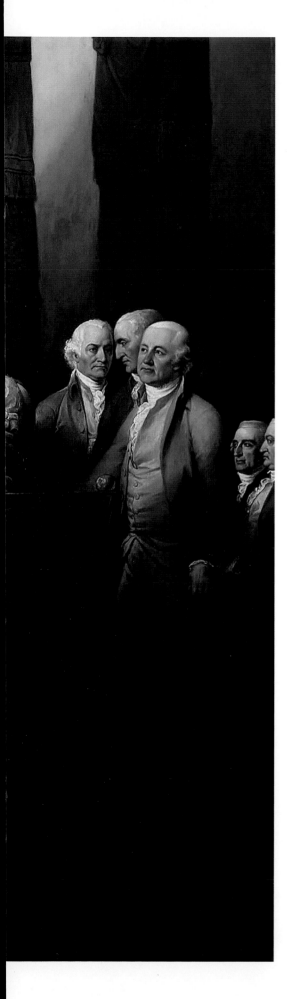

The Declaration of
Independence *(detail)*,
by John Trumbull, 1817.

Chapter Eight

Magna Carta in America: Entrenched

Joyce Lee Malcolm

By the great Charter no amerciament shall be assessed but by the oath of Honest and Lawfull men of the Vicinage. And by the Same Charter no Freeman shall be taken or imprisoned or be disseised of his Freehold or Liberties or Free Customs nor passed upon nor condemned but by lawful judgment of his Peers or by the Law of the Land.

'Instructions to their Representative', Braintree, Massachusetts Town Meeting protesting the Stamp Act (1765)

Magna Carta decreed that no man would be imprisoned contrary to the law of the land. Art. 39.

US Supreme Court, *Boumediene v. Bush*, 553 US 723 (2008)

On a winter's day in 1761, Bostonians crowded into the Massachusetts Superior Court to hear James Otis challenge the legality of the writs of assistance on behalf of sixty-three Boston merchants. The writs were general search warrants authorizing government officials to break into private homes and warehouses at any time to search for contraband. Constables and even passers-by could be required to aid in the search. Oddly, these writs had been approved by Parliament in 1660 and used successfully in England despite legal treatises questioning their legality. Yet when they began to be used in the American colonies a century later they provoked outrage. The Boston suit started when James Paxton, a Massachusetts customs official, applied to the Massachusetts Superior Court for the writ. Ordinarily James Otis, the colony's advocate general, would have been expected to support Paxton. Instead he resigned his post to represent the furious merchants.

Otis and his co-counsel, Oxenbridge Thatcher, charged, among

James Otis, engraving by C. Schlecht after J. Blackburn, 1881.

other complaints, that the writ was 'against the fundamental principles of English Law', quoting Sir Edward Coke in *Dr Bonham's Case* on that basic rule from Magna Carta: 'An act against the constitution is void. An act against natural equity is void.' Even Parliament, Coke had insisted, could not pass legislation that was against fundamental law. Otis traced that principle to Saxon laws and to Magna Carta, adding that parliaments had confirmed the Charter fifty times. Violators of Magna Carta had been executed. Otis reminded the court:

> The security of these rights to life, liberty, and property had been the object of all those struggles against arbitrary power, temporal and spiritual, civil and political, military and ecclesiastical, in every age. He asserted that our ancestors, as British subjects, and we, their descendants, as British subjects, were entitled to all those rights, by the British Constitution, as well as by the law of nature and our provincial charter, as much as any inhabitant of London or Bristol, or any part of England; and were not to be cheated out of them by any phantom of 'virtual representation', or any other fiction of law or politics, or any monkish trick of deceit and hypocrisy.

By the seventeenth and eighteenth centuries, of course, the original articles in Magna Carta had been stretched and interpreted to embrace an expanded list of individual rights, but these were no less sincerely and passionately held for all that.

The justices ruled that they had the right to issue the writ and granted Paxton's request. But Otis's insistence that the writs were a

violation of fundamental law affirmed by Magna Carta resonated throughout the colonies. This insistence on a right against unreasonable searches would be ultimately embedded in American state and federal constitutions. The claim that an act against fundamental law is void has been the foundation of American judicial review.

Magna Carta and the rights of the colonists

The quarrel over the extent to which the colonists enjoyed the liberties of Englishmen had begun much earlier. 'Let an Englishman go where he will,' Richard West, British Board of Trade counsel advised in 1720, 'he carries as much of law and liberty with him as the state of things will bear.' Differences over just how much 'law and liberty' this entailed would bring Britain and thirteen of her North American colonies to blows. Certainly the liberties that made Englishmen 'free-born' seemed straightforward to the colonists. All their charters, starting with the first in 1606 which James I granted to the planters of Virginia, promised:

> That all and every the Persons, being our Subjects, which shall dwell and inhabit within every or any of the said several Colonies and Plantations, and every of their children, which shall happen to be born within any of the Limits and Precincts of the said several Colonies and Plantations shall HAVE and enjoy all Liberties, Franchises, and Immunities, within any of our other Dominions, to all Intents and Purposes, as if they had been abiding and born, within this our Realm of England, or any other of our said Dominions.

English kings reckoned that the dangers of crossing the Atlantic and setting up residence in a wild land were so great that few of their subjects would emigrate unless they were assured they would enjoy their old liberties in their new homes. The core of these liberties were laid out in Magna Carta which, despite fits and starts, had been woven into common law over four centuries. Just at the time America was being settled there was growing fear in England that King James and his successors were bent on curbing those precious rights. That anxiety led to civil war in Britain and drove families to the colonies. This jealousy over their rights sharpened the colonists' political sensitivities. How they understood those ancient tenets of Magna Carta and entrenched them in their federal and state constitutions is the subject of this chapter. While Englishmen on both sides of the Atlantic set a high value on their rights, their manner of protecting them diverged. That divergence has arguably resulted in Magna Carta's legacy remaining more vibrant in America than in the land of its origins.

Although the colonists boasted of their liberties anchored in Magna Carta, there has been some doubt about their knowledge of its

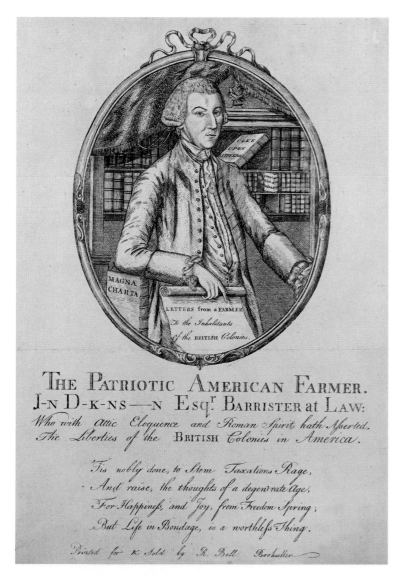

Affirming colonists' liberties rooted in Magna Carta: engraving by James Smither, 1768.

provisions – there was a serious lack of English law books in the early years, and justices and colonial assemblies ordered books from England. Yet at least the colonists' leaders knew their Magna Carta. In 1646, twenty-six years after the pilgrims set foot on the inhospitable coast of Massachusetts, the colony's legislature issued a document comparing Magna Carta, article by article, to the 'Fundamentalls of the Massachusetts' and finding parallels throughout. And to make doubly sure customary English rights were put into practice Maryland (1639), Massachusetts Bay (1641) and West New Jersey (1676) passed statutes providing for the application of common law and referring to specific chapters of Magna Carta, especially the cluster of key property and judicial rights in chapters 39 and 40 of the 1215 charter, consolidated into chapter 29 of the 1225 text:

No free man will be taken or imprisoned or disseised or outlawed or exiled or in any way ruined, nor shall we go or send against him, save by the lawful judgement of his peers and/or by the law of the land. To no one shall we sell, to no one shall we deny or delay right or justice.

English colonists often needed to be more litigious than their peers in the Mother Country because the English government was unsure how to treat its colonies and, despite all the charter promises of rights, shifted its approach from time to time. The cases that Americans brought illustrate their determination to exercise those promised rights, particularly when policies violated what the colonists considered their fundamental liberties confirmed by Magna Carta, chief among them representation in parliaments and trial by jury. In 1664, the Massachusetts Bay's assembly, in a letter to their 'Dread Soveraigne', took issue with a royal commission that accused the New England colonies of passing laws 'repugnant to the laws of England', claiming their own colony had 'an exemption to the payment of customs' imposed by the navigation acts. While other New England colonies yielded, the Massachusetts Bay assembly reminded Charles II that their charter, reconfirmed by him just two years earlier, granted

unto them their heirs, assignes, & associates forever, not onely the absolute use & propriety of the tract of land herein mentioned, but also full & absolute power of governing all the

William Penn receiving the Charter of Pennsylvania from King Charles II of England, *by Allan Stewart, 1913.*

people of this place, by men chosen by themselves, & according
to such lawes as they shall from time to time see meete to make
& establish, being not repugnant to the laws of England.

According to their charter they were to pay only the fifth part 'of the
oare of gold & silver that shall here be found for & in respect of all
duties, demands, exactions, & services whatsoever.' They even objected
to the royal commission itself: 'Wee are like to be subjected to the
arbitrary power of strangers, proceeding, not by any established lawe,
but by their owne discretions!' 'If these things goe on,' they warned,
'your subjects here will either be forced to seeke new dwellings or sinck
& faint under burdens that will be to them intolerable.' The Crown
officials withdrew the commission, but the Massachusetts assembly
refused even to answer its charges.

To bring the colonies under tighter royal control, the short-lived
Dominion of New England placed them under a royal appointee
unimpeded by colonial assemblies, and sharply curtailed their former
rights. In 1687 Governor Edmund Andros and his council levied town
taxes in Massachusetts without consulting the colony's assembly. The

Ipswich town meeting protested that these taxes were illegal and
refused to pay them. Andros arrested the leaders of the protest, the
Reverend John Wise and five others, and would not allow them habeas
corpus. When they pleaded that this was in violation of Magna Carta,
Joseph Dudley, Chief Judge of the colony, informed Wise and the
others that they must 'not think the Laws of England follow [them] to
the ends of the earth or whither [they] went', that the only privilege
they had was 'Not to be sold as a slave'. When they were found guilty
by a stacked jury, the Massachusetts assembly had their cases shifted to
the colony's Supreme Judicial Court and 'empowered that court to
exercise powers comparable to those of the courts as Westminster',
entitling them to grant habeas corpus. In 1692, the Massachusetts
assembly with a new governor passed a law similar to the English
Habeas Corpus Act of 1679. Other colonies followed and, although the
Privy Council vetoed these acts, beginning in 1710 under Queen Anne
the writ began to be extended to the colonies.

By the mid-eighteenth century Massachusetts residents had
become even more vociferous in their constitutional objections to
British policy. In response to Parliament's passing of the Stamp Act in

William Penn, early 19th-century engraving by James Posselwhite, after a print by John Hall based on a portrait by Benjamin West.

William Penn and Magna Carta

William Penn, founder of Pennsylvania, had the entire text of Magna Carta published in 1687, its first printing in the western hemisphere, to enlighten any residents of Pennsylvania 'That are strangers, in a great measure, to the true understanding of that inestimable Inheritance that every *Free-born Subject of England is Heir unto by Birth-right*, I mean that unparallel'd Priviledge of *Liberty* and *Property*'. Penn reckoned this 'happy Frame of Government … shines most conspicuously in two things: 1. PARLIAMENTS 2. JURIES.' Whoever impairs or undermines these, he wrote, strikes at the constitution of the government and should be severely punished: 'To cut down the Banks and let in the Sea, or *to poison all the springs and Rivers* in the Kingdom, could not be a greater Mischief; for this would only affect the present Age, but the other will Ruin and enslave all our *Posterity*.' Magna Carta also laid the foundation for American property law, for the notion that the government was bounded by the rule of law, and for the recognition that any act that contradicted a right it declared was no law at all. In 1701, Penn granted a Charter of Privileges to Pennsylvanians that echoed King John's promise in Magna Carta: 'Neither I, my Heirs or Assigns, shall procure or do any Thing or Things whereby the Liberties In this Charter contained and expressed, nor any part thereof, shall be infringed or broken: And if any thing shall be procured or done, by any Person or Persons, contrary to these Presents, it shall be held of no Force or Effect.'

1765, the town meeting of Braintree, Massachusetts adopted 'Instructions to their Representative' drawn up by John Adams charging that the act violated two key fundamental rights. First the tax was unconstitutional because

> By the great Charter no amerciament shall be assessed but by the oath of Honest and Lawfull men of the Vicinage. And by the Same Charter no Freeman shall be taken or imprisoned or be disseised of his Freehold or Liberties or Free Customs nor passed upon nor condemned but by Lawfull judgment of his Peers or by the Law of the Land.

Since it was 'a grand and fundamental principle of the constitution, that no freeman should be subject to any tax to which he has not given his own consent, in person or by proxy', it was contrary to 'the essential fundamental principles of the British constitution, that we

Lithograph of Sir Edmund Andros proclaiming the Dominion of New England in 1686 with himself as governor, 1898.

The Gaspee affair

The right to a local jury came up again in the 1772 case of the burning of HMS *Gaspee*, a military ship patrolling off Rhode Island to intercept smugglers. When she pursued the sloop *Hannah* out of Newport, Rhode Island, the *Hannah*'s captain lured the *Gaspee* into shallow waters where she ran aground. A group of 'patriots' rowed out to the foundering ship and took the captain and crew prisoner. Then, just before dawn the *Gaspee* was set ablaze. Furious British officials found no one willing to identify the perpetrators even after a reward was offered. The Dockyard Act passed by Parliament in April permitted persons charged with burning one of the King's ships to be tried in England on a charge of treason. To avoid summoning an American grand jury, a special commission was created, made up of the chief justices of the supreme courts of Massachusetts, New York, New Jersey, the judge of the vice-admiralty of Boston, and Stephen Hopkins, governor and chief justice of Rhode Island. Since the commission could get no evidence, it was unable to deal with the case. Chief Justice Hopkins declared that, in any event, sending the accused to England for trial violated their right to have a local jury as promised in Magna Carta.

Destruction of the schooner Gaspee,
by J. McNevin, engraved by J. Rogers, c.1872.

should be subject to any tax imposed by the British Parliament; because we are not represented in that assembly in any sense, unless it be by a fiction of law.' But 'the most grievous innovation of all', in their view, was 'the alarming extension' of admiralty courts where a judge, serving at will, presides and 'No juries have any concern there!' They charged that this would make

> an essential change in the constitution of juries, and it is, directly repugnant to the Great Charter itself; for, by that charter, 'no amerciament shall be assessed, but by the oath of honest and lawful men of the vicinage;' and, 'no freeman shall be taken, or imprisoned, or disseized of his freehold, or liberties or free customs, nor passed upon, nor condemned, but by lawful judgment of his peers, or by the law of the land.'

The Stamp Act would 'make such a distinction, and create such a difference between the subjects in Great Britain and those in America, as we could not have expected from the guardians of liberty in "both"'.

Juries were the best strategy the colonists had to protect their rights. 'A Custom House officer has no chance with a jury,' one governor of Massachusetts complained, while another grumbled, 'A trial by jury here is only trying one illicit trader by his fellows, at least his well-wishers.' The records justify this cynicism. Hundreds of defendants were charged during the 1600s and 1700s, but no more than half a dozen prosecutions were brought, and only two convictions obtained. The case of *Jonathan Sewall v. Hancock* in 1768–9 was one example. It began in June 1768, when John Hancock's sloop, *Liberty*, was seized by a British man-of-war for failing to obtain a permit to unload its cargo. The *Liberty* was condemned in August and sold in September. But the government was not finished with Hancock. In October an admiralty court filed suit against him for the enormous sum of £9,000 (in today's money, something approaching £1 million). John Adams, Hancock's attorney, argued before Judge Auchmuty that the admiralty court prosecution was against law because Hancock was deprived of his right to a jury trial. This, he argued, repealed 'Magna Charta, as far as America is concerned,' and reduced Hancock 'below the Rank of an Englishman.' Adams was successful. The trial record concludes, 'The Advocate General prays leave to Retract this information and says our Sovereign Lord the King will prosecute no further hereon.'

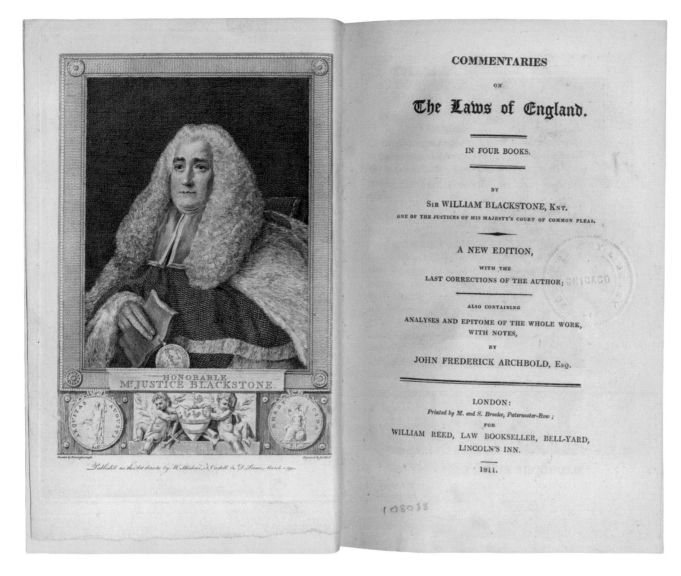

COMMENTARIES
ON
The Laws of England.

IN FOUR BOOKS.

BY
SIR WILLIAM BLACKSTONE, KNT.
ONE OF THE JUSTICES OF HIS MAJESTY'S COURT OF COMMON PLEAS.

A NEW EDITION,
WITH THE
LAST CORRECTIONS OF THE AUTHOR;

ALSO CONTAINING
ANALYSES AND EPITOME OF THE WHOLE WORK,
WITH NOTES,
BY
JOHN FREDERICK ARCHBOLD, ESQ.

LONDON:
Printed by M. and S. Brooke, Paternoster-Row;
FOR
WILLIAM REED, LAW BOOKSELLER, BELL-YARD,
LINCOLN'S INN.
1811.

Frontispiece and title-page from Commentaries on the Laws of England in Four Books *by William Blackstone, published by M. and S. Brooke, London, 1811.*

Interpreting Magna Carta: divergence and independence

Even though rights derived from Magna Carta were embedded in their statutes and in common law, Americans still worried about whether such rights were secure. The answer turned on their source. If the source were a king, what a king gave a king might take away. On the other hand, legal experts argued that Magna Carta merely confirmed existing, even inalienable, rights. The leading seventeenth-century authority on Magna Carta and common law, Sir Edward Coke, praised the 'great weightiness and weighty greatness of the matter [Magna Carta] contained ... being the fountain of all the fundamental Laws of the Realm' which 'make free men'. Coke was Chief Justice of the Court of Common Pleas under James I, until James dismissed him for insisting on the supremacy of law over royal prerogative. By 1628 when he penned his famous discussion of Magna Carta, Coke was a Member of Parliament. In the same year he was instrumental in drafting the Petition of Right reasserting Magna Carta's protections. He found Magna Carta rights 'but a confirmation or restitution of the Common Law' subsequently confirmed by English kings some thirty times. 'Judgment given against any points of the Charters of Magna Carta or the Charter of the Forest', he assured readers, 'are adjudged void, and ... if any statute be made against either of these charters it shall be void.' In another section of the *Institutes*, however, Coke wrote that Parliament could not 'be confined, either for causes or persons within any bounds'. Even so, America's founding fathers, Thomas Jefferson, John Adams, John Marshall and others schooled in Coke's works, focused on his claims that acts against Magna Carta were void, not the contradictory claim for the supremacy of Parliament.

William Blackstone's magisterial *Commentaries on the Laws of England* was an instant best-seller in America when the first volume appeared in 1765. Its publication coincided with sharply increasing fear among Americans that their rights were being trampled upon by the British government. Blackstone would be second only to Montesquieu as the author most frequently cited by the founding generation. Like Coke, Blackstone insisted that Magna Carta did not create, but merely preserved individual rights. He pointed to its tenets on religious and property rights, economic and judicial rights. Despite Magna Carta's focus on those few who were 'free men' in 1215, Blackstone explained that 'it protected every individual of the nation in the free enjoyment of his life, his liberty, and his property, unless declared to be forfeited by the judgment of his peers or the law of the land', a blessing 'which alone would have merited the title that it bears, of the *great* charter.' 'Every wanton and causeless restraint of the will of the subject, whether practiced by a monarch, a nobility, or a popular assembly,' he added, 'is a degree of tyranny.'

If the liberties of Englishmen were not created but only confirmed by Magna Carta, where did they come from? Blackstone declared that the absolute rights of individuals 'vested in them by the immutable laws of nature' were founded 'on nature and reason'. That view was useful for the English but absolutely crucial for the colonists. They were represented in their colonial assemblies but not in Parliament, where they were lumped together with Englishmen unqualified to vote and represented by proxy. Further, their colonial charters were grants from kings alone, not kings in Parliament. Whether a king promising colonists the rights of Magna Carta made those liberties more or less secure was problematic. As already noted their charters had been removed under James II's short-lived Dominion of New England, and were again when King William recalled them in 1689 and reissued them in a standardized form. There was also the worrisome example of Ireland, where the rights of residents were problematic. American fears seemed justified in 1774, when Massachusetts Bay residents were punished by a series of statutes that sharply curbed their charter rights and replaced their governor with a military officer backed by an army. If a charter were withdrawn, would its promised rights still apply? They certainly would if they were innate and inalienable. So innate they had to be.

At the dedication of a liberty tree in Providence, Rhode Island two years after the repeal of the Stamp Act, Silas Downer pinpointed the essence of the British constitution – 'that the people shall not be governed by laws, in the making of which they had no

Jonathan Mayhew, etching by Giovanni Cipriani, 1767.

Jonathan Mayhew and the colonists' 'natural right'

Bostonians sitting in the pews of the West Church to hear the fiery Jonathan Mayhew give thanks for the repeal of the Stamp Act were reminded they had 'a natural right of our own, till we have freely consented to part with it, either in person, or by those whom we have appointed to represent, and to act for us'. 'It shall be taken for granted', Mayhew added, 'that this natural right is declared, affirmed and secured to us, as we are British subjects, by Magna Charta; all acts contrary to which, are said to be *ipso facto* null and void. And that this natural, constitutional right has been further confirmed to most of the plantations by particular subsequent royal charters … the legality and authority of which charters was never once denied by either house of Parliament … till very lately.'

Thomas Paine, oil painting by Auguste Millière, 1880, after an engraving by William Sharp based on a portrait by George Romney, 1792.

hand, or have their monies taken away without their own consent', a privilege that he judged

> *inherent*, and cannot be *granted* by any but the Almighty. It is a natural right which no creature can *give*, or hath a right to take away. The great charter of liberties, commonly called *Magna Carta*, doth not *give* the privileges therein mentioned, nor doth our *Charters*, but must be considered as only declaratory of our rights, and in affirmance of them.

John Tucker, a Boston clergyman, insisted it was the people who were the source of government power. He praised the British government 'under which we have the happiness to live'. Tucker saw Magna Carta as a compact between the King and the people, the King swearing to govern 'according to these laws', but 'Beyond the extent of these then, or contrary to them he can have no rightful authority at all.'

By the time hostilities broke out Americans had come to believe that the design of government and the rights it ensured must be the work of the people as a whole. An anonymous author writing in Philadelphia in 1776 compared colonial charters that were the act of individuals to Magna Carta, which was written by a host of people and contended that charters written by an individual were 'a species of tyranny'. 'All constitutions should be contained in some written Charter, but *that* Charter should be the act of *all* not of *one man*.' Magna Carta, the pamphleteer wrote, 'was not a grant from the Crown, but only agreed or acceded to by the Crown, being first drawn up and framed by the people'. That same year Tom Paine in 'The Forester's Letters' pointed out in his cocksure style:

> The Charter which secures the freedom in England, was formed, not in the senate, but in the field; and insisted on by the people, not granted by the crown. The crown in that instance *granted nothing*, but only renounced its former tyrannies, and bound itself over to its future good behaviour. It was the compromise, by which the wearer of it made his peace with the people, and the condition on which he was suffered to reign.

Not surprisingly, when Thomas Jefferson and his committee drafted a declaration of independence they affirmed that the 'Laws of Nature and of Nature's God' entitled them to dissolve their bonds with Great Britain, that they were 'endowed by their Creator with certain unalienable Rights', and that governments were 'instituted among men, deriving their just powers from the consent of the governed.' Magna Carta rights would remain theirs even without their charters or the connection to the Mother Country. They were inalienable.

Timing, they say, is everything, and that was certainly true for the American attitude toward fundamental rights and how to preserve them. Just as the American colonies were being settled, English fears about threats to their ancient rights made colonists suspicious of any act that seemed to jeopardize theirs. Second, and equally important, customary English strategies for protecting those rights shifted during the years leading up to the American Revolution. Blackstone and his countrymen no longer subscribed to Coke's view that acts against fundamental rights are null and void. Instead they trusted Parliament to protect their liberties. Parliament, not judges consulting Magna Carta or any list of rights, determined what English liberties were or

Gilbert Burnet, engraving from A Biographical Dictionary
of Eminent Scotsmen *by Thomas Thomson, 1870.*

should be. During the Glorious Revolution of 1688, when Parliament replaced James II with William and Mary, it linked their elevation to acceptance of a bill of rights that Bishop Gilbert Burnet declared was to be no less than 'a new magna charta'. Despite Parliament's insistence that nothing had changed, this bloodless transition signalled a shift in British constitutional thinking. T. F. T. Plucknett sees the 'final expression' of judicial review of English statutes in Coke's report of Dr Bonham's Case, where he proclaimed that acts against right were void, while the Glorious Revolution marked 'the abandonment of the doctrine' that legislation must not violate either right or reason. The only check on Parliament's actions was that its legislation be rational. Blackstone said so. In the first eight editions of his *Commentaries on the Laws of England*, he wrote that Parliament could 'change and create afresh even the constitution of the kingdom and of parliaments themselves'. It could, in his famous phrase, 'do every thing that is not naturally impossible'. He did concede that 'acts of parliament that are impossible to be performed are of no validity; and if there arise out of

them collaterally any absurd consequences, manifestly contradictory to common reason, they are, with regard to those collateral consequences void.' But if Parliament were clear about its intent, however unreasonable, 'No court has power to defeat the legislature.' Blackstone became concerned about the implications of this unchecked power over the English rights he was so proud of and, by the ninth and final edition of the *Commentaries*, he qualified the statement of its power to read: 'But if parliament will positively enact a thing to be done which is unreasonable, I know of no power in the ordinary forms of the constitution that is vested with authority to control it.'

Americans, on the other hand, remained wedded to Sir Edward Coke's assurance that a royal command or parliamentary statute that violated a right was void. No one need, or ought to obey it. This view was especially compelling for Americans, since they opposed those parliamentary statutes infringing on promised rights and resented having no representation in that body. The American mindset, therefore, remained fixed on early seventeenth-century ideas that fundamental liberties embedded in Magna Carta and in common law needed to be jealously guarded and the appropriate means to protect them. These means included individual challenges and civil disobedience; the refusal of officials to carry out acts repugnant to rights; judges ready to declare any violation of a right against law; and finally nullification by juries.

Americans were suspicious of the scope of unbounded parliamentary sovereignty. To the question 'What do you think of the British constitution of government?' John Lland in 'The Yankee Spy' answered:

There is no constitution in Britain. It is said, in England that there are three things unknown, viz. the prerogatives of the crown – the privileges of parliament – and the liberty of the people. These things are facts, for although they consider the seventy-two articles of the Magna Charta as the basis of their government, yet from that basis they have never formed a constitution to describe the limits of each department of government. So that precedents and parliamentary acts are all the constitution they have.

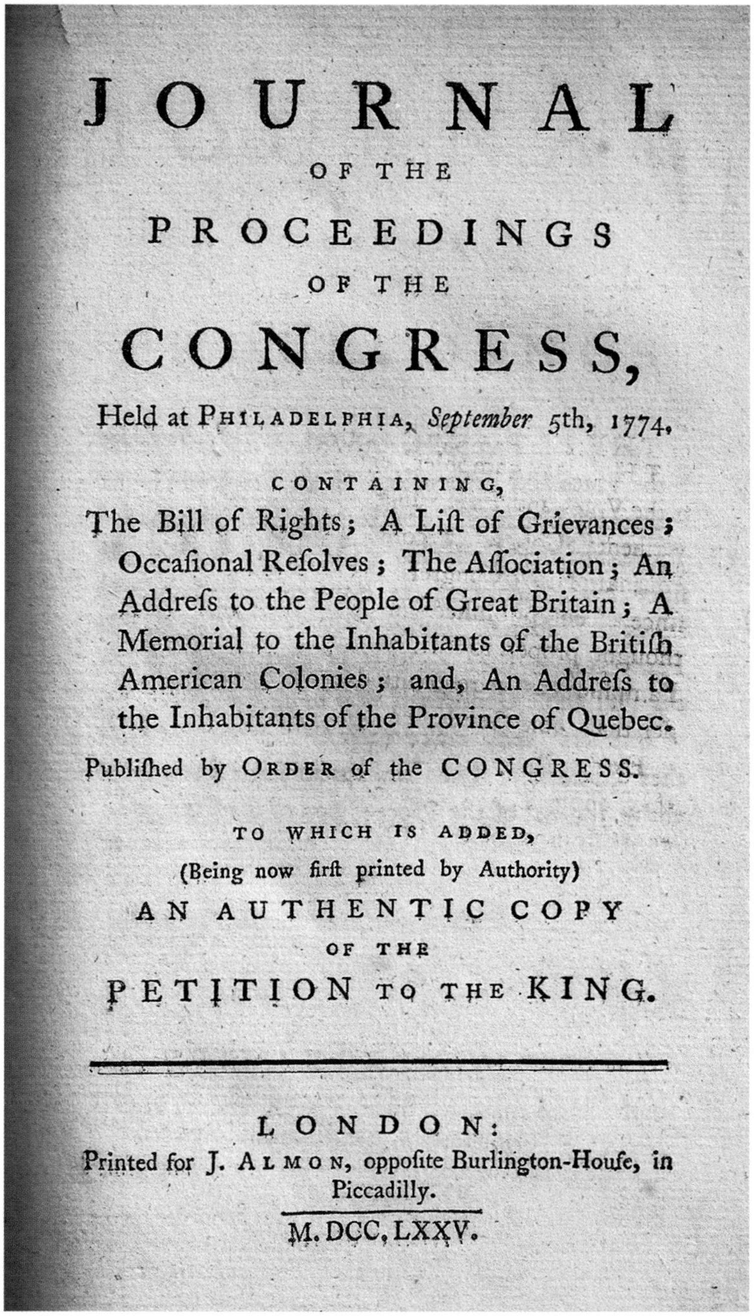

JOURNAL
OF THE
PROCEEDINGS
OF THE
CONGRESS,

Held at PHILADELPHIA, September 5th, 1774,

CONTAINING,

The Bill of Rights; A Lift of Grievances; Occaſional Refolves; The Affociation; An Addreſs to the People of Great Britain; A Memorial to the Inhabitants of the Britiſh American Colonies; and, An Addreſs to the Inhabitants of the Province of Quebec.

Publiſhed by ORDER of the CONGRESS.

TO WHICH IS ADDED,

(Being now firſt printed by Authority)

AN AUTHENTIC COPY

OF THE

PETITION TO THE KING.

LONDON:

Printed for J. ALMON, oppoſite Burlington-Houſe, in Piccadilly.

M. DCC. LXXV.

Title-page of the Journal of the Continental Congress containing the colonists' petition to the King, published 1775.

Magna Carta and state constitutions

The colonists' turn to fashion a frame of government for themselves came as soon as they issued the Declaration of Independence. As independent states their charters were invalid, so they had to draft constitutions of their own. The Continental Congress which operated under the Articles of Confederation during the war found the scheme inadequate, and in 1787 the task of producing a revised framework fell to a special convention. It is instructive to see how the states and the federal government sought to incorporate and protect their Magna Carta and common law legacy.

Many states incorporated paraphrases of parts of Magna Carta as well as common law in their constitutions but rejected the British notion of a sovereign Parliament, explicitly exempting basic rights from any alteration by their legislatures. Article 24 of Delaware's constitution was typical: 'The common law of England, as well as so much of the statute law as has been heretofore adopted in practice in this State, shall remain in force, unless they shall be altered by a future law of the legislature' except any laws 'repugnant to the rights and privileges contained in this constitution, and the declaration of rights'. New Jersey's article 22 read:

> That the common law of England, as well as so much of the statute law, as have been heretofore practiced in this colony, shall still remain in force, until they shall be altered by a future law of the Legislature; such parts only excepted, as are repugnant to the rights and privileges contained in this Charter; and that the inestimable right of trial by jury shall remain confirmed as a part of the law of this colony, without repeal, forever.

Georgia's preamble claimed for citizens 'the rights and privileges they are entitled to by the laws of nature and reason', followed by several articles including the pledge from the English Bill of Rights that 'excessive fines shall not be levied, nor excessive bail demanded', the right to habeas corpus and to 'trial by jury' which was 'to remain inviolate forever'. Over and over again, trial by jury was accorded special reverence and variously described as 'one of the best securities of the rights of the people' (North Carolina), which 'ought to remain sacred and inviolable' (Pennsylvania, South Carolina) and 'to be held sacred' (Vermont).

The seal of the colony of Massachusetts, 1775: freedom (libertas) is represented by Magna Carta brandished in the figure's left hand.

Some constitutions included distinct bills of rights, others relied instead upon the incorporation of common law and references to fundamental rights. Since the states were republics, not monarchies, there was a strong sense that their governments were limited only to specifically designated powers and had no authority to trample on their liberties. A list of rights might even be a danger since it implied government powers in those areas. Further, rights that were inadvertently omitted would be unprotected. Other Americans, with English practice in mind, argued that any government tended to threaten rights and a list was crucial. But whether or not specific lists of rights were included in their first constitutions, over the years Americans became convinced of the value of articulating and embedding in them and their statute books the rights in Magna Carta.

Incorporation of Magna Carta in state statute books

The following list gives those states that have the text of Magna Carta included in their statute books along with the date of that inclusion.

South Carolina 1836	Idaho 1900
North Carolina 1837	Colorado 1910
Georgia 1845	New York 1910 (does not have full version)
Maryland 1870	
Kentucky 1873	Nevada 1912
Nebraska 1893	Oklahoma 1912
Illinois 1896	Michigan 1915
Wisconsin 1898	New Jersey 1937
Wyoming 1899	North Dakota 1943

Still more states included an article in their constitution based on chapters 39 and 40 of the 1215 version of Magna Carta subsequently consolidated in chapter 29 of the 1225 version: 'No person shall be deprived of life, liberty, or property, without due process of law.'

State constitutions with a 'due process' provision

Alaska 1959	Missouri 1945
Arizona 1912	Montana 1889
Colorado 1876	Nebraska 1875
Florida 1887	Nevada 1864
Georgia 1945	New Mexico 1912
Hawaii 1959	New York 1939
Illinois 1870	Oklahoma 1907
Iowa 1857	South Carolina 1895
Louisiana 1921	South Dakota 1889
Michigan 1964	Utah 1896
Minnesota 1857 as amended 1904	Washington 1889
	West Virginia 1872
Mississippi 1890	Wyoming 1890

Four additional states have a similar 'due process' provision in the context of criminal prosecutions (California, Connecticut, Idaho, North Dakota) while in another five states the provision is limited to the accused in criminal prosecutions (Alabama, Delaware, Kentucky, Pennsylvania, Rhode Island).

Virginia is the only state that has separate provisions for criminal and property prosecutions, stating, for example, that 'No person shall be deprived of his property without due process of law'.

Nor was this merely for show. State courts have referred to Magna Carta on numerous occasions for guidance in cases on questions of inheritance, property rights, due process, corporations and other subjects. For example, the opinion in *Griffith v. Griffith's Executors* (General Court of Maryland, 1798), mentions Magna Carta eight times.

Right: The Declaration of Independence.
Below: George Washington at the Constitutional
Convention, by Junius Brutus Stearns, 1856.

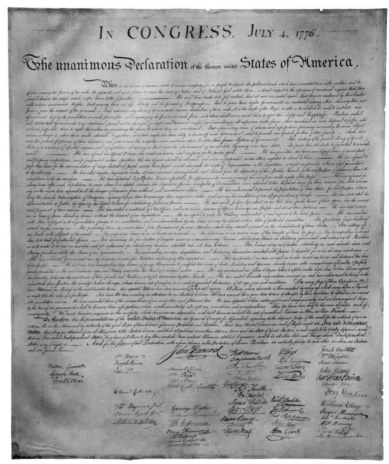

The federal Constitution

The federal government's own effort to craft a constitution began with the Declaration of Independence, in which the Continental Congress proclaimed that all men were endowed by their Creator with certain inalienable rights and substituted for 'property' in the great British triad of life, liberty and property 'the pursuit of happiness'. The first federal Constitution, the Articles of Confederation, did not concern itself with rights. It had very limited judicial responsibility, could not tax directly, or otherwise interfere with the internal governments of what were sovereign states. Protection of rights was left to the states themselves. However, in 1787, when the Continental Congress passed the Northwest Ordinance laying out the manner in which that territory would be governed, it did include a list of rights. Article 2 of the Northwest Ordinance sets out the fundamental rights of residents including a battery of what Americans considered the crucial Magna Carta rights. Inhabitants, it proclaimed,

> shall always be entitled to the benefits of the writ of habeas corpus, and of trial by jury, of a proportionate representation of the people in the legislature, and of judicial proceedings according to the course of the common law … No man shall be deprived of his liberty or property, but by the judgment of his peers or the law of the land.

Compensation was to be given if private property were taken by the government or personal services demanded.

When a revised, more vigorous federal constitution was drafted in 1787, the Framers limited the new central government to specifically designated powers and gave it no authority to infringe on cherished rights. For prudence's sake, though, they included in the body of the document core rights they felt it essential to set down. In section 9 of Article I, which spells out the powers of Congress, the Framers, assuming the population had the writ of habeas corpus and due process of law, lay down the rule that the writ 'shall not be suspended, unless when in Cases of Rebellion or Invasion the public Safety may require it'. This is followed by a prohibition against bills of attainder, which were then still permitted in the British Parliament, and a prohibition against *ex post facto* laws. Section 2 of Article III, which established the judicial branch, promised: 'The Trial of all Crimes, except in Cases of Impeachment, shall be by Jury; and such Trial shall be held in the State where the said Crimes shall have been committed.' This short list left out many traditional liberties and did not touch on the expanded rights Americans had come to cherish as a result of their political struggles with the Mother Country – freedom of religion, freedom of speech and of the press.

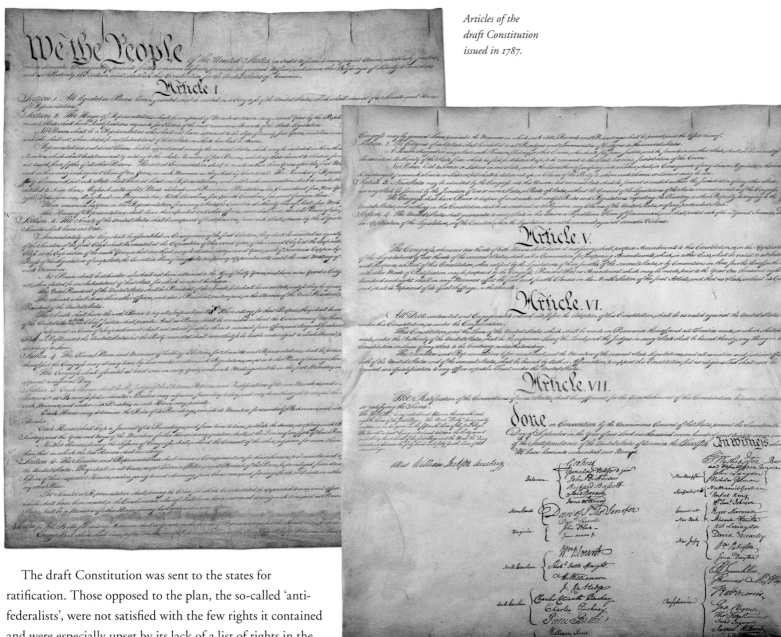

Articles of the draft Constitution issued in 1787.

The draft Constitution was sent to the states for ratification. Those opposed to the plan, the so-called 'anti-federalists', were not satisfied with the few rights it contained and were especially upset by its lack of a list of rights in the British fashion. Everyone agreed rights must be protected, but those who favoured the document as it was, insisted rights were safe without a list, indeed probably safer. The anti-federalists had many objections to the great powers the new constitution gave the central government, but trained most of their fire on the lack of a bill of rights. Thomas Jefferson agreed. He was ambassador to France when the Constitutional Convention met but was sent a copy of the final document. In a famous response to James Madison, the so-called Father of the Constitution, Jefferson was frank: 'I will now add what I do not like. First the omission of a bill of rights.' He argued 'that a bill of rights is what the people are entitled to against every government on earth, general or particular, and what no just

government should refuse, or rest on inference'.

Despite Jefferson's concerns and those of the anti-federalists the Constitution was ratified without a list of rights. But the vote in favour of ratification was so close in Massachusetts that only the promise by the proponents that a bill of rights would be added once the new Congress met persuaded that state's convention to approve the document. The remaining states relied on that promise as well. Jefferson hoped Madison would take up the task and wrote again urging him to press for a bill of rights. The Constitution 'forms us into one state as to certain objects, and gives us a legislative and executive body for these objects', Jefferson pointed out. 'It should therefore guard us against their abuses of power within the field submitted to them.' Weighing all the pros and cons of listing rights Jefferson concluded:

> There is a remarkeable difference between the characters of the Inconveniences which attend a Declaration of rights, and those which attend the want of it. The inconveniences of the Declaration are that it may cramp government in its useful exertions. But the evil of this is shortlived, moderate, and reparable. The inconveniences of the want of the Declaration are permanent, afflicting and irreparable: they are in constant progression from bad to worse.

When the first congress convened Madison pressed the members to approve amendments, and despite their reluctance these were drafted and sent to the states for ratification. They included protection against unreasonable search and seizure, the right to assemble and to petition the government, to keep and bear arms, protection against self-incrimination and a variety of specific judicial rights. The Eighth Amendment was taken verbatim from the English Bill of Rights: 'Excessive bail shall not be required, nor excessive fines imposed, nor cruel and unusual punishments inflicted.' The Ninth Amendment sought to allay fears about any right inadvertently omitted: 'The enumeration in the Constitution of certain rights shall not be construed to deny or disparage others retained by the people.' The Tenth Amendment left powers not delegated to the central government to the states or the people. The list also included, indeed started out with the then novel rights prohibiting Congress from establishing a religion, or abridging the freedom of speech and of the press.

The Constitution's amendment process presents a formidable barrier to the removal of any of these rights. Of course, like common law itself, the understanding of Magna Carta rights in America has evolved and broadened through case law and judicial decisions, but centuries after the barons wrung those concessions from King John the basic rights enshrined in Magna Carta and in the American Constitution still stand as barriers against the pretensions of government. Their preservation against infringement, as Jefferson recognized, requires constant vigilance – a government mindful of its limits, individuals ready to challenge any violation, judges prepared to resort to first principles. While the British Parliament by a simple

The anti-federalist Richard Henry Lee, widely held to be the author of The Federal Farmer, *late 18th-century hand-coloured engraving.*

majority vote can limit the use of juries or abolish the hereditary House of Lords, no American Congress or president has the power to alter the Constitution or to abolish a constitutional right. Magna Carta remains the touchstone it has been for eight centuries. The United States Supreme Court continues to cite Magna Carta in decisions, and has now done so on well over two hundred occasions.

The author of *The Federal Farmer*, writing during the debate over the American Constitution in 1788, explains how our freedom depends upon keeping in view that legacy of Magna Carta:

> That the people might not forget these rights, and gradually become prepared for arbitrary government, their discerning and honest leaders caused this instrument to be confirmed near forty times, and to be read twice a year in public places, not that it would lose its validity without such confirmations, but to fix the content of it in the minds of the people, as they successively come upon the stage. Men, in some countries do not remain free, merely because they are entitled to natural and unalienable rights, men in all countries are entitled to them, not because their ancestors once got together and enumerated them on paper, but because, by repeated negociations and declarations, all parties are brought to realize them, and of course to believe them to be sacred … I might shew the wisdom of our past conduct, as a people in not merely comforting ourselves that we were entitled to freedom, but in constantly keeping in view, in addresses, in bills of rights, in newspapers, &c. the particular principles on which our freedom must always depend.

The sealing of Magna Carta, stained-glass window in the dining room at Mansion House, London, by Alexander Gibbs, 1868.

Chapter Nine

Magna Carta in the Nineteenth Century

Miles Taylor

The Great Charter… Here commences the history of the English nation.

Thomas Babington Macaulay, *The History of England from the Accession of James the Second* (1848)

The whole of the constitutional history of England is little more than a commentary on Magna Carta.

William Stubbs, *Constitutional History of England* (1875–8)

The six hundredth and seven hundredth anniversaries of the signing of Magna Carta were overshadowed by war. On 15 June 1815 allied British, Dutch and Prussian forces were making their final preparations to fight Napoleon at Waterloo. One hundred years later, Magna Carta day fell as the Second Battle of Ypres drew to a bloody conclusion. On both occasions, celebrations of Magna Carta in the peaceful meadows of Runnymede were thwarted by carnage on Flanders fields.

In 1815, preparations for publishing an extravagant illuminated edition of Magna Carta were delayed. A 'gold' edition of *Magna Carta Regis Johannis* had been intended for George III and selected nobility by the printer and publisher John Whittaker, illustrated by John Harris father and son (only two copies have survived, both from a later date). However, the only memorial event of note was a 'grand baronial entertainment' hosted by the Duke of Norfolk at his castle in Arundel, Sussex, where a ball and dinner heralded the installation of a new 'Baron's Chamber' and a stained-glass depiction of Hugh Bigod, the 3rd Earl of Norfolk, presenting the Charter to King John. A century later, plans for an international conference of scholars, organized by the Royal Historical Society, were abandoned, and a collection of essays – notable for its lack of German contributors – was produced instead.

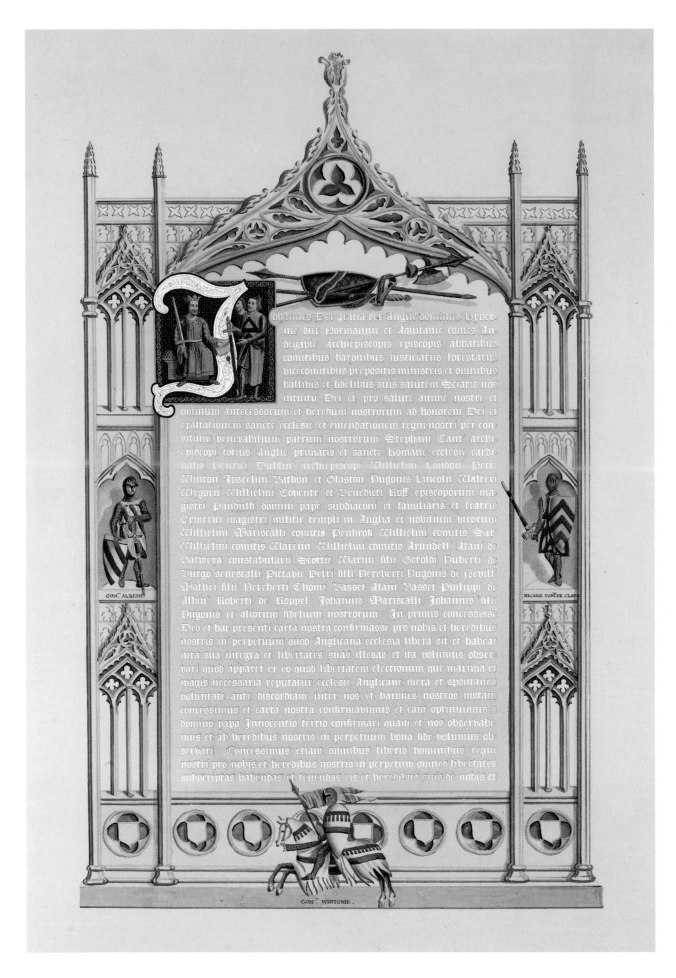

Left: Opening page of the Magna Carta text in John Whittaker's 'gold' edition, 1870. Right: The Lords Chamber, from Charles Barry's Gothic design (1840–7), showing seven of the eighteen statues of barons and bishops ranged between the windows and above the dais.

The fascination of Magna Carta

Despite these inauspicious anniversaries, Magna Carta – or 'Magna Charta' as it now tended to be known – enjoyed an unrivalled reputation as a constitutional icon in Regency and Victorian Britain, only coming in for more scrutiny and questioning towards the end of the nineteenth century and into the Edwardian era (1901–10). In a country notorious for having no written constitution, Magna Carta became an essential element, along with the 1689 Bill of Rights, in the 'the grand palladium of English liberty', a copy of which, one author suggested, should be in every British home. Like a biblical tablet of stone, the famous Charter provided a unique historical reference point

for a nation moving rapidly through decade on decade of social and political change, and imperial expansion. Magna Carta began the period as the first act of the comprehensive *Statutes of the Realm*, published by the Record Commission in nine volumes between 1810 and 1829. A facsimile of the Charter by A. P. Harrison of Brighton was displayed in the 'Paper, Printing and Bookbinding' section of the Great Exhibition at the Crystal Palace in Hyde Park in 1851. Effigies of the barons who were present at Runnymede were ordered by the Fine Art Commission for inclusion in Charles Barry's new Houses of Parliament at Westminster, which were formally opened in 1852. Mansion House, the home of the Lord Mayor of London, was fitted out with a Magna Carta window during refurbishments in the 1860s.

Lord Byron, by Henry Meyer after James Holmes, 1818.

Byron's complaint

Magna Carta did not sweep up everyone. In 'Thoughts Suggested by a College Examination' (1806) the poet Lord Byron complained that young men at university knew more of the classical republicanism of ancient Athens and Rome than the history of English liberties:

> Though marvelling at the name of Magna Charta,
> Yet well he recollects the laws of Sparta;
> Can tell, what edicts sage Lycurgus made,
> While Blackstone's on the shelf, neglected laid;
> Of Grecian dramas vaunts the deathless fame,
> Of Avon's bard, rememb'ring scarce the name.

However, when we consider the ubiquity of references to Magna Carta in late Hanoverian and Victorian print and visual culture, Byron's concern seems wide of the mark.

Everyone wanted to be seen with the document or associated with its history. Facing imprisonment in the Tower of London in 1810, the radical MP Sir Francis Burdett posed for a portrait by John Raphael Smith reading Magna Carta to his son upon his knee. In 1820, Queen Caroline, the estranged consort of George IV, was caricatured by the radical publisher, William Hone, as a perhaps unlikely defender of the principles of 1215. William IV (r. 1830–7) was depicted twice in portraits by Robert Bowyer clutching Magna Carta, and Queen Victoria (r. 1837–1901) was known to enjoy 'barons of beef' (a hearty English dish which in the nineteenth century became specifically associated with the events of 1215) for her Christmas lunch. As professional scholars extended their research on constitutional history beyond the seventeenth century so beloved by earlier generations of Whig historians, and into Saxon and Norman England, Magna Carta came to represent the seed of the national political genius. It was the 'earliest monument of English liberty', according to J. R. Green in his *Short History of the English People* (1874); it was 'the first great public act of the nation, after it has realised its own identity', wrote William Stubbs, Regius Professor of History at the University of Oxford, in his *Constitutional History of England* (1874–8).

'Magna Charta', illustration from William Hone's The Political House That Jack Built, 1819.

William IV holding Magna Carta, by Robert Bowyer, 1830.

caused confusion and poor arithmetic. James Lonsdale's memorial window for the Duke of Norfolk showed only twelve, the Fine Art Commission came up with sixteen barons and two bishops for the new Palace of Westminster, whilst later Victorian estimates ran variously to twenty-three, twenty-five and twenty-six.

Similarly, Georgians and Victorians skated over the complexities of a document written in manuscript in the Latin language six centuries previously. For much of the nineteenth century, commentaries on the Charter relied heavily on its earlier interpreters, especially Edward Coke (1552–1634), William Blackstone (1723–80) and Daines Barrington (c.1727–1800). In doing so, they became fixated with the struggle between the King and peers, as though 1215 was merely a dry-run for the 'Glorious Revolution' of 1688–9. They showed little interest in the subsequent charters of the thirteenth century which did so much to consolidate the original settlement, and they tended to focus on certain clauses in the Charter, such as 39 ('No free man …') and 12 and 14 (scutage), which were taken to be early versions of trial by jury and no taxation without representation. These were political rights which were very familiar to modern readers, but less obviously part of the fabric of medieval law. Not until the work of Stubbs in the 1870s, and in much greater depth, the research of F. W. Maitland beginning in the 1880s, and William Sharp McKechnie's major study of 1905, were many of these simplistic assumptions challenged and myths surrounding the Charter dispelled. Until then, the popular understanding of Magna Carta was bound up with a quaint view of the olden time, in which a despotic monarch (not unlike the Hanoverian Georges) and a noble aristocracy (not unlike the Whig party in the age of reform) vied to establish representative government. The theatre played its part too in this rendition of medieval England for modern audiences. Shakespeare's King John was a perennial favourite on the London stage, along with lighter dramas and comedies set in medieval times, such as *Punch's Pantomime, or, Harlequin King John, and the Magna Carta* performed at Covent Garden in January 1843, and Alfred Bate Richards's *Runnymede: or the Magna Charta. An Historical Tragedy in Five Acts* (1846).

Why did Magna Carta as a piece of history fascinate nineteenth-century Britons so, whilst failing to excite their curiosity as a historical document? It is a question worth posing. After all, there was little to connect the nineteenth century with the thirteenth. Ancestral links

By mid-century, invocations of Magna Carta had become so commonplace and so hackneyed as to invite the satire of Charles Dickens, who included the Great Charter in Josiah Bounderby's 'moral infection of clap-trap' in *Hard Times* (1854) and William Thackeray, who in his *Rebecca and Rowena* (1850) – a spoof on Walter Scott's *Ivanhoe* – had a disguised knight, Sir Wilfrid Ivanhoe, as the hero of the piece, with not a baron in sight.

For all their certainty about its status, commentators in the nineteenth century remained surprisingly ignorant or at best lacking in curiosity about the precise facts surrounding the conflict between King John, the barons and the bishops. Take, for example, the historic site of Runnymede. Various illustrators at different times depicted King John signing the Charter under a tree (Hamilton Mortimer, 1813), in an open field (John Leech, 1872), in a tent (James Doyle, 1864), and by a tent under a tree (Ambrose William Warren, c.1830s). Confusion also remained as to whether the ceremony took place on the island in the Thames or on the meadow – not helped by the fact that by the 1850s the river had silted up and William Clifford, the owner of the estate, built a causeway to connect the bank of the Thames to the island and also erected a mock-Tudor 'Barons' Chamber', where a dining-room awaited tourists. The number of barons assembled on the mede also

Runnymede as imagined in the 19th century: King John under a tree, by Hamilton Mortimer, 1813 …

… in an open field, by John Leech, 1872 …

… in a tent, by James Doyle, 1864 …

… and by a tent under a tree, by Ambrose William Warren, c.1830s.

Magna Charta, and the Charter of the Forests signed by King John.

A 19th-century engraving based on James Londale's design for the Duke of Norfolk's memorial window.

like those of the Duke of Norfolk were the exception not the rule by 1800 (and his descent came through the female line). It was often noted – most pointedly by Bernard Burke (of Burke's Peerage fame) in his *Vicissitudes of Families* (1860) – that there were no living descendants of the Runnymede barons in the Victorian House of Lords. Moreover, in legal terms Magna Carta had increasingly less relevance to modern British jurisprudence. Successive revisions of statute law (particularly those of 1829, 1863 and 1879), together with a zeal for legal codification, meant that much of the Charter had been repealed away or amended by the end of the century. Some of this modernization – for example, the repeal of the clauses respecting customary forestry and fishing rights – provoked opposition. However, apart from pockets of resistance amongst workers in the Forest of Dean, and periodic attempts to halt the progress of the 'salmon laws', law reformers and free-traders were allowed to march through the clauses of the Charter unchecked. Noting its demise as law, some historians have concluded that Magna Carta also disappeared as fable. Not so. Throughout the nineteenth and early twentieth centuries the complex tale of a Norman king struggling with a Pope, an archbishop and assorted English knights for a Latin roll, took on new meaning and relevance as Britain forged ahead, whilst constantly looking to the past.

'Brougham's Reform Cordial': a bottle produced in 1832 in honour of Lord Brougham, the Lord Chancellor who played a key role in persuading the House of Lords to accept the Reform Act. Brougham is depicted clutching 'The Second Magna Charta'.

Manipulating the Charter

Magna Carta proved so enduring because it could be deployed to suit most standpoints in the party and ecclesiastical politics of the nineteenth century. Across the spectrum – from Tories to Whigs to radicals and socialists, and on to the suffragettes – the Charter provided legitimacy and precedent to those seeking to change, correct or conserve the constitutional status quo. And the uses of Magna Carta were not confined to Parliament. The Church of England, and the English Catholic Church too, resorted to the history of Magna Carta in the thirteenth century to reinforce their claims in the nineteenth. In this way the utility of Magna Carta did not diminish with the Utilitarians of the 1830s, as some historians have argued. Rather, it enjoyed a heyday as a handmaiden to the arguments of reformers and anti-reformers down to the First World War.

The most famous appropriation of Magna Carta in the nineteenth century was the 1832 Reform Act, described by one of its Whig supporters, the historian Thomas Babington Macaulay, as 'the Great Charter'. When the Act was finally passed in June 1832, *The Times* named it the 'new Magna Carta' and called for national celebrations to take place on Magna Carta day the following week. Other nicknames given to the reform bills of 1831–2 also pointed to a historic lineage: the 'New Charter', the 'People's Charter' and the 'Maxima Charta'. Although as historians Whigs such as Macaulay and Henry Hallam steered clear of the medieval period, and located constitutional modernity in the Protestant succession after 1688, to politicians the analogy between 1832 and 1215 was too good to pass up. The sculptor Francis Chantrey was commissioned by Thomas Coke of Holkham Hall in Norfolk (direct descendant of the Coke of Coke's *Institutes*) to depict William IV granting the Act to Whig peers in the style of John and the barons at Runnymede. And even those who felt that the

Disraeli and Magna Carta

One young Tory, making his way in post-Reform Act Britain, was Benjamin Disraeli, and he latched upon the moral of Magna Carta as his strapline. In his *Letters of Runnymede* (1836), and in journalism of the period, he sketched a picture of pre-lapsarian England in which the Church and nobility sided with the people, contrasting it with the self-interested oligarchy of mercantile wealth and the great landowners which comprised the Whig ascendancy. However, in contesting the Whigs' monopoly of Magna Carta, Disraeli was soon outshone by the Chartist movement.

Benjamin Disraeli, by Sir Francis Grant, 1852.

Whigs' reforms did not go far enough drew from a similar stock of stories, arguing that the nobility of the thirteenth century would have been truer to the wishes of the people, than the modern peers whose titles were created since 1688. As one supporter of the radical Birmingham Political Union put it in 1831, 'The old Peers who led our fathers on to conquest and liberty, the descendants of those who wrested Magna Charta from the tyrant John – these men, I say, behold with indignation the warfare which the Pittite creations carry on against the liberty of the people'. One pamphleteer, Henry Francis (Lord Teynham), argued that the barons at Runnymede, having 'obtained the great Charter from the tyrant John', then did little for the people, an inference obvious to any critic of the Whigs. Conversely, those politicians who knew their Magna Carta better than the Whigs could use the same text to fulminate against any change in the constitution. For example, Sir Charles Wetherell, Tory MP for Boroughbridge and one of the most doughty opponents of the reform bills, challenged Lord John Russell, one of its Whig architects (and a sometime historian), by attacking his ignorance of the corporate rights guaranteed by Magna Carta. In 1831, Russell had been given a gold box, inscribed with the words 'Magna Carta and reform' by the Corporation of the City of London. Wetherell told Russell that if he supported Magna Carta, 'he must give up reform', for the 1215 document had given many of the parliamentary constituencies the Whigs wished to disfranchise their original charters which had enabled them to send representatives to the first Parliament of 1265 (a neat argument, though not necessarily a sound or scholarly one).

Indeed, the Whigs' manipulation of Magna Carta in 1832 brought them more criticism than praise. In addition to Tory invective there was the far more potent Chartist movement, which in 1838 issued its totemic six points of parliamentary reform in the shape of *The People's Charter*, an evocation both of 1215 and of 1832 which merits closer investigation in order to unravel its multiple meanings.

Although there were Chartists such as John Watkins, whose *Five Cardinal Points of the People's Charter* (1839) found in Magna Carta historical precedents for physical force, the Chartists' appeal to the first charter rested on two other distinct grounds. First, *The People's Charter* of 1838 was offered as a corrective to the Whigs' self-styled 'Great Charter' of 1832. The intervening years, for many radical and Chartist opponents of the Whigs, had seen divisive class legislation in the form

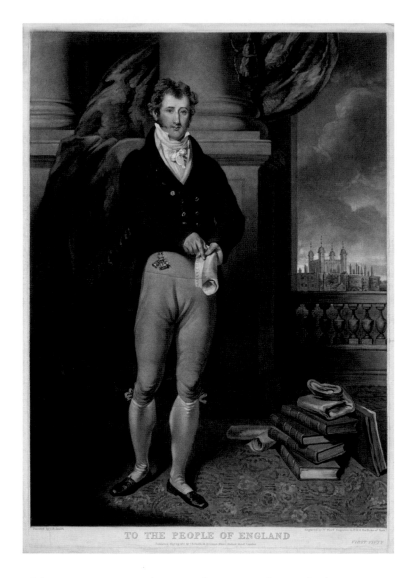

TO THE PEOPLE OF ENGLAND

Sir Francis Burdett holding Magna Carta, with the Tower of London in the background, by William Ward after John Raphael Smith, 1811.

R. J. Richardson, threatened to march into the city with one hundred thousand men, copies of Magna Carta in their hands, to demand the liberation of the imprisoned orator Joseph Rayner Stephens.

In the 1830s and 1840s – the age of reform – Magna Carta was thus open to all political persuasions, and the sole preserve of none. Magna Carta could indicate reverence for unreformed Britain and leaving things the way they were, or be a manifesto for change, or a restatement of immemorial civic rights. It was Magna Carta's availability for appropriation and misappropriation which guaranteed its traction in political rhetoric, just as it was losing its place in the statute book.

In this way Magna Carta in the Victorian period could be as much part of a forward-looking liberal pluralism, as a backward glance at gothic glory. Nowhere is this clearer than in the religious uses to which the story of Magna Carta was put. That Magna Carta had been drawn up and signed in a Catholic England, and its sentiments (if not the manner of its enactment) supported by Pope Innocent III, had sometimes been regarded as irrelevant, but took on new meaning in the nineteenth century as Catholics in Britain and Ireland sought emancipation from the civil disabilities to which they had been subject since the late seventeenth century. During the three major Catholic controversies of the first half of the nineteenth century – Catholic emancipation, the funding of Maynooth College in Ireland, and the Ecclesiastical Titles Bill of 1851 – Magna Carta was turned to frequently by liberal politicians keen to counter the strident and exclusive association of English liberty with Protestantism. Supporters of Catholic emancipation before 1829 often cited the case of the Duke of Norfolk, descended indirectly from a baronial family of 1215, but belonging to a Catholic faith now proscribed from enjoying various of the rights enshrined in Magna Carta. In 1845, when the Earl of Winchelsea led several fellow peers and bishops in opposition to the decision to use state funding to support the Maynooth Catholic training college in Ireland – lamenting that the legislation was being passed on Magna Carta day, 'the anniversary of the day on which the barons of England wrested from King John the charter of English liberty' – he was rebuked by the Lord Chancellor for failing to specify that they had been Roman Catholic barons. Then in 1851, a wave of anti-Catholicism spread through Britain, fuelled by Pope Pius IX's claim of jurisdiction over British Catholics. Several liberal MPs

of the new Poor Law and a new police system, but no further constitutional change such as the introduction of secret voting by ballot. Disillusioned with the Whigs, Chartist leaders concluded in 1838 that whilst the 'barons of old' had got their charter in 1215, and the middle classes theirs in 1832, now a separate 'people's charter was needed for the working classes'. So the Chartist movement sought, like Disraeli, to seize the mantle of Magna Carta from the Whigs, rather than simply appealing to it as a blueprint for reform. Secondly, the Chartists, like many radicals before them, looked to clause 39 ('No free man …') as one of the most significant rights enjoyed by British people, and found it to be enshrined in Magna Carta. Just as Sir Francis Burdett MP had famously appealed to Magna Carta on the eve of his incarceration in the Tower of London in 1810, and Henry Hunt had done so in 1819, Chartists greeted each arrest of their outspoken leaders in the years 1839–42 as a breach of habeas corpus, and in so doing invoked Magna Carta. For instance, the Manchester Chartist, pointed to the long history of Catholic loyalty to the British state, starting with Magna Carta. Nonetheless, a zealous Protestant backlash followed, and for a while Magna Carta was identified solely with the Church of England. It was seen as the beginning of the English reformation: the first moment when an English king was rendered independent of Rome. Catholic historians struck back. One writer sought to vindicate King John completely, arguing that the Charter was a French conspiracy designed to weaken the English Crown. In 1875, Cardinal Manning, the recently appointed archbishop of Westminster, argued that without the support of the Pope, Magna Carta might have been set aside altogether.

Against this backdrop of stalwart Anglicanism at home and ultramontanism abroad, anti-Catholicism reared its head once more during one of the strangest incarnations of Magna Carta in modern times. This was the 'Magna Carta Association' of 1875, established by a barrister, Dr Edward Kinealy, after his unsuccessful defence of an Australian butcher's claim to be the missing English Catholic heir, Sir Roger Tichborne, presumed drowned in a shipwreck in 1854. Arthur Orton, the Tichborne claimant, was convicted of perjury, and

Kinealy's conduct during the trial – his attacks on the judge and the witnesses, as well as his anti-Catholic prejudice (he turned on the Tichborne family who he claimed had conspired against Orton) – was widely condemned and he was disbarred. Kinealy then organized a nationwide movement ostensibly to muster support for Orton, although clearly designed to clear Kinealy's own name and pave the way for his entry into Parliament, in which he succeeded at the Stoke by-election of 1875. The Potteries hustings were overrun by sectarian rhetoric as Kinealy mobilized the traditional anti-Irish feeling of the local electorate. The Association also issued a twenty-point programme, a hotchpotch of radical measures, including the demand for the restitution of the full powers of the Privy Council. Kinealy proved an ineffective MP. Orton emerged from prison in 1884, and the Magna Carta Association lingered on until 1886. It was a curious episode, in which many of the disparate features of nineteenth-century Magna Carta worship – popular Protestantism, legal procedure and baronial pedigree – were mixed into a heady brew.

Gradually, however, the mid-Victorian decades saw the emergence of a more moderate understanding of the religious history of the

Magna Carta (left) and the death warrant of Charles I (right) on Tom Brown's wall, frontispiece to the 1885 Macmillan edition of Tom Brown at Oxford.

Tom Brown's mixed message

In his *Tom Brown at Oxford* (1861), Thomas Hughes captured the ambiguous status enjoyed by Magna Carta when he had his eponymous hero, eager to flaunt his new views on 'universal democracy', place a picture of the Charter on his mantelpiece ahead of his father's visit, only for his father to commend his choice, but show alarm by the accompanying portrait of a copy of the death warrant of Charles I. Magna Carta sent out mixed messages: there was no one undisputed understanding of what the famous parchment meant.

One of a series of 'Cartoons in Model' at the Women's Political and Social Union exhibition held in
May 1909: 'King John Asquith' is compelled by suffragettes to sign the Women's Magna Carta.

Charter. Stephen Langton, the archbishop of Canterbury in 1215, became central to these new accounts, especially in the work of Edward Conybeare and Arthur Hassall, as they claimed that the national Church was in the vanguard of progress, and not the enemy of liberty as sometimes supposed. Both Conybeare and Hassall drew on professional historians to substantiate their claims, finding support in the work of J. R. Seeley, the Regius Professor of History at Cambridge, and in the pioneering research of the liberal churchman, Stubbs, at Oxford. By the turn of the new century, Magna Carta was sitting as calmly and comfortably in the iconography of the Church of England as it was in the historical topography of English local life. The six-day St Edmundsbury Pageant of 1907, in which the Charter played a prominent role, was matched the following year by a Church of

England event of equal length at Lambeth Palace (where Stubbs had been the librarian prior to the call from Oxford). Magna Carta came halfway through the chronological sweep of historical re-enactments which stretched from Constantine to the acquittal of the seven bishops in 1688.

The last significant outing of Magna Carta as a political tool came with the women suffragettes of the early twentieth century. Women were notable by their omission from the history of 1215, although they are referred to in several of the clauses of the Charter. There were obvious resonances to be exploited. When the Liberal government of Herbert Asquith introduced 'Cat and Mouse' legislation in 1909, interning suffragette leaders, the Women's Political and Social Union depicted Asquith at an exhibition as King John trying to set aside

Helena Normanton, champion of Magna Carta

Helena Normanton's was an ingenious and timely intervention. She fought her own personal battle to break the male monopoly on the English bar, becoming one of the first woman barristers in the country in 1922. And she led the movement launched in 1923 to preserve Runnymede as a national monument to Magna Carta, joining with the Vicar of Egham and the Marquess of Lincolnshire to save the Mede from private sale after the First World War. In 1929, the appeal was vindicated when Lady Fairhaven and her sons, the owners of the Runnymede estate, donated the 188-acre site to the National Trust. History had come full circle. Omitted from the full story of Magna Carta across the ages, women finally made their mark, ensuring that a permanent memorial eventually came to the 1215 site.

Helena Normanton in 1949.

habeas corpus. In January 1911, the suffragette newspaper *Votes for Women* drew on the example of the 'militant methods' employed by the Magna Carta barons to justify their shock tactics. And four years later, at the time of the seven hundredth anniversary, Helena Normanton, a member of the Women's Freedom League, crafted a much more substantial account of 'Women and Magna Carta' in an article in the *Englishwomen's Review*. Normanton showed how English noblewomen such as Isabel de Clare and Matilda de Braose had been part of the opposition to King John, and so it was fair 'to infer that we owe Magna Carta partly to our never-forgotten forefathers, and partly to our seldom-remembered foremothers'. She also demonstrated that women's rights were implicit in Magna Carta. Trial by a jury of one's peers might include women jurors, as there was no definition of freeholders as male until 1832. Indeed, she showed that protection of women was explicit in the Charter. By clauses 7, 8, 11 and 26 'all the best practices of the day were confirmed in their [i.e. women's] favour', that is to say, the right to own property independent of marriage and the freedom to remarry. Normanton found only one 'unchivalrous clause' in Magna Carta: clause 54, that no man accused of murder could be arrested or imprisoned upon the appeal of a woman, unless the victim was her husband.

Magna Carta across the British empire

As a symbol of common law custom, political pluralism and religious toleration, the ideals of Magna Carta were, like many commodities of Victorian Britain, ripe for export overseas as well as for consumption at home. Here lies another explanation of the continuing relevance of Magna Carta in the nineteenth century: its extension throughout the English-speaking world as a symbol of the rights which were the peculiar entitlement of those peoples subject to British dominion. The colonial branch of the Magna Carta industry was strongest in the American colonies before 1776, and no less prevalent in the new republic. At the time of the centennial of American independence, an attorney, John Cleland Wells, traced the lineage of his country's legal tradition back to the Charter of 1215 and its ratification under Henry III and Edwards I, II and III. American genealogists also reworked neglected seams connecting the modern world to the nobility of the thirteenth century. No one did this more avidly than Charles

Magna Carta Place, Canberra.

Magna Carta in Australia

Genealogical descent from Runnymede was of course only possible for a chosen few. In other parts of the nineteenth-century world still formally part of the British empire, where aristocratic connections were weaker, Magna Carta provided a set of live political principles. The new Australian colonies are a good case study of just how amphibious claims for the rights of Englishmen could be. In the crown colony of New South Wales in the 1820s, despite the convict origins of many of the settlers, Magna Carta was frequently invoked as one of the sources of their political freedoms. In 1827 reformers in Sydney petitioned for the establishment of representative assembly to protect them from unfair taxation which was 'contrary to Magna Carta', and

four years later when the unpopular Governor Ralph Darling left his post in the colony, a local newspaper office was emblazoned with a transparency which included 'a corn-stalk sustaining a Crown, with these words, 'GOD SAVE THE KING! MAGNA CARTA!' Through to the 1850s and 1860s, when representative government began to be rolled out in Australia, New Zealand and the colonies of southern Africa, and consolidated in Canada, Magna Carta could supply a ready template for political redress for small property-owners, tax-payers and jurors who in their own country lacked the kind of institutions enjoyed back in Britain. The past still echoes in the present in modern-day Canberra, the capital of Australia, where the Parliament building faces out onto Magna Carta Place.

Browning, author of *The Magna Carta Barons and their American Descendants* (1898). He not only proved that most of the baronial families were related by marriage, but also that many had distant relatives across the United States. The research of enthusiasts such as Browning paved the way in 1898 for the establishment of the Philadelphia-based 'Baronial Order of Runnymede' (later renamed the 'Baronial Order of Magna Carta'), membership of which was open to anyone who could prove a link to the barons of 1215.

Magna Carta offered the cloak of protection not only to colonial settlers but also to subject peoples in the British empire. The clauses of Magna Carta which related to forestry (including those in the supplementary Charter of the Forest of 1217) and to rivers, were broadly interpreted by advocates of the interests of indigenous peoples, especially in North America and in New Zealand. Customary forest rights included grazing, foraging for fuel and enjoyment of pasture-land. These rights were not limited to woods, but could be extended to fields, moors and other places inhabited by 'freemen'. Protection of common access to rivers and coastal waters, through the removal of fish-weirs, was also covered by a flexible application of clause 33. In this way, the common rights to the land and to the waters conventionally exercised by free aboriginal people came under the remit of Magna Carta. In British Canada, the Proclamation of 1763 became known as the 'Magna Carta' of native Indian tribes, for the manner in which it pledged to respect their territories. And in the Treaty of Waitangi of 1840, established fishing and farming rights were guaranteed to the Maori iwi, in such a way that the annexation of New Zealand – one of

Sikhs aboard the Komagata Maru, *Vancouver, 1914.*

The case of the Komagata Maru

The racial turn in the appropriation of Magna Carta had much wider ramifications, not in Britain itself, but overseas in its empire. In 1914 a large group of Punjabi Sikhs sought entry to the Canadian province of British Columbia from the Japanese steamship *Komagata Maru*. Kept in detention and not allowed into Canada, they sought to test Canadian immigration laws by using Magna Carta in their defence. In London the Court of Appeal upheld the Canadian refusal to allow the *Komagata Maru* to disembark in Vancouver. *The Times* was triumphant: 'The judgment finally disposes of the idea … that British citizenship in itself confers an unrestricted right of entrance into any part of the British Dominions' (9 July 1914). On the eve of its seven hundredth birthday Magna Carta was no longer so ready for export – it really had become an island story.

the few acts of British colonization to be concluded by a treaty – rested on what were believed to be the maxims of Magna Carta.

Nowhere in the nineteenth-century British empire was Magna Carta applied with more political consequences than in India. In 1858, the government of India was transferred from the East India Company to the Crown, with Queen Victoria as the titular head of a vast dominion in the Subcontinent. The new government was formally proclaimed in November of that year, and the document announcing the transfer was carefully worded in order to assuage and appease the princes and people after the Indian rebellion (or 'mutiny' as the British public termed it). The 'Queen's Proclamation' confirmed that the peoples of India would enjoy the same status as other subjects of British dominion, and with that large promise the Proclamation was dubbed the 'Magna Carta of Indian liberties'. In a narrow sense the Proclamation confirmed the principle of religious toleration and recognized the titles of the native chiefs. However, much more was read into the Proclamation than this. It seemed to imply that the Indian legislature, civil service, law courts and officer classes of the army would be opened up to meritorious Indians, and that a large measure of local government would also be introduced. When the Indian National Congress was formed in 1885, its leaders were quick to make the 1858 'Magna Carta' an issue of breach of promise, as so little administrative and constitutional reform had been undertaken by the British. And further afield in the empire – in the Cape Colony – a young Gujarati lawyer, Mohandas Gandhi, was to use a similar argument to uphold the rights of indentured Indian labourers brought before the courts there. Despite the lip-service paid to the Queen's pledge, the Magna Carta of Indian liberties proved an enduring rallying cry.

These colonial variations on the theme of Magna Carta may seem far removed from Runnymede. However, English statute law – or imperial legislation – did remain relevant overseas, with only small measures of discretion given to colonial administrations to interpret the ways of Westminster in local cases, with the Privy Council always acting as a last court of appeal. Hence the universal scope of the medieval Magna Carta, in effect encompassing all British or formerly British territory, remained powerful enough to mobilize liberal and nationalist movements, the tactics and demands of which were otherwise modern and forward-looking. With that in mind, it is worth noting how much of the new professional scholarship on Magna Carta in the later nineteenth century focused on the Charter as a peculiar product of the English race, rather than its realm – on biology, and not the law. Popular accounts of Magna Carta had already begun to strike this chord in the middle of the nineteenth century, referring to the Charter as the outcome of a fusion or blending of the Norman and Saxon population. Stubbs, Green and Freeman picked up this theme in their histories, and by the time McKechnie produced his magnum opus in 1905, the suggestion that those principles which became enshrined in the 1215 Charter and its further refinements later in the same century were the particular property of the 'English tribes' was offered without comment or qualification (even from a Scot). So when Viscount Bryce, the President of the Royal Historical Society, penned his prefatory remarks for the seven hundredth commemoration volume of 1917, few would have dissented from his observation that 'the Charter of 1215 was the starting-point of the constitutional history of the English race, the first link in a long chain of constitutional instruments which have moulded men's minds and held together free governments not only in England, but wherever the English race has gone and the English tongue is spoken'. Similarly, when the Defence of the Realm Act was rolled out in the anniversary year, replacing habeas corpus in some cases with military tribunals, noble Lords in Parliament dismissed constitutional niceties, declaring that 'the rights of the individual have to give way when it is a case of maintaining the existence of our race'.

Magna Carta entered modernity in the long nineteenth century. It became memorialized and depicted as never before. It supplied all shapes and size of campaigns inside and outside Parliament with text and pretext. And as never before it became the subject of historical investigation. Magna Carta remained deeply contested across the span of the 1815–1915 period. Around the turn of the twentieth century it could be seen variously as libertarian – the 1896 abolition of the mandatory flagged speed limits for cars was nicknamed the 'Magna Carta of motorists' – or as collective: the Parish Councils Act of 1894 became the 'villagers' Magna Carta' – and, as G. K. Chesterton pointed out in his *Short History of England* (1907), it could be deemed a conservative and not a democratic measure. Between its sixth and seventh centenaries Magna Carta truly was all things to all peoples. At least until all peoples became inconvenient to the national narrative.

Chapter Ten

The sealing of Magna Carta, frieze over the main entrance of Middlesex Guildhall, now the Supreme Court of the United Kingdom, by Henry Charles Fehr, 1913.

From World War to World Heritage: Magna Carta in the Twentieth Century

Nicholas Vincent

When the long tally is added, it will be seen that the British nation and the English-speaking world owe far more to the vices of John than to the labours of virtuous sovereigns; for it was through the union of many forces against him that the most famous milestone of our rights and freedom was in fact set up.

Winston Churchill, *A History of the English-Speaking Peoples* (published 1956–8)

Law, scholarship and legend

Like many other totems, Magna Carta did not pass unscathed through the twentieth century. Law reform under the Victorians had already butchered the majority of the Charter's clauses that had survived in English statute law. In 1966, Parliament repealed the clauses (Magna Carta 1215 clauses 20–2, 1225 clause 14) relating to amercements and fines owed to the King, first heard of as long ago as 1100 in Henry I's Coronation Charter. Attempts were made thereafter to repeal what remained, but these stalled on the opposition of lawyers anxious to retain at least some of the dignified as well as the efficient parts of the British Constitution. As a result, four clauses (clauses 1, 13, 39 and 40 of the 1215 Magna Carta, represented by clauses 1, 9, 29 and part of 37 of the 1225 Charter) still have effect in English law. The principles that they enunciate, however, are so general as to render it unlikely that they will ever be tested specifically in the English law courts.

At the same time as the Charter's legal corpse was being dissected, academic historians sought to demystify the circumstances of its issue.

In 1905, the Glasgow lawyer William Sharp McKechnie published the first full commentary on the Charter to have been attempted since the work of Richard Thomson in 1829. In its second and extended edition, of 1914, McKechnie's commentary remains, even today, the lengthiest (and quite possibly the dullest) exposition of the Charter. It is still the only published book to offer a clause by clause explanation of what Magna Carta 1215 was intended to achieve. Of a very different stamp, J. C. (later Sir James) Holt's *Magna Carta*, first published by Cambridge University Press in 1965, republished in a revised second edition in 1992, remains the most definitive of the twentieth-century attempts to explain the Charter's context and meaning. Holt's book was timed to coincide with the Charter's 750th anniversary. This same anniversary also produced a sprightly survey by Sir Ivor Jennings, perhaps the greatest and certainly the most prolific of English constitutional lawyers, himself one of those responsible for drafting the recent constitutions of the newly independent Sri Lanka and Malaysia. As Jennings acknowledged, and despite the fact that 'the celebration of an anniversary … tends towards exaggeration', the influence of Magna Carta remains of 'psychological' significance, even if its direct or practical effects upon modern law remain intangible.

Commonwealth Heads of State arriving at the Thanksgiving service at St Paul's Cathedral, London, held to mark the 750th anniversary of the sealing of Magna Carta, 1965.

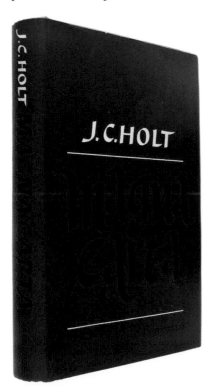

First edition of Holt's great work on Magna Carta.

As this suggests, not everything in Magna Carta's modern history has run smoothly. Even so, at a more popular level, the legend of Magna Carta has continued to spread. It can be found alive and well in modern British and American political rhetoric, in the appeal to some essentially 'Anglo-Saxon' tradition of liberty to be defended against the leviathan of the modern state. It has invaded Hollywood, most recently and anachronistically in Ridley Scott's 2010 version of *Robin Hood*. Here an entirely fictitious Robin forces an equally fictitious Magna Carta upon bad King John. In the Second World War, as we shall see, Magna Carta came into its own as an embodiment of all that needed to be defended against the menace of Nazi Germany. At the same time, not only Magna Carta the myth but Magna Carta the museum piece enjoyed burgeoning celebrity. As a physical artifact, the Charter has been collected and treasured since at least the seventeenth century. Only in the past hundred years, however, has this collecting mania extended to America and Australia. In the process, it has transformed Magna Carta into the most expensive single piece of parchment ever offered for sale.

The First World War and beyond

Let us begin with the Charter's seven hundredth anniversary in 1915. This had been planned as a major celebration. An anniversary committee was established in April 1914, chaired by Lord Bryce, a Liberal politician and professor of law, from 1907 to 1913 British ambassador to the United States. The committee comprised more than fifty of the great and the good, including the archbishop of Canterbury, and a Roman Catholic cardinal. Unfortunately, by June 1915, circumstances had changed. The year 1915 witnessed the first use of poison gas in France. In May came the sinking of the *Lusitania* by German U-boat and the first aerial bombardment of London. Major campaigns at Ypres and Gallipoli led to the loss of hundreds of thousands of lives. Rather than press ahead with public celebrations, Lord Bryce instead commissioned a volume of 'Commemoration' essays eventually published under the auspices of the Royal Historical Society in 1917. Nine historians were invited to contribute, three of them American, one Spanish (and therefore a wartime ally), another (Mr, later Sir Hilary Jenkinson) an officer in the Royal Artillery serving on the western front. In June 1915, the anniversary itself passed

Russell Crowe as Robin Hood, champion of Magna Carta, in Ridley Scott's fanciful reimagining of the Charter's story.

virtually unnoticed. The only public demonstration came from the Church Reform League, via a printed circular demanding that Magna Carta clause 1 be used to lobby for 'a reasonable measure of self-government' for the Anglican Church. Meanwhile, from 1914 to 1918, the Defence of the Realm Act effectively suspended both the letter and the spirit of Magna Carta. Arbitrary arrest and detention without trial became the final resorts of a state geared towards total warfare.

For Magna Carta, the aftermath of the First World War was felt chiefly at Runnymede, the meadow between Staines and Windsor. The agent of change here, Cara Leland Broughton, was an American heiress, daughter of Henry Huttleston Rogers, one of the co-founders of Rockefeller's Standard Oil Company. In 1895, she had married Urban Hanlon Broughton, an English sewerage engineer employed to bring modern sanitation to the town of Fairhaven in Massachusetts. Returning to England in 1912, Broughton had spent the First World War as Conservative MP for Preston, drumming up support for the Anglo-American alliance. He had been recommended for a peerage only a few weeks before his death in 1929. As a result, his widow was permitted to succeed to the newly created title as Lady Fairhaven. In December that year, she gifted 188 acres of land at Runnymede to the National Trust, commissioning Sir Edwin Lutyens, recently architect of both the Cenotaph in London and the Indian capital at New Delhi, to build a pair of lodges there in tribute to her late husband.

Developments at Runnymede

Since 1929 the site of Runnymede has undergone yet further developments, not all of them felicitous. After the Second World War, an Air Forces Memorial was raised, intended to commemorate the twenty thousand men and women of the British empire killed in air operations during the war. The architect was Sir Edward Maufe, best known for his design of Guildford Cathedral, itself brought to worldwide fame as a location used in the classic horror film *The Omen*. In 1957, again with Maufe as architect, the American Bar Association commissioned a Magna Carta Memorial. This takes the form of a domed rotunda in 'classical' style, surrounding a granite pillar inscribed to Magna Carta, 'Symbol of Freedom Under Law'. In 1965, the 750th anniversary of Magna Carta was marked by the Queen's unveiling at Runnymede of the John F. Kennedy Memorial, approached by fifty irregular granite steps and bearing

a stone tablet carved with words from the President's inaugural address, promising to spare no efforts 'In order to ensure the survival and success of liberty'. All of these monuments are of significance, not least as reminders of the relations between England and America. In visual terms, they would none of them disgrace a suburban crematorium.

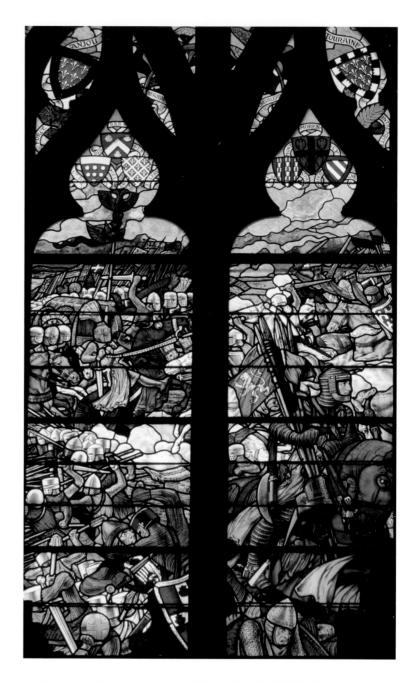

Stained-glass window in the Church of St Pierre in Bouvines, commemorating the battle of 1214.

The Second World War

Having been eclipsed by the First World War, Magna Carta fared rather better in the Second. As early as 1939, the Charter had come to embody everything that the English, and by extension Americans, valued about Western democracy, now menaced by Hitler and the rape of Eastern Europe. Leaving Berlin in September 1939 after the outbreak of war, Sir Nevile Henderson, former British Ambassador and by many identified as the most craven of appeasers, sent a final dispatch to the Foreign Office. In it, he quoted Abraham Lincoln on 'government of the people, by the people, for the people', defined by Henderson as 'the abiding principle of the Magna Carta … [that] constitutes in fact the warp and woof of Anglo-Saxon or British history'. At much the same time, General Alan Brooke, future wartime Chief of the Imperial General Staff (and future Viscount Alanbrooke), was stationed in northern France only a few miles from the site of the Battle of Bouvines. In December 1939, he is to be found in his *Diaries* musing on the circumstances in which King John was made to sign Magna Carta. For the next few months, Brooke conducted numerous visiting British generals on whistle-stop tours of Bouvines. This was perhaps not the most auspicious precedent for a campaign that was shortly to end in German invasion and the fall of France.

Meanwhile, Magna Carta was enjoying even greater impact in the United States. Early in 1939, some months before the outbreak of war, the Dean and Chapter of Lincoln had bowed to pressure from the British government and agreed that their original of the 1215 Charter, since the time of its first issue stored in the Lincoln Cathedral archives, should be allowed to travel out of England for public display at that year's New York World's Fair. The government paid for it to be insured against loss or damage up to a value of £100,000, clearly in the hope that so remarkable an object, exhibited in the USA, might foster closer Anglo-American co-operation. As it transpired, the Lincoln Charter arrived in America just as the European political crisis reached its climax. Hitler's threatened invasion of Poland, the Nazi–Soviet pact, and the fact that no official alliance existed by which Britain and France could call upon American assistance in the event of an outbreak of war, raised Anglo-American relations to the very top of the British political agenda.

It was on the eve of this crisis, in June 1939, that a letter was received at 10 Downing Street, addressed to the British Prime Minister, Neville Chamberlain, by the prominent Conservative politician and former government minister for the Colonies, Leo Amery. Amery had himself received a letter from an American citizen, J. W. Hamilton, Secretary to the International Magna Carta Day Association. What Hamilton proposed, and what Amery now supported, was that the Lincoln Magna Carta be permanently gifted by Great Britain to the United States of America. There, so Hamilton suggested, 'It might do more finally to obliterate all recollection of previous disagreements by reasserting the common origin of our liberties than anything that could be imagined.' To offset any financial loss, it was suggested that the Dean and Chapter be offered sufficient compensation to repair the fabric of their Cathedral, considered in imminent danger of collapse. Chamberlain's response, sent at the end of July 1939 and effectively dictated by officials at the British Foreign Office, was that 'Such a gift would merely be represented in malevolent quarters as a clumsy bribe to gain American goodwill'. So the matter rested, at least for the time being.

By the time that the New York World's Fair closed, in the autumn of 1939, Britain and Germany were at war. Rather than risk the Lincoln Magna Carta to the high seas now patrolled by German U-boats, the Charter was deposited for safekeeping in the Library of Congress, in Washington D.C. The occasion was marked by a suitably patriotic speech by the British Ambassador, Lord Lothian, who reminded his listeners that

> Inscribed on the musty parchment before us, we see the nucleus of most of our liberties, of trial by jury, of habeas corpus, of the principles of [no] taxation without representation, of the Bill of Rights and of the whole constitution of modern democracy…
> The principles which underlay Magna Carta are the ultimate foundations of your [American] liberties no less than ours.

Not everyone was so enthusiastic. Amongst the advocates of American isolation, General Hugh Johnson, whose vividly expressed opinions were syndicated across the newspapers of North America, was prepared to accept the dependence of the United States Constitution upon a legal tradition reaching back to Magna Carta, but remained deeply suspicious of British motives. 'Would it seem to be too much like mooching', General Johnson wrote, 'to suggest that, instead of just letting us hold this one, they give it to us outright?'

In April 1940, the Charter once again made the journey between Washington and New York, to be displayed in the British Pavilion of the 1940 New York World's Fair. It was whilst the Charter was thus displayed in New York that Britain was confronted by the sudden escalation of hostilities in Europe. In May 1940, Germany invaded France. Within a matter of a few weeks the British army, or what remained of it, had been evacuated from the beaches of Dunkirk, and France itself had capitulated. It was at this moment of crisis, amidst the darkest of threats not merely to Britain but to the entire future of

democracy, that J. W. Hamilton, Secretary to the International Magna Carta Day Association, again wrote to England, this time to the King, George VI. Hamilton suggested that 15 June be celebrated each year throughout the English-speaking world as Magna Carta Day. Furthermore, he recommended, the Lincoln Magna Carta, still on exhibition in New York, should be presented to the people of the United States once the World's Fair ended later that year.

On 10 October 1940, John Colville, private secretary to the Prime Minister, wrote to the Foreign Office backing the idea of a gift of Magna Carta to the American people, reporting that it had already excited the personal interest of Mrs Churchill. Once again, however, the Foreign Office prevaricated. The Charter itself was due to return in December 1940 to safekeeping in the Library of Congress. But proposals were afoot in the United States for a coast-to-coast touring exhibition, taking in ten leading universities, with the city of Cleveland, Ohio, offering to meet any additional insurance premium. Canada had also expressed an interest in hosting such a tour. On 17 December, a reluctant approach was made from the Foreign Office to the Dean of Lincoln, but with the openly expressed hope that the Dean and Chapter would refuse permission for Magna Carta to travel. This is precisely what happened, with the Dean, R. A. Mitchell, writing on 3 January 1941 that no permission would be granted for the Charter to tour America unless he could be assured that the tour was 'a matter of urgent national importance'.

The idea that the Charter might be gifted to the American people nonetheless continued to gather momentum. On 13 March 1941, in the immediate aftermath of the Lend-Lease Act intended to bring American aid to the British war effort, a private American citizen, T. North Whitehead, once again raised the idea of such a gift. He suggested that the Dean and Chapter of Lincoln be compensated for the loss of their charter by the grant either of £100,000 in war bonds and one of the British Museum originals of the 1215 Magna Carta, or with £250,000 in war bonds in full settlement of all claims, the gift to be announced by the King or Prime Minister, Winston Churchill, in a broadcast address to the American people. Now, for the first time, the British Foreign Office began to change tack from cautious disapproval to lukewarm support. Propelled by the lobbying of both Duff Cooper, Minister of Information, and Rab Butler, junior minister in the Foreign Office, the idea was rapidly passed from departmental level to

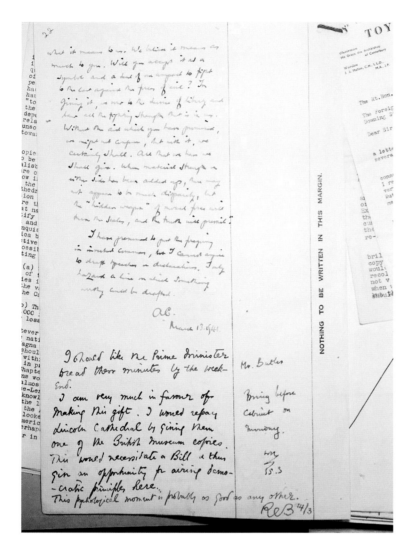

*Discussion of offering the Lincoln 1215 Magna Carta as a gift to the
United States: Alexander Cadogan's memorandum of 13 March 1941,
with Churchill's annotation 'Bring before Cabinet on Monday'.*

The War Cabinet discussed the affair, but opinion was now divided.
If an original Magna Carta were to be given to the United States,
might not Australia, Canada, New Zealand and South Africa expect
similar gifts? The transfer to Lincoln Cathedral of one of the British
Museum Magna Cartas would necessitate an Act of Parliament. Leo
Amery, in a letter to Churchill of 18 March 1941, demanded not only
that the gift of Magna Carta to America be made but that it be made
as soon as possible, suggesting 15 June 1941, Magna Carta Day, as a
suitable date and urging that preliminary discussions be held to ensure
that President Roosevelt have a speech of welcome for the Charter
already prepared. Churchill himself has marked in red ink here, in a
memorandum dated 21 March 1941, 'I prefer this, as it gives more
time.' At this point, however, cold reality began to dawn.

So far, no one seems to have considered that the Lincoln Magna
Carta was not the British government's property to give away. In
particular, no approach whatsoever had been made to the Dean and
Chapter of Lincoln to establish how they might view such a gift. As
soon as this approach was made, it became apparent that the scheme
was unworkable. By the second week of April 1941, Churchill had
decided to back off. 'Better leave it alone,' he minuted to Butler.
Although the idea of giving a Magna Carta to the United States had by
no means been dropped, the prevailing view remained that such a gift
was better left until the war was over. The entry of the United States

Downing Street and thence to the British War Cabinet. As Sir
Alexander Cadogan, Permanent Undersecretary at the Foreign Office,
minuted in a form of words subsequently adopted as the official
Foreign Office communiqué to the Prime Minister's office on 18
March 1941:

> I have always wanted to do this. I should like to say to the
> Americans, 'You are giving us aid on a scale which makes it
> almost impossible for us materially to repay. Any material
> repayment we could offer can only look insignificant. We shall
> owe you a debt which can never be discharged. May we give
> you – at least as a token of our feeling – something of no
> intrinsic value whatsoever: a bit of parchment, more than 700
> years old, rather the worse for wear. You know what it means
> to us. We believe it means as much to you. Will you accept it as
> a symbol and a seal of our compact to fight to the last against
> the forces of evil?'

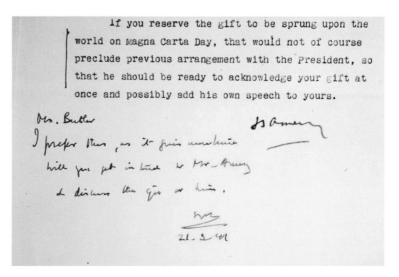

The Lincoln 1215 Magna Carta is packed for return to England from the United States, 1946.

The Lincoln Charter's troubled return

There is a rather sad postscript to the tale of the Lincoln Charter's American travels. On 5 April 1946, a special service held in Lincoln Cathedral to welcome back the Charter was interrupted by an unknown woman who stood up at the back of the Cathedral, shouting: 'I denounce Magna Carta: it is a relic, and relics are denounced in the Bible.' Whether or not this denunciation was heeded by the Almighty, it was soon afterwards noticed that the Lincoln Charter was showing signs of fading. By December 1950, it was judged necessary to break into the armour-plated case and to send the Charter to the Public Record Office for conservation. There, a minor disaster occurred. The Deputy Keeper of the Record Office, Sir Hilary Jenkinson, the same man who in 1917 had contributed to the Magna Carta Commemoration essays, was forced to admit that the Charter had suffered 'indubitable and regrettable' damage. This he blamed upon 'internal deterioration from some organic cause, for example a fungoid affection which might have developed in the long period during which it was, as I understand, immured between sheets of glass'. In reality, the blame here almost certainly lay not with some imaginary fungus, but with the fact that the Charter had been deliberately and perhaps carelessly dampened in the Record Office in order that it might be re-backed with modern parchment.

into the war in December 1941, in the aftermath of the attacks on Pearl Harbor, merely confirmed this assessment.

After a period when, together with other national treasures, the Lincoln Charter was sent from Washington to Fort Knox for safekeeping, the saga of how to gift Magna Carta to the United States resumed in January 1945. By this time the librarian of Congress had begun to wonder whether the loan of the Lincoln Magna Carta to Washington might be continued after the war, perhaps by the replacement of the Lincoln Charter with one of the other originals still in the UK, perhaps on an indefinite basis. The return of the Lincoln Charter to England was still being discussed a year later, by which time the Library of Congress was proclaiming that 15 million Americans had taken the opportunity to view it. Sailing on the *Queen Elizabeth* from New York on 18 January 1946, the Charter returned to England in the same bronze and armour-plated case, weighing 60 lbs, in which it had previously been displayed in Congress, now presented as a token of thanks to the Dean and Chapter of Lincoln. The ship docked at Southampton on 23 January.

The Lacock Charter: America denied again

Meanwhile, no sooner did one Magna Carta return to England, than another prepared to cross the Atlantic in the opposite direction. The 1225 issue of Magna Carta sent into Wiltshire had been committed by the knights of the shire to keeping in Lacock Abbey, a nunnery which at the Dissolution in the sixteenth century passed into the hands of the Fox-Talbot family. In 1939, the then-owner of Lacock, Miss Talbot, had carefully buried the Charter under one of the Abbey floors. There it lay until 1945, wrapped in a box inside flannel, the whole enclosed in a metal container. Following discussions with the British Museum, it was now proposed that the Lacock Magna Carta be sent to Washington in place of the Lincoln Charter, this time on loan for a fixed period of two years. This proposal was accompanied by further suggestions, backed by the newly promoted Lieutenant-Commander Douglas Fairbanks Jr that 15 June be set aside as a public holiday throughout the English-speaking world.

The loan of the Lacock Charter necessitated a special Act of Parliament, introduced to the House of Lords in May 1946 in a debate chiefly memorable for their lordships inability to agree whether Magna C(h)arta should be spelt with or without an 'h'. In December the Charter and Miss Talbot were both transported across the Atlantic at the British taxpayer's expense, although in those days of post-war austerity, it was determined that Miss Talbot herself should be maintained whilst in America on an allowance to cover subsistence set at the hardly princely figure of three dollars a day, rising to eight dollars only if she should have to stay in a hotel. This despite the fact that in 1945 Miss Talbot had gifted Lacock Abbey and its entire estate village to the National Trust, at the same time donating her Magna Carta to the British Museum. As James Lees-Milne, secretary of the National Trust, recorded on first visiting Lacock in December 1943:

> [Miss Talbot] is a dear, selfless woman, and extremely high-minded. She has the most unbending sense of duty towards her tenants and the estate, to the extent that she allows herself only a few hundreds [of pounds] a year on which to live. She spends hardly a farthing on herself, and lives like an anchorite … [The abbey] was warm and smelled sweet and cosy. Miss Talbot said 'I hate fresh air. It is the cause of most of our ills in England.'

The fate of 'Magna Carta Day'

Like the proposal to present the United States with a Magna Carta, the idea that 15 June should be celebrated throughout the English-speaking world as Magna Carta Day was thwarted by official objections. It had been hoped in some quarters that such a celebration might serve as propaganda in the nascent Cold War. Set against this, however, were the misgivings of the Ministry of Education, which pointed out that most American schools were on vacation by 15 June, so that the proposed day of celebrations could have little or no impact in the indoctrination of American youth. Moreover, far from combating communism, the proposal might actively encourage communist sympathies. As the British Foreign Office official E. J. Perowne pointed out, the Charter had been issued not to the common people but to the much more restricted class of 'free men'. Communists would therefore be prejudiced against it. Worse still, a senior civil servant, K. W. Blaxter of the Colonial Office, minuted in February 1947 that there was a risk that Magna Carta might be interpreted by 'Colonial peoples' not as a symbol of British authority, but in some way as a guarantee of popular rights. As Blaxter pointed out: 'There is a danger that the Colonial peoples might be led into an uncritical enthusiasm for a document which they had not read but which they presumed to contain guarantees of every so-called "right" they might be interested at the moment in claiming.' There can have been few more honest, yet few more extraordinary statements ever penned by a British writer on Magna Carta. Thus did the brave initiatives of the early 1940s decline into economies with the truth.

In December 1948, two years after its arrival in the United States, and despite attempts to prolong its stay including yet further suggestions that it be gifted to the American nation, the Lacock Magna Carta returned to England in the custody of A. J. Collins of the British Museum, arriving on New Year's Day. For the moment, the USA was once again without a document which the librarian of Congress, writing to the British Foreign Secretary, had recently described as possessing 'Fully as much significance for citizens of the United States as it does for the citizens of the United Kingdom'.

The Bruton/Canberra Magna Carta

Meanwhile, just as America was denied possession of an original Magna Carta, Australia entered the arena. In the spring of 1951, one of the governors of a small and impoverished private school in the English West Country, the King's School at Bruton, went up to London carrying with him a peculiar document that he wished to be examined by experts in the British Museum. It was an original Magna Carta, of the 1297 issue. In 1951, it was one of only two such 1297 Magna Cartas known to exist, the other being held by the Corporation of the City of London. Quite how Bruton School had come to acquire the Charter was never properly explained. Local tradition suggested that it had been found in a boy's desk in 1936. Certainly it was in the school's possession by 1939, when it appeared as the very earliest of the documents in a privately printed catalogue of the school muniments. At some point before 1939 it seems to have been shown to Jenkinson at the Public Record Office, in order that its seal could be repaired. In 1950, it had been publicly displayed as part of the school's four hundredth anniversary celebrations. The Charter was undoubtedly genuine. On arrival in London, it excited the keenest of interest from the British Museum and in particular from the Keeper of Western Manuscripts there, A. J. Collins.

Collins saw immediately that the 1297 Magna Carta could be made to plug a gap in the Museum's collection. The Museum had long prided itself on its display case, the Magna Carta Cabinet, in which were exhibited not only the Articles of the Barons and the two 1215 Magna Cartas that had once belonged to Sir Robert Cotton, but since the late 1940s, the 1225 Magna Carta from Lacock Abbey recently gifted to the nation. If only the 1297 Charter could be added to this collection then, as Collins realized, the collection could be considered not just unique but complete. There was only one stumbling block here, and as usual that stumbling block was money. The headmaster of Bruton School wanted to sell his Magna Carta at the highest possible price. His school was poor, and the money potentially vital to its survival. Although Collins already judged the Bruton Charter to be, in his own words, 'supremely important', he could imagine offering no more than £2,000–2,500 to obtain it. When, in July 1951, the headmaster removed it from the British Museum to have it independently valued, and when that valuation was placed at the, then,

BEING HANDED TO THE AUSTRALIAN HIGH COMMISSIONER, SIR THOMAS WHITE (LEFT), BY LORD BLACKFORD: THE COPY OF MAGNA CARTA BOUGHT BY AUSTRALIA.
The thirteenth-century copy of Magna Carta, which has been bought by the Australian Commonwealth National Library from King's School, Bruton, Somerset, was handed to the Australian High Commissioner, Sir Thomas White, by Lord Blackford, who was representing the Governors of the school, at Australia House, London, on October 24. The High Commissioner gave Lord Blackford a cheque for £11,000—the balance of the purchase price of £12,500. The document is a copy of Edward I's confirmation of Magna Carta, and is dated October 12, 1297.

The Bruton Charter about to depart for Australia, photograph from the Illustrated London News, *1 November 1952.*

unprecedented figure of £10,000 (£12,500 with seller's commission), Collins remained adamant. The charter must come to the Museum, but at a reasonable price, and not at the valuation price which he dismissed as 'excessive'.

There followed an unseemly row within the British government committee established to advise on the sale and export of items of historic significance. By November 1951, the school governors, acting via Sotheby's the auctioneers, had begun to sound out the possibility of selling the document to Australia. The matter was discussed before the Library Committee of the Australian Parliament and a press campaign was initiated in support of such a sale. In Britain, various proposals were considered, including the possibility that the Bruton Magna Carta be licensed for export to Australia but that the London 1297 Charter be placed on permanent display in the British Museum. The proposal was made in full knowledge that the then Lord Mayor of London, Sir Leslie Boyce, was an Australian by birth and therefore likely to support anything that might benefit his homeland. Once again, however, as with the Lincoln Charter in 1940, no one had fully

The Bruton Charter on display in Canberra.

thought through the implications of government officials giving away what was in reality private property. In the end, the Bruton Charter was exported to Australia. Sotheby's, acting for Bruton School, was paid the £12,500 asking price. The London Charter of 1297 remains in the archives of the Corporation of London, and the British Museum remains, despite Collins' best endeavours, without any original of the 1297 Magna Carta. There is, however, a sequel to this story, only recently uncovered.

In 1951, it had been noticed that there were a number of unique features to the Bruton Charter, amongst them that it was inscribed on the fold *Com Surr*, suggesting that it was the exemplar of the 1297

Magna Carta originally sent to the county of Surrey. Reporting to the Trustees of the British Museum in May 1951, Collins had already noted that the headmaster and governors of Bruton School had no real idea of how they had acquired their Magna Carta. Certainly it was odd that a school in Somerset, in the English south-west, should have come into possession of a charter addressed to the county of Surrey, far away in the English south-east. One theory was voiced, but almost immediately suppressed. According to the senior civil servant chairing the exports committee, writing to Rab Butler, Chancellor of the Exchequer, on 2 April 1952: 'Nobody knows how the Charter came into the possession of Bruton School, but I am told the best guess is

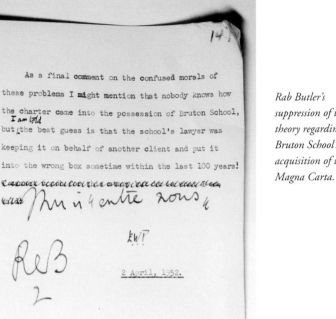

Rab Butler's suppression of the theory regarding Bruton School's acquisition of its Magna Carta.

The British Library's 1297 Forest Charter, companion piece to the Magna Carta now in Canberra (see page 85).

daughter of Edward Quekett, a banker at Langport in Somerset. Drayton lies only twenty miles from Bruton.

Although proof here is never likely to be absolute, the following scenario seems to represent the most plausible reconstruction of a very tangled history. Both the Magna Carta and the Forest Charter sent into Surrey in 1297 were delivered to the sheriff of Surrey and Sussex who, we can surmise, deposited them for safekeeping with the nuns of Easebourne Priory in Sussex. In just this way, the Wiltshire Magna Carta of 1225 had been handed over by the knights of the shire for keeping in the nunnery of Lacock. After the dissolution of the monasteries in the 1530s, by means as yet unknown, a substantial number of the deeds of Easebourne Priory, including the 1297 Forest Charter and Magna Carta, passed into the possession of a family that in due course employed the services of John Louch of Drayton as their solicitor. Either in Louch's strong-room, or subsequently, one of these deeds, the 1297 Magna Carta, escaped from Louch family custody, lost, sold or given away. As a result, when John Louch's son granted the rest of his father's charters to the British Museum, in 1905, the 1297 Magna Carta was not amongst them. Instead, by means still unknown, it lay undiscovered for the next thirty years, resurfacing only in the late 1930s in the possession of Bruton School. By such means was Magna Carta eventually brought to Australia, where the Bruton Charter is today displayed.

The totems that a nation or legal system chooses to adopt tell us much about that nation's underlying psychology. To this extent, it is perhaps no bad thing that the English system of common law should be founded on totems and myths so strongly associated with the idea of 'liberty'. That the mighty be made legally responsible for their actions is by no means the worst principle to enshrine in constitutional law. As I hope to have shown here, and as others have shown throughout this book, Magna Carta is a multi-faceted thing. It is both document and law, story and statute, principle and myth. It has been as much lauded by the political right as by the revolutionary left. To some it seems to place the King under the law. To others it can be interpreted as proving that law itself comes from kings. It has no simple explanation, and a highly complicated posterity. Winston Churchill praised it as the foundation stone of liberty. In 1941, as we have seen, Churchill even considered gifting it to America. But let us end on a rather different, but nonetheless resonant note. As is well

that the school's lawyer was keeping it on behalf of another client and put it into the wrong box some time within the last 100 years.'

Next to this statement, in red crayon, Butler has marked, 'This is "entre nous" RB'. Not until 2007 did confirmation of the basic accuracy of this report emerge from the British Library. There, a previously unnoticed copy of the 1297 Forest Charter came to light, companion piece to the 1297 Bruton Magna Carta. Not only was this particular copy (British Library Additional Charter 53712) a unique survival, there being no other known originals of the 1297 reissue of the Forest Charter, but it was written in the same hand, sealed in the same way, and most significantly bore the same subscription on its foot (*Surr' exam*[*inatur*]) as the Bruton/Canberra Magna Carta, itself intended for Surrey. The British Library's 1297 Forest Charter formed part of a small collection of documents from the archives of the nunnery of Easebourne near Midhurst in Sussex, gifted to the British Museum (later the British Library) in 1905. According to the British Library's printed catalogue, the author of this gift was a 'Mr F. Quekett Zouch'. About him nothing further appeared to be known. The trail seemed to go cold. Only in 2010 was it noticed that the Library's printed catalogue was itself in error. There was never any such donor as 'F. Quekett Zouch'. Instead, into his place stepped a Mr Francis Quekett Louch (1856–1922), born at Drayton in Somerset as the eldest of four children of John Louch (1825–1905), an attorney and solicitor at Drayton, and his wife Lucy Isabel Quekett, herself the

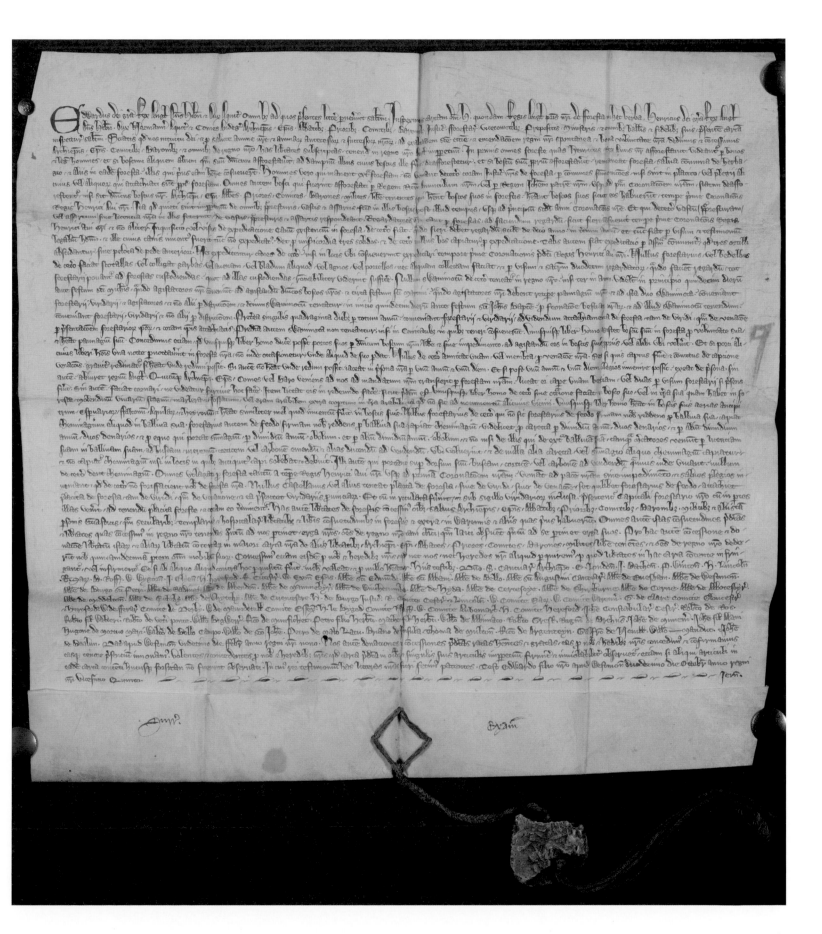

Churchill and George VI on VE Day, 8 May 1945.

known, as wartime Prime Minister, Churchill did not always see eye to eye with his own sovereign, King George VI, father of the present Queen Elizabeth. The *Diaries* of Sir Alan Lascelles, the King's private secretary, record these differences between King and Prime Minister. On Friday 16 June 1944, only a fortnight after the D-Day landings that both the King and Churchill had sought personally (but failed to obtain permission) to lead, Lascelles takes up the story. The King and he were travelling home from London, late at night:

> We left the train at Staines and reached Windsor about 11.30pm. On this drive the King inveighed, with some bitterness, against the governmental interference to which he was constitutionally liable. Suddenly, he threw his arm out the window and exclaimed, 'And that's where it all started!' We were passing Runnymede.

Or as another English imperialist, Rudyard Kipling, had put it, in his poem on *The Reeds of Runnymede*, first published in 1911:

> And still when Mob or Monarch lays
> Too rude a hand on English ways,
> The whisper wakes, the shudder plays,
>   Across the reeds at Runnymede.
> And Thames, that knows the moods of kings,
> And crowds and priests and suchlike things,
> Rolls deep and dreadful as he brings
>   Their warning down from Runnymede!

Washington acquires a Magna Carta

The odyssey of the Bruton Charter is by no means the last of the wanderings to which Magna Carta has been subject. In 1976, at the time of the American bicentennial, proposals were seriously entertained, reviving those of 1940, that one of the British Library's two 1215 Magna Cartas be gifted to the American people. These came to nothing, thanks both to resistance in London and to the unwillingness of the Library of Congress to participate in a transaction that had grave implications for the future custody not only of the British but of all world heritage. Instead, Congress was presented with a gift considered more appropriate: a replica of Magna Carta on gold leaf, housed within a gold and enamel case. The tastes of 1976 being unlike those of other times, the golden Magna Carta, although still displayed in the Rotunda of Congress, is upstaged there by a number of more significant artifacts. Amongst these is yet another original of the 1297 Magna Carta, itself only recently brought to light. It was at precisely the time of the 1976 bicentennial that we first read of the efforts being made by the Chief Justice of the United States, Warren Earl Burger (Chief Justice 1969–86), acting in concert with the Director of the Folger Shakespeare Library in Washington, to obtain purchase of an original Magna Carta, of the 1297 issue, for permanent display in the United States.

The Charter referred to here had been unearthed amongst the

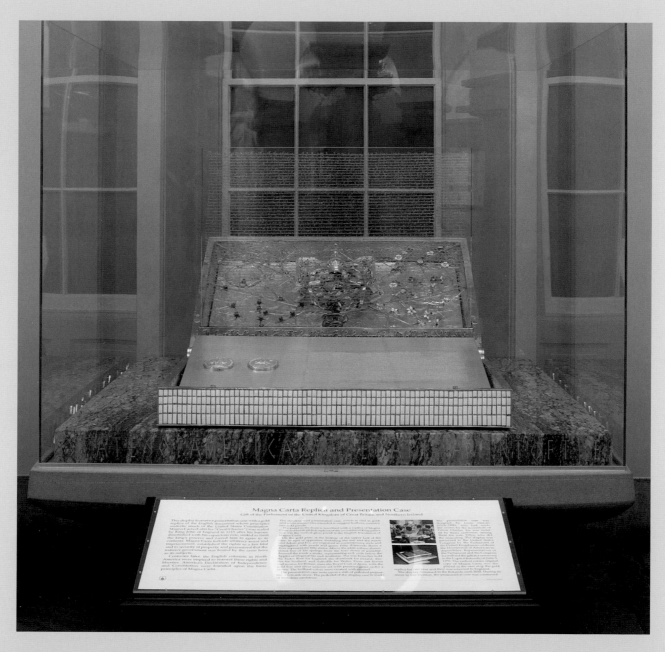

Right: The gold-leaf replica Magna Carta in a gold and enamel case presented to Congress in 1976. Left: The auction of Ross Perot's Deene Park Charter at Sotheby's, New York, 18 December 2007.

collections of the Brudenell family of Deene Park in Northamptonshire. The Brudenells, earls of Cardigan, one of whose ancestors had played a prominent but notorious role in the Charge of the Light Brigade of 1854, enjoyed an ancient association with the county of Buckinghamshire, to which the Deene Park 1297 Magna Carta had undoubtedly been sent. A sixteenth-century Brudenell had been a historian with keen antiquarian interests. Perhaps it was he who first acquired Magna Carta for the family. In any event, after further discussions over an export licence, the Deene Park Charter was sold in 1983 to the American billionaire and two-times presidential candidate, Ross Perot. Perot had it exhibited in the National Archives in Washington until in 2007 he in turn sold it, at auction in New York, for the unprecedented sum of $21.3 million. The new buyer, David Rubenstein, co-founder of the Carlyle Group, has since restored it to the National Archives, in 2011 gifting a further $13.5 million to pay for a new gallery and visitors' centre. By such means has Magna Carta come not only to Australia but to Washington.

Chapter Eleven

Twenty-First Century Magna Carta

Richard Goldstone

> *I never thought I would be in the House of Commons on the day Magna Carta was repealed.*
>
> Tony Benn, 11 June 2008, in response to the extension of detention without charge for terror suspects to forty-two days

The preceding chapters have described the extraordinary character of Magna Carta and its influence over the past eight hundred years. In this concluding chapter, I consider the influence of this remarkable document in the twentieth and twenty-first centuries. That it should still retain relevance after eight centuries justifies the frequently cited statement by Lord Denning that it is 'the greatest constitutional document of all times – the foundation of the freedom of the individual against the arbitrary authority of the despot.' It is that freedom that is enshrined and celebrated as 'the rule of law' that is now recognized as the foundation of democracy not only by the people of England but indeed throughout the democratic world. The rule of law has increasingly become not only the bedrock of domestic democracy but also the basis of a fair and democratic international order.

Applying the rule of law

The 'rule of law' has not been susceptible to precise definition. At the very least it incorporates the requirement that the law must be applied fairly and impartially to all people, the powerful and the weak, the rich and the poor. In order to ensure its efficacy there must be an independent judiciary to interpret and apply the law.

As suggested by Lord Denning, the freedom recognized in Magna Carta is that of ordinary citizens and it is from the power of the

US President Barack Obama signs an executive order to close the 'War on Terror' prison at Guantanamo Bay, 22 January 2009.

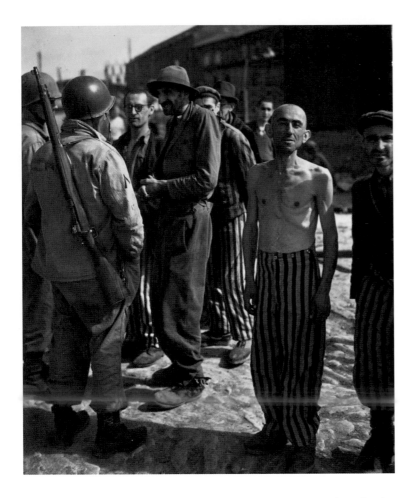

American soldiers with survivors of Buchenwald concentration camp, 18 April 1945.

the consequent scarcity of resources. Modern technology has facilitated the enhanced control and surveillance of citizens. The need for increased taxes has grown exponentially because of demands to furnish taxpayers with everyday expectations of basic comforts and more. And, in many countries, there has been the massive cost of maintaining armies and supplying them with hugely expensive modern weaponry. It is these, and other changes that tend to be taken for granted, that have encouraged governments to demand ever-increasing intrusion into the lives of their citizens. These developments make the protections provided by the rule of law essential to retaining democratic forms of government.

As appears from the early history of Magna Carta, its terms were originally relevant only to the King and the barons. Ordinary citizens were not in any way beneficiaries of its provisions. However, the rights included in Magna Carta committed the sovereign to the exercise of due process in criminal proceedings. Over the centuries, those rights have been progressively extended to all people and today incorporate the rights of women, minorities and persons who in the eleventh century were not considered worthy of possessing any rights at all.

It is with this changing application of the rule of law that this chapter is concerned. I shall first consider the influence of Magna Carta in the international arena and then its legacy in the domestic law of democratic nations.

sovereign that they require protection. In 1199, King John of England inherited supreme and absolute power and was subject to no law at all. Yet he was forced by the political reality of his time to yield that power not to any competing authority, but to the law itself. This was indeed the birth of the rule of law.

The scope of the rule of law and the nature of the protection to which citizens are entitled at any time will depend upon prevailing political and social conditions. Since the second half of the twentieth century, the meaning and application of the rule of law have been influenced and shaped by the catastrophic violations of fundamental human rights perpetrated during the Second World War. That war wrought havoc for many millions of people. One consequence was the recognition in the Charter of the United Nations that human rights must be protected. The Universal Declaration of Human Rights and its progeny followed. In successive wars around the globe, governments sought additional powers.

In today's world, some leaders claim that there is a permanent state of war and that enhanced powers are required indefinitely in order to combat the enemy. Those increased powers have also been justified by the societal dislocations resulting from ever-growing populations and

One of the most controversial initiatives aimed at protecting citizens: US President Ronald Reagan announces the Strategic Defense Initiative ('Star Wars Program'), 23 March 1983.

The influence of Magna Carta in the global community

The application of the rule of law in the global community is of recent origin. It has been manifested in two ways. The first is directed to the relationship between individual citizens and states, and the second to the relationship between states themselves. As will emerge, in some aspects there is an overlap between the two. I shall consider each in turn.

Until the middle of the twentieth century, international law regulated only the relationship between sovereign states. The rights of individuals in their own states were not within the domain of international law. That changed radically in reaction to the scourge of Nazism and its egregious violations of the human rights of millions of people. It was reflected in the preamble of the Charter of the United Nations that was unanimously adopted by the nations assembled on 26 June 1945 in San Francisco. They resolved 'to reaffirm faith in fundamental human rights, in the dignity and worth of the human person, in the equal rights of men and women and of nations large and small'. They determined that one purpose of the organization was the promotion and encouragement of the 'respect for human rights and for fundamental freedoms for all without distinction as to race, sex, language, or religion'. In this way the protection of individuals against the power of the sovereign that lay at the heart of Magna Carta was adopted by the global community as the means to ensure respect for the fundamental human rights of all people.

What was absent from that first formulation was the recognition that those fundamental human rights required enforcement. In other words, that they were dependent on the application of the rule of law. The United Nations General Assembly took this next step in Paris on 10 December 1948, when it adopted the Universal Declaration of Human Rights. This was drafted by the Human Rights Commission of the United Nations. Its chair and indefatigable champion was Eleanor Roosevelt. In her speech to the General Assembly on 10 December 1948 she said:

We stand today at the threshold of a great event both in the life of the United Nations and in the life of mankind. This declaration may well become the international Magna Carta for

Eleanor Roosevelt with the Universal Declaration of Human Rights, 1 January 1949.

all men everywhere. We hope its proclamation by the General Assembly will be an event comparable to the proclamation in 1789 [the French Declaration of the Rights of Man and of the Citizen], the adoption of the Bill of Rights by the people of the US, and the adoption of comparable declarations at different times in other countries.

Whilst not a legally binding document, it was the first expression of the rights to which all human beings were entitled for no reason other than being members of humankind. The Universal Declaration recalls in its Preamble that

Whereas disregard and contempt for human rights have resulted in barbarous acts which have outraged the conscience of mankind, and the advent of a world in which human beings shall enjoy freedom of speech and belief and freedom from fear and want has been proclaimed as the highest aspiration of the common people,

Whereas it is essential, if man is not to be compelled to have recourse, as a last resort, to rebellion against tyranny and oppression, that human rights should be protected by the rule of law.

Human rights, and their adherents

The **International Convention on the Elimination of All Forms of Racial Discrimination 1969** defines 'racial discrimination' as

> Any distinction, exclusion, restriction or preference based on race, colour, descent, or national or ethnic origin which has the purpose or effect of nullifying or impairing the recognition, enjoyment or exercise, on an equal footing, of human rights and fundamental freedoms in the political, economic, social, cultural or any other field of public life.

Article 2 requires States Parties to take wide and far-reaching steps to implement the provisions of the Convention. These include taking 'effective measures to review governmental, national and local policies, and to amend, rescind or nullify any laws and regulations which have the effect of creating or perpetuating racial discrimination wherever it exists'. In addition, each State Party shall prohibit and bring to an end, by all appropriate means, including legislation as required by circumstances, racial discrimination by any persons, group or organization. **Only forty-five nations have ratified this Convention**.

The **International Convention on the Eradication of Discrimination against Women 1979** defines discrimination against women as

> Any distinction, exclusion or restriction made on the basis of sex which has the effect or purpose of impairing or nullifying the recognition, enjoyment or exercise by women, irrespective of their marital status, on a basis of equality of men and women, of human rights and fundamental freedoms in the political, economic, social, cultural, civil or any other field.

States that join the Convention oblige themselves to make its provisions enforceable. **It has been ratified by 187 nations**.

The **Convention against Torture and Other Cruel, Inhuman or Degrading Treatment 1984** commits its parties to prohibit any form of torture or cruel, inhuman or degrading treatment in their jurisdictions. Torture is defined as

> Any act by which severe pain or suffering, whether physical or mental, is intentionally inflicted on a person for such purposes as obtaining from him or a third person, information or a confession, punishing him for an act he or a third person has committed or is suspected of having committed, or intimidating or coercing him or a third person, or for any reason based on discrimination of any kind, when such pain or suffering is inflicted by or at the instigation of or with the consent or acquiescence of a public official or other person acting in an official capacity. It does not include pain or suffering arising only from, inherent in or incidental to lawful sanctions.

A total of 154 nations have ratified this Convention. Apart from those nations that have ratified the Convention, the prohibition of torture has become accepted in customary international law and is binding on all nations. So, too, is the prohibition against genocide.

However, in 1948 members of the international community were not ready to oblige themselves to protect those human rights. Hence, the Universal Declaration was adopted as an aspirational document that did not require any Member State to translate it into binding domestic law. They nonetheless accepted the obligation 'to promote respect for these rights and freedoms and by progressive measures, national and international, to secure their universal and effective recognition and observance, both among the peoples of Member States themselves and among the peoples of territories under their jurisdiction'.

It was only in the 1960s that nations began to accept legally enforceable obligations to respect and enforce fundamental human rights. In 1966, the United Nations General Assembly adopted the International Covenant on Civil and Political Rights (ICCPR) and the International Covenant on Economic, Social and Cultural Rights (ICESCR) which entered into force ten years later. These covenants made many of the provisions of the Universal Declaration of Human Rights effectively binding on governments. As of October 2013, the ICESCR had been ratified by 161 states and the ICCPR by 167 states. The Universal Declaration and the two covenants have become known as the 'International Bill of Rights'.

The **Convention on the Rights of the Child 1989** incorporates the full range of rights applying to children, defined as people under the age of eighteen years. These include civil, cultural, economic, political and social rights. As described by the United Nations:

> The Convention sets out these rights in 54 articles and two Optional Protocols. It spells out the basic human rights that children everywhere have: the right to survival; to develop to the fullest; to protection from harmful influences, abuse and exploitation; and to participate fully in family, cultural and social life. The four core principles of the Convention are non-discrimination; devotion to the best interests of the child; the right to life, survival and development; and respect for the views of the child. Every right spelled out in the Convention is inherent to the human dignity and harmonious development of every child. The Convention protects children's rights by setting standards in health care; education; and legal, civil and social services.
>
> By agreeing to undertake the obligations of the Convention (by ratifying or acceding to it), national governments have committed themselves to protecting and ensuring children's rights and they have agreed to hold themselves accountable for this commitment before the international community. States Parties to the Convention are obliged to develop and undertake all actions and policies in the light of the best interests of the child.

This Convention has been ratified by **every member of the United Nations except Somalia and the United States**.

According to Article 2 of the ICCPR, States Parties commit to respecting all rights enumerated in the Convention and ensuring that persons whose rights are violated have an 'effective remedy'. Competent authorities are obliged to 'enforce such remedies when granted'. In contrast, Article 2 of the ICESCR only requires States Parties to 'take steps, individually and through international assistance and cooperation … to the maximum of [their] available resources, with a view to achieving progressively the full realization of the rights recognized in the present Covenant by all appropriate means'. In other words, the rights recognized in both covenants are in principle

UN Secretary-General Kofi Annan at the UN headquarters in New York, 30 December 2004.

Kofi Annan on the rule of law

In his Report of 23 August 2004 to the Security Council, the then Secretary-General Kofi Annan referred to the rule of law as being at the very heart of the organization's mission. He stated:

> It [the rule of law] refers to a principle of governance in which all persons, institutions and entities, public and private, *including the State itself*, are accountable to laws that are publicly promulgated, equally enforced and independently adjudicated, and which are consistent with international human rights norms and standards. It requires, as well, measures to ensure adherence to the principles of law, equality before the law, accountability to the law, fairness in the application of the law, separation of powers, participation in decision-making, legal certainty, avoidance of arbitrariness and procedural and legal transparency.

The Secretary-General was conflating the rule of law as a protection of the rights of individual citizens and the relationship of states between themselves.

However, the application of the rule of law between states is increasingly gaining traction.

*Competition in space: a 1973 poster produced in the Soviet
Union to mark Cosmonauts' Day, depicting Yuri Gagarin,
the first man in space; a 1969 poster issued by NASA to mark
the Apollo 12 mission, the second to land on the moon.*

judicially enforceable, but the rights protected by the ICCPR are
directly enforceable whilst the rights protected by the ICESCR were to
be progressively implemented. It should come as no surprise that in
very few countries are the social and economic rights justiciable.
Increasingly, civil society is pressuring governments to recognize and
enforce those social and economic rights.

There are now also a number of regional human rights treaties that,
with varying strength of provisions for enforcement, guarantee
individuals the right to hold their own governments accountable for
human rights violations. They are the European Convention on
Human Rights 1950, the American Convention on Human Rights
1969, the African Convention on Human and Peoples' Rights 1981,
and the Arab Convention on Human Rights 1994. By far the most
advanced system is that under the European Convention, with
thousands of individual complaints coming to the European Court of
Human Rights each year. Indeed, that Court has recently been
over-burdened with an unmanageable caseload.

King John could just about conceive of citizens having rights arising
from international commerce (Magna Carta 1215 clauses 41–2). He
could not possibly have imagined States requiring protection from the
conquest of space. Yet, the principles that were included in Magna
Carta translate without conceptual difficulty to these modern
incarnations of international law. There are conventions relating to
commerce between citizens of different states. The Convention on the
Limitation Period in the International Sale of Goods 1974 establishes
uniform rules governing the period of time within which a party under
a contract for the international sale of goods must commence legal
proceedings against another party to assert a claim arising from the
contract or relating to its breach, termination or validity. The United
Nations Convention on the Carriage of Goods by Sea 1978 establishes

a uniform legal regime that governs the rights and obligations of
shippers, carriers under contracts of carriage of goods by sea. There are
complex international laws relating to the carriage of goods and
persons by air. In the preceding half-century, space exploration has
made significant advances. The potential for competition and even
violent contest with regard to the benefits of such scientific endeavours
has resulted in far-reaching international treaties.

The need for international lawmaking is well illustrated by the
failure thus far to reach agreement on the provisions of a global
telecoms treaty that would impose controls over the use of the
Internet. Negotiations recently broke down because of disagreement
over whether the Internet should be within the scope of regulation at
all and whether the treaty should include language recognizing a
right to access telecommunication services. In March 2014, Sir Tim
Berners-Lee, inventor of the World Wide Web, called specifically for
'an online Magna Carta' to protect the Web's independence and the
rights of its users.

There are today in excess of 150,000 international treaties registered
with the United Nations. The interpretation and procedures with
regard to such international treaties are governed by the provisions of
the Vienna Convention on the Law of Treaties, 1969. This Convention
has been ratified by 114 nations. A number of nations that have not
ratified the Convention, such as the United States, accept that its
provisions now represent customary international law and are thus
binding on them.

A more difficult situation obtains with regard to enforcement of
orders of international criminal courts. One need look no further than
the conduct of Sudan and Libya in failing and indeed refusing to
comply with orders issued by the International Criminal Court. The
referrals of those two situations to the Court were made by the
Security Council under peremptory resolutions issued pursuant to the
provisions of Chapter VII of the Charter of the United Nations. Sudan
and Libya are thus also in violation of their Charter obligations. The
Security Council has not taken any action in response.

On the other hand, during the later 1990s, political and economic
pressure exerted by the United States against Serbia and Croatia
resulted in those nations sending senior members of their governments
and militaries for trial before the United Nations International
Criminal Tribunal for the former Yugoslavia. As that tribunal comes

to the end of its mission, every single one of those indicted has faced trial in The Hague. International criminal law and the tribunals that enforce it have effectively limited the previous regime of impunity for war criminals.

In a recent law journal article, Professors Oona Hathaway and Scott Shapiro describe the ways in which international legal norms are enforced – not usually by force but by denying violators the benefits that a myriad of international treaties provide for States Parties. It is this process that the authors describe as 'outcasting'. For example, violations of the rules of the World Trade Organization and its compulsory dispute resolution system will result in specific retaliatory trade measures and might also deprive offending nations of the benefits of the General Agreement on Tariffs and Trade. A failure to comply with orders of the European Court of Human Rights could result in suspension of membership in the European Union. Then there are unofficial sanctions brought about by international organizations 'naming and shaming' violators and bringing often effective pressure on other governments to take retaliatory steps to encourage compliance.

The rule of law as applied in the global context has advanced in ways and to a degree that would have been unimaginable half a century ago.

Former Yugoslav president Slobodan Milošević on trial at The Hague, 12 February 2002.

The influence of Magna Carta in the domestic laws of democratic nations

In the second half of the twentieth century democratic government spread to many new nations in the aftermath of the egregious human rights violations that accompanied the rise of fascism in Germany, the commission of widespread war crimes during the Second World War, and the end of colonialism. In this way, the influence of Magna Carta became truly international.

In the older democracies there was no consistency with regard to the codification of constitutional principles. In Britain, Australia and Canada those principles are to be found in a number of constitutional documents whilst in the United States and France they are incorporated in one. Israel did not follow the more recent trend. The terms of a bill of rights became controversial in the early years of statehood and the Israeli Parliament (the Knesset) opted for a series of 'Basic Laws' instead.

For some decades there have been vigorous debates concerning the application of 'the rule of law' in the domestic context. Whatever the differences, there is general agreement that the core principles for democratic government include the separation of powers between the legislature, executive and judiciary, an independent judiciary, an independent legal profession, equality before the law, and due process. Those principles are expressly or implicitly to be found in Magna Carta. They are also enshrined in the constitutions of all democracies, though they are not all strictly observed in all democratic states.

There are many examples of overlap between different branches of government, even in well-established democracies. In the United States, the Vice President, second in authority to the President in the executive branch, is also the presiding officer of the Senate, one of the two chambers of the legislative branch. In the United Kingdom, the Constitutional Reform Act of 2005 removed some of the more glaring overlaps. Until then, the most senior member of the judiciary, the Lord Chancellor, was a member of all three branches. In addition to serving on the Appellate Committee of the House of Lords, which was the highest court of appeal, he presided over the House of Lords itself, and was a senior member of the Cabinet. The reforms of 2005 created an independent Supreme Court with its own building in London, and removed the legislative and judicial functions of the Lord Chancellor.

Nelson Mandela casts his vote in the first free elections in post-Apartheid South Africa, 1994.

The Lord Chancellor is now only a member of the Cabinet, where he or she serves as the Secretary of State for Justice.

In all systems, competition between the three branches has to be kept in equilibrium through systems of checks and balances. For instance, the appointment of judges is not left to the whim of the executive or legislative branch. In many countries, including the United Kingdom, South Africa and Israel, judges are appointed on the recommendation of an independent appointments committee. This method is now also being introduced in India. The United States invests appointment powers in the legislative and executive branches, which are expected to work together. The President nominates judicial candidates who must then be confirmed by the Senate.

In countries where the judiciary has the power to review legislation, the political branches have a crucial interest in knowing and evaluating the views of potential judges prior to their appointment. These political ramifications frequently follow nominees onto the bench. That has become the norm in the United States where the Senate confirmation process has become intensely drawn out, partisan and often acrimonious.

It has often been said that the judiciary is by far the weakest branch of government. That follows from its reliance on the executive branch to enforce its orders and the legislative branch to provide its resources.

The orders made by the courts, and the judicial reasoning on which they are based, might well be anathema to the government of the day. This notwithstanding, it is crucial for democratic governance that final orders of the courts are implemented. This is especially important in new democracies. In the early days of South Africa's democracy, the Constitutional Court declared executive orders relating to the then forthcoming local government election to be unconstitutional and void. President Nelson Mandela's response was to state that the Court was carrying out its constitutional mandate and duty. Notwithstanding inconvenience and expense, he recalled Parliament to enact the laws in a manner consistent with the Constitution. That deference to the functions and powers of the courts has continued, and orders of the South African courts are respected and enforced.

The most serious danger to the application of the rule of law in democracies in the second decade of the twenty-first century arises from inroads into the principles of the equal protection of the law and due process. This situation has arisen in response to the fears arising out of acts and threats of terrorism, and has become exacerbated since the catastrophic events of 11 September 2001. The dilemma facing governments in democracies arises from the tension between the necessity to combat terrorism, on the one hand, and the resort to means that are not consistent with the rule of law, on the other.

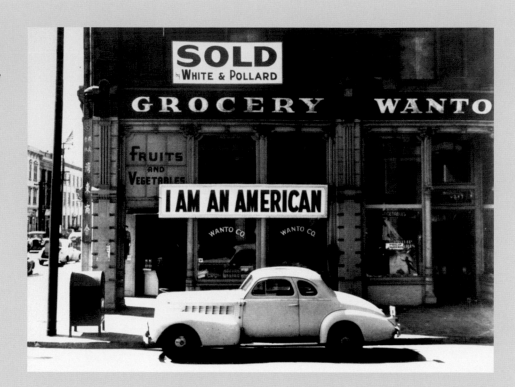

Below: Fred T. Korematsu, photographed c.1940.
Right: An American grocery store bearing the sign
'I am an American', placed on the front window the
day after the Pearl Harbor attack. The store was sold
after its owner, a University of California graduate
of Japanese descent, followed evacuation orders.

Reaction to Pearl Harbor

One compelling example of a State's overreaction in wartime is that of the United States to the attack on Pearl Harbor in 1941. Over 110,000 Japanese Americans were interned in 'War Relocation Camps'. In the case of *Korematsu v. The United States*, a sharply divided United States Supreme Court upheld a conviction of the appellant, a Japanese American, for failing to report for relocation. In a strong dissent, Justice Jackson was reported as follows:

> Much is said of the danger to liberty from the Army program for deporting and detaining these citizens of Japanese extraction. But a judicial construction of the due process clause that will sustain this order is a far more subtle blow to liberty than the promulgation of the order itself. A military order, however unconstitutional, is not apt to last longer than the military emergency. Even during

that period a succeeding commander may revoke it all. But once a judicial order rationalizes such an idea to show that it conforms with the Constitution, or rather rationalizes the Constitution to show that the Constitution sanctions such an order, the Court for all time has validated the principle of racial discrimination in criminal procedure and of transplanting American citizens.

In 1980, a commission appointed by President Jimmy Carter found little evidence to support allegations of Japanese disloyalty. In 1988 Congress apologized for the internment and made provision for the payment of reparations to those who had been interned and their heirs. In the legislation, Congress candidly admitted that the government action had been the result of 'racial prejudice, wartime hysteria, and a failure of political leadership.' The political victim of these actions was the rule of law itself.

The tendency of governments to overreact to situations of danger is hardly a new phenomenon. In times of war governments in democracies have not hesitated to violate the fundamental rights of their citizens. Justice William Brennan of the United States Supreme Court referred to this tendency in the following words:

There is considerably less to be proud about, and a good deal to

be embarrassed about, when one reflects on the shabby treatment civil liberties have received in the United States during times of war and perceived threats to national security … After each perceived security crisis ended, the United States has remorsefully realized that the abrogation of civil liberties was unnecessary. But it has proven unable to prevent itself from repeating the error when the next crisis came along.

The twin towers of the World Trade Center ablaze, New York, 11 September 2001.

The words of Justice Brennan proved to be prescient. Legislation designed to combat terrorism has been introduced in the vast majority of nations. Indeed, the Security Council required such legislation in the terms of a peremptory resolution on 28 September 2001. Of the democratic nations, the United States and United Kingdom have passed the most far-reaching legislation. In what follows, I will consider only those two countries.

In the aftermath of the terrorist attacks of September 2001, the administration of President George W. Bush rushed through legislation that violated the fundamental principles underlying the rule of law, through a wholly acquiescent Congress. Less than a week after 9/11, Congress adopted a resolution authorizing the President to

use all necessary and appropriate force against those nations, organizations, or persons he determines planned, authorized, committed, or aided the terrorist attacks that occurred on September 11, 2001, or harbored such organizations or persons, in order to prevent any future acts of international terrorism against the United States by such nations, organizations or persons.

This resolution was passed pursuant to the provisions of section 5(b) of the War Powers Resolution of 1973, giving the President the authority to use military force as he might determine. The President used that authority to empower himself to determine that any individual, not being a United States citizen, was a member of Al Qaeda who had participated in terrorist activities and who should be dealt with in accordance with the provisions of the order. Thus began 'the war on terrorism' – a war without an end.

From this followed the series of policies and acts pursuant to them that has so seriously weakened the application of the rule of law in the United States. Hundreds of people, by order of the President, have been detained at Guantanamo Bay and deprived of access to federal courts. That they were there subjected to forms of torture appears with horrifying detail from the leaked report of 14 February 2007 to the United States Government from the International Committee of the Red Cross.

Conduct that violates the provisions of the Torture Convention had earlier been authorized by the infamous torture memorandum that was issued by the then Assistant Attorney-General of the United States. It was also later leaked to the media. Photographs of the attacks on the fundamental dignity of the unfortunate prisoners at Abu Ghraib Prison were broadcast around the world. The Military Commissions Act of 2006 in effect made provision for two systems of law – one for United States citizens and another for aliens. The former were to be tried by the ordinary courts, the latter by specially constituted military tribunals. An unknown number of people detained by the United States have been held incommunicado in prisons outside the United States controlled by the Central Intelligence Agency. Some of those

The infamous image of prisoner Satar Jabar, hooded and attached to electrical shocking devices, at Abu Ghraib Prison, February 2006.

Royal Ulster Constabulary and British Army personnel shooting and reloading rubber bullets in a clash with Catholic demonstrators, Belfast, 1981.

detained were handed to foreign governments for purposes of interrogation. These acts were kept secret and placed those subject to them in a highly vulnerable position.

The United Kingdom has had over thirty years of experience of responding to terrorism emanating from Northern Ireland. The reaction of the British government was to treat acts of terrorism as criminal conduct. Legislation made provision for broad police powers of search and arrest. Membership of proscribed terrorist organizations was made a criminal offence. The freedom of movement of people could be restricted without judicial intervention. Prior to 2000, the European Court of Human Rights held that the United Kingdom, even though it had lawfully derogated some provisions of the Convention, had violated fundamental provisions of the European Convention on Human Rights. These included violations of the rights to life, liberty, fair trial and protection against torture. In 2000, the United Kingdom's laws were tightened and the definition of 'terrorism' broadened under the provisions of the Terrorism Act. Legislation allows the authorities surveillance powers over many kinds of communication subject to warrants issued by a court.

In reaction to the events of 9/11, the British Parliament passed the 2001 Anti-Terrorism, Crime and Security Act. Like its United States counterpart, this legislation was passed with dramatic speed and hardly any debate in Parliament. The legislation confers wide and far-reaching powers on the government that seriously implicate rights of liberty and privacy. These powers are not restricted to acts of terrorism. Providers of telecommunications are required to supply information on private communications when so ordered by the authorities. Non-nationals may be designated 'suspected international terrorists' and subjected to deportation. If the individual might be

US drone over southern Afghanistan, 29 November 2008.

Obama and the war on terrorism

Some, but by no means all, of America's subversions of the rule of law were reversed when President Obama came into office. The promise to close the prison on Guantanamo Bay was not fulfilled, although the number of people held there has been reduced. On the other hand, the Obama Administration has substantially expanded the use of drones to assassinate suspected terrorists. It has also continued the vast spy network of the National Security Agency that operates both internationally and domestically. With regard to these programmes, no effective oversight has been disclosed by the Administration.

subject to torture in his or her own country and therefore cannot be lawfully deported, the person may be detained without trial and without recourse to the ordinary courts. The United Kingdom adopted laws far more draconian in nature than those of any other member of the European Union. In *A and others v. Secretary of State for the Home Department*, a majority of the Appellate Committee of the House of Lords held that the detention of foreign prisoners without trial under the 2001 Act was a violation of the European Convention, because it discriminated between nationals and foreign nationals. In a separate concurring judgement, Lord Hoffman stated that the whole scheme was contrary to the United Kingdom Constitution. He expressed himself as follows:

> This is a nation which has been tested in adversity, which has survived physical destruction and catastrophic loss of life. I do not underestimate the ability of fanatical groups of terrorists to kill and destroy, but they do not threaten the life of the nation. Whether we would survive Hitler hung in the balance, but there is no doubt that we shall survive Al-Qaeda. The Spanish people have not said that what happened in Madrid, hideous crime as it was, threatened the life of their nation. Their legendary pride would not allow it. Terrorist violence, serious as it is, does not threaten our institutions of government or our existence as a civil community.

> … Others of your Lordships who are also in favour of allowing the appeal would do so, not because there is no emergency threatening the life of the nation, but on the ground that a power of detention confined to foreigners is irrational and discriminatory. I would prefer not to express a view on this point. I said that the power of detention is at present confined to foreigners and I would not like to give the impression that all that was necessary was to extend the power to United Kingdom citizens as well. In my opinion, such a power in any form is not compatible with our constitution. The real threat to the life of the nation, in the sense of a people living in accordance with its traditional laws and political values, comes not from terrorism but from laws such as these. That is the true measure of what terrorism may achieve. It is for Parliament to decide whether to give the terrorists such a victory.

Lord Hoffman's concerns were prescient. In response to this ruling, Parliament enacted the Prevention of Terrorism Act, 2005, which granted the government extensive powers of surveillance and detention over both citizens and non-citizens alike. The Act was not repealed until 2011.

Terrorism and the reaction to it by democracies demonstrate yet again the need for the principles that underlie Magna Carta to be constantly nurtured and protected. If terrorism is indeed to remain a permanent feature of life in the twenty-first century, then the stark choice facing democracies is whether to abandon these principles or to find means of fighting terrorism that are consistent with the rule of law. I would suggest that terrorists should not be given the victory to which Lord Hoffman refers.

Richard Goldstone at the UN Office at Geneva, 7 July 2009.

The role of the rule of law in democracies can hardly be overstated. As we have seen, in leading democracies it has been violated from time to time, especially in times of actual or perceived threats to the nation. The need for vigilance by the legislature and civil society cannot be overstated.

No leader of a democratic state, and few even of oppressive societies, has publicly renounced the centrality of the principles of the rule of law. Their adherence to the doctrine is a deterrent to wider violations and is tribute to the endurance of the concept. For all people who support a democratic form of government, there is much to celebrate in 2015 on Magna Carta's eight hundredth anniversary.

Magna Carta: The 1215 Text

John, by the grace of God King of England, lord of Ireland, duke of Normandy and Aquitaine, count of Anjou, sends greetings to the archbishops, bishops, abbots, earls, barons, justices, foresters, sheriffs, reeves, ministers and all his bailiffs and faithful subjects. You should know that, at the prompting of God and for the salvation of our soul and the souls of all our ancestors and heirs, for the honour of God and for the exaltation of holy Church and the repair of our realm, through the counsel of our venerable fathers Stephen archbishop of Canterbury, primate of all England and cardinal of the holy Roman Church, Henry archbishop of Dublin, William bishop of London, Peter bishop of Winchester, Jocelin bishop of Bath and Glastonbury, Hugh bishop of Lincoln, Walter bishop of Worcester, William bishop of Coventry and Benedict bishop of Rochester, Master Pandulf papal subdeacon and familiar, brother Aimery master of the knighthood of the Temple in England, and the noble men William Marshal earl of Pembroke, William earl of Salisbury, William earl Warenne, William earl of Arundel, Alan of Galloway constable of Scotland, Warin fitz Gerald, Peter fitz Herbert, Hubert de Burgh seneschal of Poitou, Hugh de Neville, Matthew fitz Herbert, Thomas Basset, Alan Basset, Philip d'Aubigné, Robert of Ropsley, John Marshal, John fitz Hugh and others of our faithful subjects

1. We have, in the first place, granted to God and by this our present charter confirmed for ourselves and our heirs in perpetuity that the English Church is to be free and have its rights in whole and its liberties unimpaired, and we wish that this be observed as is evident from the fact that of our own free will, before the dispute that arose between us and our barons, we granted and confirmed by our charter freedom of elections, reputed to be of great importance and most necessary to the English Church, and obtained confirmation of this from the lord Pope Innocent III, which we shall observe and which we wish to be observed by our heirs in perpetuity in good faith.

We have also granted to all the free men of our realm for ourselves and our heirs in perpetuity all the liberties written below, to have and hold to them and their heirs from us and our heirs:

2. If any of our earls or barons* or others holding of us in chief by knight service should die, and at his death his heir is of full age and owes relief,* he will have his inheritance by the ancient relief, namely the heir or heirs of an earl £100 from a whole earl's barony, the heir or heirs of a baron £100 for a whole barony,* and the heir or heirs of a knight at most 100 shillings from a whole knight's fee, and anyone who owes less will give less according to the ancient custom of fees.

3. If, however, the heir of any such person happens to be under age and in custody, when he comes of age he will have his inheritance without relief and without fine.

4. The keeper of the land of such an heir who is under age will not take from the land anything other than the reasonable issues and reasonable customs and reasonable services, and this without destruction or waste of men or goods. And if we entrust the custody of any such land to a sheriff or to any other who is answerable to us for its issues, and he causes destruction or waste of the custody, we shall take amends of him, and the land will be committed to two lawful and discreet men of that fee who answer to us for the issues or to him to whom we shall have assigned them. And if we shall

give or sell to anyone the custody of any such land, and he causes destruction or waste, he will lose the custody and it will be transferred to two lawful and discreet men of that fee who will be similarly answerable to us as is aforesaid.

5. The keeper, however, so long as he has custody of the land, will maintain the houses, parks, fishponds, ponds, mills and other things pertaining to that land from the issues of the same land, and he will restore to the heir, when he comes of full age, all his land stocked with ploughs and wainage* such as the season of wainage (i.e. the agricultural season) demands, and such as the issues of the land can reasonably support.

6. Heirs will be married without disparagement, save that before a marriage is contracted it be made known to the heir's close kin.

7. After her husband's death, a widow will have her marriage portion and her inheritance at once and without any difficulty, nor will she pay anything for her dower, for her marriage portion or for her inheritance which she and her husband held on the day of the said husband's death, and she may stay in her husband's house for forty days after his death, within which period her dower will be assigned to her.

8. No widow will be compelled to marry so long as she wishes to live without a husband, provided that she give security that she will not marry without our consent if she shall hold of us, or without the consent of her lord of whom she holds, if she shall hold of another.

9. Neither we nor our bailiffs shall seize any land or rent in payment of a debt so long as the chattels of the debtor are sufficient to repay the debt, nor will the sureties of the debtor be distrained* so long as the chief debtor himself is capable of paying the debt, and if the chief debtor defaults in the payment of the debt, having nothing wherewith to pay it, the sureties will be answerable for the debt, and if they wish, they may have the lands and revenues of the debtor until they have received satisfaction for the debt they previously paid on his behalf, unless the chief debtor shows that he has discharged his obligations to the sureties.

10. If anyone who has borrowed from the Jews any amount, great or small, dies before the debt is repaid, it will not carry interest so long as the heir is under age, of whomsoever he holds, and if such debt falls into our hands, we shall take nothing except the chattel specified in the bond.

11. And if a man dies owing a debt to the Jews, his wife is to have her dower and pay nothing for the debt, and if he leaves children under age, their needs will be met in a manner in keeping with the holding of the deceased, and the debt will be paid out of his residue, saving the service due to the lords. Debts owing to others than Jews will be dealt with likewise.

12. No scutage* or aid* is to be levied in our realm except by the common counsel of our realm, unless it is for the ransom of our body, the knighting of our eldest son, or the first marriage of our eldest daughter, and for these only a reasonable aid is to be levied. Aids from the city of London are to be treated likewise.

13. And the city of London is to have all its ancient liberties and free customs both by land and water. Furthermore, we will and grant that all other cities, boroughs, towns and ports will have all their liberties and free customs.

14. And to obtain the common counsel of the realm for the assessment of an aid, except in the three cases aforesaid, or a scutage, we will have archbishops, bishops, abbots, earls and greater barons summoned individually by our letters, and we shall also have summoned generally through our sheriffs and bailiffs all those who hold of us in chief, for a fixed date, with at least forty days' notice, and to a fixed place, and in all letters of this summons we shall state the cause for the summons. And when the summons has thus been made, the business will go forward on the day assigned according to the counsel of those present, even if not all those summoned have come.

15. Henceforth we shall not grant anyone that he may take an aid from his free men except to ransom his person, to make his eldest son a knight or to marry his eldest daughter for the first time, and for these purposes only a reasonable aid is to be levied.

16. No man will be compelled to perform more service for a knight's fee or for any other free tenement than is due therefrom.

17. Common pleas will not follow our court but will be held in some fixed place.

18. Recognizances of *novel disseisin,* *mort d'ancestor* and *darrein presentment* will not be held elsewhere than in the court of the county in which they occur, and in this manner: we, or if we are out of the realm, our chief justiciar,* shall send two justices through each county four times a year, who with four knights of each county chosen by the county will hold the said assizes in the county court on the day and in the place of meeting of the county court.

19. And if the said assizes cannot all be held on the day of the county court, so many knights and freeholders of those present in the county court on that day will remain behind as will suffice to make judgements according to whether the business be great or small.

20. A free man will not be amerced* for a trivial offence except in accordance with the degree of the offence, and for a serious offence he will be amerced according to its gravity, saving his livelihood, and a merchant likewise, saving his merchandise. In the same way, a villein* will be amerced saving his wainage, if they fall into our mercy, and none of the aforesaid amercements will be imposed save by the oath of reputable men of the neighbourhood.

21. Earls and barons will not be amerced except by their peers and only in accordance with the degree of the offence.

22. No clerk will be amerced on his lay tenement except in the manner of the others aforesaid, and without reference to the extent of his ecclesiastical benefice.

23. No vill or man will be forced to build bridges at river banks, except those who ought to do so by tradition and law.

24. No sheriff, constable, coroner or others of our bailiffs will hold pleas of our crown.*

25. All shires, hundreds,* wapentakes* and ridings will be at the ancient farms, without any increment, except our demesne* manors.

26. If anyone holding a lay fief of us dies, and our sheriff or bailiff shows our letters patent of summons for a debt which the deceased owed to us, the sheriff or our bailiff will be allowed to attach* and list the chattels of the deceased found in lay fee to the value of that debt, by view of lawful men, so that nothing is removed until the evident debt is paid to us, and the residue will be relinquished to the executors to

carry out the will of the deceased. And if he owes us nothing, all the chattels will be accounted as the deceased's, saving their reasonable shares to his wife and children.

27. And if any free man dies intestate, his chattels are to be distributed by his nearest relations and friends, under the supervision of the Church, saving to everyone the debts which the deceased owed him.

28. No constable or any other of our bailiffs will take any man's corn or other chattels unless he pays cash for them at once or can delay payment with the agreement of the seller.

29. No constable is to compel any knight to give money for castle guard, if he is willing to perform that guard in his own person or by another reliable man, if for some good reason he is unable to do it himself, and if we take or send him on military service, he will be excused the guard in proportion to the period of his service in our army.

30. No sheriff or bailiff of ours or anyone else is to take horses or carts of any free man for carting without the free man's agreement.

31. Neither we nor our bailiffs shall take other men's timber for castles or other work of ours without the agreement of the owner of the wood.

32. We shall not hold the lands of convicted felons for more than a year and a day, after which the lands will be returned to the lords of the fiefs.

33. Henceforth all fish-weirs* will be completely removed from the Thames and the Medway and throughout all England, except on the sea coast.

34. The writ* called 'praecipe'* will not in future be issued to anyone in respect of any holding whereby a free man might lose his court.

35. Let there be one measure of wine throughout our realm, and one measure of ale and one measure of corn, namely the London quarter, and one width of cloth whether dyed, russet or halberjet,* namely two ells within the selvedges.* Let it be the same with weights as with measures.

36. Henceforth, nothing will be given or taken for the writ of inquisition of life or limb, but it will be given freely and not refused.

37. If anyone holds of us by fee-farm, by socage* or by burgage,* and holds land of someone else by knight service, we shall not, by virtue of that fee-farm, socage or burgage, have custody of his heir or of land of his that belongs to the fief of another, nor shall we have custody of that fee-farm or socage or burgage unless such fee-farm owes knight service. We shall not have custody of the heir or land of anyone who holds of another by knight service by virtue of any petty serjeanty* which he holds of us by the service of rendering to us knives or arrows or the like.

38. Henceforth, no bailiff will put anyone on trial by his own unsupported allegation, without bringing credible witnesses to the charge.

39. No free man will be taken or imprisoned or disseised* or outlawed or exiled or in any way ruined, nor shall we go or send against him, save by the lawful judgement of his peers and/or by the law of the land.

40. To no one shall we sell, to no one shall we deny or delay right or justice.

41. All merchants are to be safe and secure in leaving and entering England, and in staying and travelling in England both by land and by water, to buy and sell free from all bad tolls, by the ancient and rightful customs, except in time of war and if such merchants come from a land at war against us. And if such are found in our land at the outbreak of war, they will be detained without damage to their persons or goods until we or our chief justiciar know how the merchants of our land are treated in the country at war against us, and if ours are safe there, the others will be safe in our land.

42. Henceforth anyone, saving his allegiance due to us, may leave our realm and return safe and secure by land and water, save for a short period in time of war on account of the general interest of the realm and excepting those imprisoned and outlawed according to the law of the realm, and natives of a land at war against us, and merchants who will be treated as aforesaid.

43. If anyone dies who holds of some escheat* such as the honours of Wallingford, Nottingham, Boulogne or Lancaster or of other escheats which are in our hands and are baronies, his heir will not give any relief or do any service to us other than what he would have done to the baron if that barony had been in a baron's hands, and we shall hold it in the same manner as the baron held it.

44. Henceforth men who live outside the forest* will not come before our justices of the forest upon a general summons, unless they are impleaded or are sureties for any person or persons who are attached for forest offences.

45. We shall not make justices, constables, sheriffs or bailiffs who do not know the law of the land and wish to observe it well.

46. All barons who have founded abbeys of which they have charters of the kings of England or ancient tenure will have custody thereof during vacancies as they ought to have.

47. All forests which have been afforested in our time will be disafforested at once, and river banks which we have enclosed in our time will be treated similarly.

48. All evil customs of forests and warrens, foresters and warreners, sheriffs and their servants, river banks and their wardens are to be investigated at once in every county by twelve sworn knights of the same county who are to be chosen by worthy men of the county, and within forty days of the inquiry such bad customs are to be abolished by them beyond recall, provided that we or our justiciar, if we are not in England, first know of it.

49. We shall restore at once all hostages and charters delivered to us by Englishmen as securities for peace or faithful service.

50. We shall dismiss completely from their offices the relations of Girard d'Athée that henceforth they will have no office in England, (namely) Engelard de Cigogné, Peter and Guy and Andrew de Chanceaux, Guy de Cigogné, Geoffrey de Martigny with his brothers, Philip Mark with his brothers and his nephew Geoffrey and all their followers.

51. Immediately after restoring peace, we shall remove from the realm all alien knights, crossbowmen, sergeants and mercenaries who have come with horses and arms to the injury of the realm.

52. If anyone has been disseised or deprived by us without lawful judgement of his peers of lands, castles, liberties or his right, we shall restore them to him at once, and if any disagreement arises on this, then let it be settled by the judgement of the twenty-five barons referred to below in the clause securing the peace. But for all those things of which anyone was disseised or deprived without lawful judgement of his peers by King Henry (II) our father or by King Richard (I) our brother, which we hold in our hand or which are held by others under our warranty, we shall have respite for the usual crusader's term,* excepting those cases in which a plea was begun or inquest made on our order before we took the cross. When we return, however, from our pilgrimage, or if perhaps we do not undertake it, we shall at once do full justice in these matters.

53. We shall have the same respite, and in the same manner, in doing justice on disafforesting or retaining those forests which Henry (II) our father or Richard (I) our brother afforested, and concerning custody of lands which are of the fee of another, the which custodies we have hitherto by virtue of a fee held of us by knight's service, and concerning abbeys founded on fees other than our own, in which the lord of the fee claims to have a right. And as soon as we return, or if we do not undertake our pilgrimage, we shall at once do full justice to complainants in these matters.

54. No one will be taken or imprisoned upon the appeal of a woman for the death of anyone except her husband.

55. All fines which were made with us unjustly and contrary to the law of the land, and all amercements imposed unjustly and contrary to the law of the land, will be completely remitted or else they will be settled by the judgement of the twenty-five barons mentioned below in the clause securing the peace, or by the judgement of the majority of the same, along with the aforesaid Stephen archbishop of Canterbury if he can be present, and others whom he wishes to summon with him for this purpose. And if he cannot be present, the business will nevertheless proceed without him, provided that if any one or more of the aforesaid twenty-five barons are implicated in such a suit, they will stand down in this particular judgement and will be replaced by others chosen and sworn in by the rest of the same twenty-five for this case only.

56. If we have disseised or deprived Welshmen of lands, liberties or other things without lawful judgement of their peers in England or in Wales, they are to be returned to them at once, and if a dispute arises over this, it will be settled in the March* by judgement of their peers for tenements in

England according to the laws of England, and for tenements in Wales according to the laws of Wales, and for tenements in the March according to the law of the March. The Welsh are to do the same for us and ours.

57. For all those things, however, of which any Welshman has been disseised or deprived without lawful judgement of his peers by King Henry (II) our father or King Richard (I) our brother, which we have in our hands or which others hold under our warranty, we shall have respite for the usual crusader's term, excepting those cases in which a plea was begun or inquest made on our order before we took the cross. However, when we return, or if perhaps we do not go on pilgrimage, we shall at once give them full justice in accordance with the laws of the Welsh and the aforesaid regions.

58. We shall restore at once the son of Llewylyn and all the hostages from Wales and the charters delivered to us as security for peace.

59. We shall treat with Alexander King of the Scots concerning the return of his sisters and hostages and his liberties and rights in the same manner in which we act towards our other barons of England, unless it ought to be otherwise because of the charters which we have from William his father, formerly King of the Scots, and this will be determined by the judgement of his peers in our court.

60. All these aforesaid customs and liberties which we have granted to be held in our realm as far as pertains to us towards our men will be observed by all men of our realm, both clerks and lay, as far as pertains to them towards their own men.

61. Since, moreover, we have granted all the aforesaid things for God, for the repair of our realm and the better settling of the dispute which has arisen between us and our barons, wishing these things to be enjoyed fully and undisturbed in perpetuity, we give and grant them the following security, namely that the barons will choose any twenty-five barons of the realm they wish, who with all their might ought to observe, maintain and cause to be observed the peace and liberties which we have granted and confirmed to them by this our present charter, so that if we or our justiciar or our bailiffs or any other of our ministers offend against anyone in any way, or transgress any of the articles of peace or security, and the offence is indicated to four of the aforesaid twenty-five barons, those four will come to

us or our justiciar, if we are out of the realm, and will bring it to our notice and ask that we have it redressed without delay. And if we, or our justiciar, should we be out of the realm, do not redress the offence within forty days from the time when it was brought to the notice of us or our justiciar, should we be out of the realm, then the aforesaid four barons will refer the case to the rest of the twenty-five barons, and those twenty-five barons with the commune of all the land will distrain and distress* us in every way they can, namely by seizing castles, lands and possessions, and in such other ways as they can, saving our person and those of our queen and of our children, until, in their judgement, amends have been made, and when it has been redressed, they are to obey us as they did before. And anyone in the land who wishes may take an oath to obey the orders of the said twenty-five barons in the execution of all the aforesaid matters, and to join with them in distressing us to the best of his ability, and we publicly and freely permit anyone who wishes to take the oath, and we shall never forbid anyone to take it. Moreover, we shall compel and order all those in the land who of themselves and of their own free will are unwilling to take an oath to the twenty-five barons to distrain and distress us with them, to take the oath as aforesaid. And if any of the twenty-five barons dies or leaves the land or is otherwise prevented from discharging these aforesaid duties, the rest of the aforesaid barons will on their own decision choose another in his place who will take the oath in the same way as the others. In all matters the execution of which is committed to those twenty-five barons, if it should happen that the twenty-five are present and disagree amongst themselves on anything, or if any of them who has been summoned will not come or cannot come, whatever the majority of those present may provide or order is to be taken as fixed and settled as if the whole twenty-five had agreed to it, and the aforesaid twenty-five are to swear that they will faithfully observe all the aforesaid and will do all they can to secure its observance. And we will procure nothing from anyone, either personally or through another, by which any of these concessions and liberties will be revoked or diminished, and if any such thing is procured it will be null and void, and we shall never use it either ourselves or through another.

62. And we have fully remitted and pardoned to all any ill will, grudge or rancour that has arisen between us and our subjects, clerk or lay, from the time of the dispute. Moreover, we have fully remitted and pardoned to all, clerk and lay, as far as pertains to us, all offences occasioned by the said dispute from Easter in the sixteenth year of our reign to the conclusion of peace. And moreover we have caused letters patent of the lord Stephen, archbishop of Canterbury, and the lord Henry, archbishop of Dublin, the aforesaid bishops and Master Pandulf to be made for them on this security and the aforesaid concessions.

63. Wherefore we wish and firmly command that the English Church will be free, and the men in our realm will have and hold all the aforesaid liberties, rights and concessions well and peacefully, freely and quietly, fully and completely for themselves and their heirs of us and our heirs in all things and places for ever, as is aforesaid. Moreover, an oath has been sworn, both on our part and on the part of the barons, that all these things aforesaid will be observed in good faith and without evil intent. Witness the abovementioned and many others. Given by our hand in the meadow that is called Runnymede between Windsor and Staines, on the fifteenth day of June in the seventeenth year of our reign.

Glossary

aid (cc.12, 14, 15): a monetary payment charged by the King or other lord

amercement (cc.20, 21, 22, 55): a fine payable for breach of procedure or other offence

attachment (cc.26, 44): the legal procedure by which property is seized to ensure enforcement of a judgement

baron/barony (cc.1, 2, 14, 21, 43, 46, 52, 55, 59, 61, 63): the holder/landholding of a lord holding directly of the King as a tenant in chief (i.e. without intermediary lord between landholder and King)

burgage (c.37): form of tenure enjoyed by a burgess (i.e. townsman), generally in return for a fixed annual rent

crusader's term (cc.52, 57): the privileged length of time extended to all vowed to go on crusade, during which they were protected against legal proceedings and certain forms of taxation

darrein presentment (c.18): a legal procedure for the recovery of the patronage of churches to which the litigant claims the right of presentation

demesne (c.25): the land retained in a lord's direct possession, when the rest of his estate was 'farmed' (i.e. rented) out to knights or lesser men

disseisin (cc.39, 52, 56–7): the forced dispossession of property

distraint (cc.9, 61): forced seizure of property in lieu of unpaid rent or other debt

distress (c.61): procedure akin to distraint

ells within the selvedges (c.35): specified distance (*c.*18 inches) from one edge of a piece of cloth to its opposite edge

escheat (c.43): a landholding that has reverted to its overlord for lack of heirs within the tenant family

fish-weirs (c.33): large traps, essentially a network of wooden staves sunk in rivers, into which fish swim but from which they cannot escape

forest (cc.44, 47, 48, 53): land not necessarily wooded but set aside for the King's hunt under special law intended to protect game animals and their habitat

halberjet (c.35): a type of cloth

hundred (c.25): an administrative unit of land into which the shire or county was divided

justiciar (cc.18, 41, 48, 61): the King's chief law officer, responsible for the working of the King's law courts

March (c.56): the border region dividing two realms, here the 'Welsh Marches'

mort d'ancestor (c.18): a legal procedure for the recovery of land rightfully inherited

novel disseisin (c.18): a legal procedure for the recovery of land recently seized

pleas of the crown (c.24): certain categories of legal procedure, involving such offences as murder, homicide, rape and arson, reserved for hearing in the royal as opposed to manor courts or the courts of lesser lords

praecipe (c.34): a standard legal writ, sent by the King to the sheriff, ordering him to 'command' (i.e. from the Latin verb 'praecipere') a lord to transfer a case from his own court to that of the King

relief (cc.2, 3, 43): the payment to the King owed by a knight or baron for succession to his inherited lands

scutage (cc.12, 14): a money payment made in lieu of personal military service (literally 'shield money')

serjeanty (c.37): landholding in return for service, often for performance of a regular duty such as keeping a lord's falcons, polishing his weapons, etc

socage (c.37): form of tenure enjoyed by a 'soke man', generally in return for a fixed annual rent

villein (c.20): an unfree tenant, i.e. a peasant or 'serf', bonded to his or her land

wainage (cc.5, 20): service of carts or other agricultural transport

wapentake (c.25): the northern English equivalent to the southern 'hundred'

writ (cc.34, 36): a letter or other written instruction, required to initiate legal action in the King's courts

Section of the Dering Roll, c.1270–80, the oldest extant English roll of arms.

Appendix Two

The Magna Carta Sureties

The identity of the twenty-five barons appointed in 1215 as enforcers of Magna Carta is disclosed to us by the thirteenth-century chronicler Matthew Paris, and also by a contemporary list, now in Lambeth Palace Library, that supplies not only their names but lists of the numbers of knights who were to serve with them – from the two hundred promised by Geoffrey de Mandeville or William Marshal the younger, all the way through to the relatively humble ten knights offered by such men as Roger de Mowbray and William Malet. The total number of knights offered comes to 1,183. As for the barons themselves, thanks to the descent of their lands to their heirs, the dates of their deaths are generally known. Their dates of birth, by contrast, are either unknown or can only be established approximately.

William de Aubigny (*c*.1174–1221), lord of Belvoir

Roger Bigod (*c*.1143–1221), earl of Norfolk, lord of Framlingham

Hugh Bigod (d. 1225), son of the above, briefly earl of Norfolk

Henry de Bohon (*c*.1175–1220), earl of Hereford, lord of Trowbridge

Richard de Clare (d. 1217), earl of Hertford, lord of Tonbridge, Clare and Glamorgan

Gilbert de Clare (*c*.1180–1230), son of the above, future earl of Hertford

John fitz Robert (d. 1241), lord of Whalton

Robert fitz Walter (d. 1235), lord of Dunmow and Baynard's Castle

William de Forz (*c*.1191–1241), earl of Aumale, lord of Holderness and Skipton

William Hardel (dates unknown), mayor of London

William of Huntingfield (d. *c*.1225), lord of Huntingfield

John de Lacy (*c*.1192–1241), constable of Chester, lord of Pontefract, future earl of Lincoln

William de Lanvaley (d. 1215), lord of Walkern

William Malet (*c*.1175–1215), lord of Curry Mallet

Geoffrey de Mandeville (*c*.1190–1216), earl of Essex and Gloucester, lord of Pleshy

William Marshal the younger (*c*.1190–1231), future earl of Pembroke, lord of Chepstow

Roger de Montbegon (d. 1226), lord of Hornby

Richard de Montfiquet (d. 1267), lord of Stansted Montfichet

William de Mowbray (*c*.1173–*c*.1224), lord of Thirsk

Richard de Percy (d. 1244), lord of Petworth

Saher de Quincy (d. 1219), earl of Winchester, lord of Leuchars in Fife

Robert de Ros (*c*.1182–1226/7), lord of Helmsley

Geoffrey de Say (d. 1230), lord of West Greenwich

Robert de Vere (d. 1221), earl of Oxford, lord of Hedingham

Eustace de Vescy (*c*.1170–1216), lord of Alnwick

Further Reading

Chapter One
Introduction

The classic academic study of Magna Carta remains that of J. C. Holt, *Magna Carta* (Cambridge, 1965; 2nd edn 1992). See also N. Vincent, *Magna Carta: A Very Short Introduction* (Oxford, 2013), and forthcoming from David Carpenter, *Magna Carta* (London, 2015). For general histories of England in the Middle Ages, see D. Carpenter, *The Struggle for Mastery: Britain 1066–1284* (London, 2003), and N. Vincent, *A Brief History of Britain 1066–1485* (London, 2012).

Chapter Two
Law before Magna Carta: The Anglo-Saxon Law Codes and Their Successors before 1215

J. Crick, '*Pristina Libertas*: Liberty and the Anglo-Saxons Revisited', *Transactions of the Royal Historical Society*, 6th ser., 14 (2004), pp. 47–71

J. Hudson, *The Formation of the English Common Law* (London, 1996)

———— *The Oxford History of the Laws of England II: 871–1216* (Oxford, 2012)

F. W. Maitland (and F. Pollock), *History of English Law*, 2 vols (Cambridge 1898, several times since reprinted)

B. O'Brien, *God's Peace and King's Peace: The Laws of Edward the Confessor* (Philadelphia, 1999)

P. Wormald, *The Making of English Law: King Alfred to the Twelfth Century* (Oxford, 1999)

———— *The First Code of English Law* (Canterbury, 2005)

Chapter Three
Plantagenet Tyranny and Lawmaking

M. Aurell, trans. D. Crouch, *The Plantagenet Empire* (London, 2007)

A. Duggan, *Thomas Becket* (London, 2004)

Glanvill, *The Treatise on the Laws and Customs of the Realm of England Commonly Called Glanvill*, ed. G. D. G. Hall (Oxford, 1965, reprinted 2002)

J. Guy, *Thomas Becket* (London, 2012)

J. E. A. Jolliffe, *Angevin Kingship* (London, 1955)

D. M. Stenton, *English Justice Between the Norman Conquest and the Great Charter 1066–1215* (London, 1965)

N. Vincent (ed.), *Henry II: New Interpretations* (Woodbridge, 2007)

W. L. Warren, *Henry II* (London, 1973)

Chapter Four
The Tyranny of King John

In addition to works cited above, see:

S. D. Church (ed.), *King John: New Interpretations* (Woodbridge, 1999)

J. C. Holt, *The Northerners* (Oxford 1961, 2nd edn 1992)

W. L. Warren, *King John* (London, 1961, 2nd edn 1964)

Chapter Five
Magna Carta: Defeat into Victory

P. Brand, *The Making of the Common Law* (London, 1992)

D. A. Carpenter, *The Minority of Henry III* (London, 1990)

———— *The Reign of Henry III* (London, 1996)

J. C. Holt, *Magna Carta and Medieval Government* (London, 1985)

I. Jennings et al, *The Great Charter: Four Essays on Magna Carta* (New York, 1965)

J. R. Maddicott, 'Magna Carta and the Local Community 1215–1259', *Past and Present*, 102 (1984), pp. 25–65

———— *The Origins of the English Parliament 924–1327* (Oxford, 2010)

R. V. Turner, *The King and His Courts* (Ithaca, NY, 1968)

Chapter Six
Magna Carta in the Later Middle Ages

J. H. Baker (ed.), *Readings and Moots at the Inns of Court II*, Selden Society, 105 (London, 1990)

M. Clanchy, *From Memory to Written Record: England 1066–1307* (2nd edn; Oxford, 1993)

C. Given-Wilson et al (eds), *The Parliament Rolls of Medieval England* (Leicester, 2005)

A. Harding, *Medieval Law and the Foundations of the State* (Oxford, 2002)

G. Harriss, *The New Oxford History of England: Shaping the Nation, England 1360–1461* (Oxford, 2005)

J. C. Holt, *Magna Carta* (2nd edn; Cambridge, 1992)

R. W. Kaeuper (ed.), *Law, Justice and Governance: New Views on Medieval Constitutionalism* (Leiden, 2013)

A. Musson, *Medieval Law in Context: The Growth of Legal Consciousness from Magna Carta to the Peasants' Revolt* (Manchester, 2001)

———— 'Constitutional Discourse in Illuminated English Law Books', in D. Nicolas, B. S. Bachrach and J. M. Murray (eds), *Comparative Perspectives on History and Historians* (Kalamazoo, 2012), pp. 189–214

The National Archives, Special Collections, Ancient Petitions (SC 8)

S. Phillips, *Edward II* (New Haven and London, 2011)

M. Prestwich, *The New Oxford History of England: Plantagenet England, 1225-1360* (Oxford, 2005)

G. O. Sayles (ed.), *Select Cases in the Court of King's Bench*, Selden Society, 88 (London, 1971)

F. Thompson, *Magna Carta: Its Role in the Making of the English Constitution 1300–1629* (Minneapolis, 1948)

Chapter Seven
From *Liber Homo* to 'Free-born Englishman': How Magna Carta Became a 'Liberty Document', 1508–1760s

B. Bailyn, *The Ideological Origins of the American Revolution* (Cambridge, MA, 1967)

———— *The Origins of Independence* (New York, 1968)

C. L. Becker, *The Declaration of Independence: A Study in the History of Political Ideas* (New York, 1942)

A. D. Boyer, *Law, Liberty and Parliament: Selected Essays on the Writings of Sir Edward Coke* (Indianapolis, 2004)

G. Burgess, *The Politics of the Ancient Constitution: An Introduction to English Political Thought 1603–1642* (Basingstoke, 1992)

A. H. Cash, *John Wilkes: The Scandalous Father of Civil Liberty* (New Haven and London, 2007)

J. Greenberg, *The Radical Face of the Ancient Constitution: St Edward's 'Laws' in Early Modern Political Thought* (New York, 2001)

C. Hill, *The Intellectual Origins of the English Revolution* (Oxford, 1965, rev. 1997)

P. B. Kurland and R. Lerner (eds), *The Founder's Constitution* (Chicago, 1987)

J. G. A. Pocock, *The Ancient Constitution and the Feudal Law* (Cambridge, 1957)

Richard L. Perry and John C. Cooper (eds), *Sources of Our Liberties* (Chicago, 1952), pp. 338–40

J. Sommerville, *Royalists and Patriots, Politics and Ideology, 1603–1640* (London, 1999)

Chapter Eight

Magna Carta in America: Entrenched

W. Blackstone, *Commentaries on the Laws of England*, 4 vols (1765–9; repr. Chicago, 1979)

S. Botein, *Early American Law and Society* (New York, 1983)

R. F. Bowden, 'The Colonial Bar and the American Revolution', *Marquette Law Review*, 60 (1976), pp. 1, 10 n. 27

J. P. Greene (ed.), *Great Britain and the American Colonies, 1606–1763* (Columbia, 1970)

A. E. D. Howard, *The Road from Runnymede: Magna Carta and Constitutionalism in America* (Charlottesville, 1968)

C. S. Hyneman and D. S. Lutz (eds), *American Political Writing during the Founding Era: 1760–1805* (Indianapolis, 1983)

P. B. Kurland and R. Lerner (eds), *The Founders' Constitution*, 5 vols (Chicago, 1987)

L. Levy, *Origins of the Bill of Rights* (New Haven, 1999)

P. Linebaugh, *Magna Carta Manifesto: Liberties and Commons for All* (Berkeley, 2008)

J. L. Malcolm, 'Doing No Wrong: Law, Liberty, and the Constraint of Kings', *Journal of British Studies*, 38 (April 1999), pp. 161–86

J. Quincy, *Massachusetts Bay Reports, 1761–1777* (Boston, 1865)

E. Sandoz (ed.), *Political Sermons of the American Founding, 1730–1805*, 2 vols (Indianapolis, 2nd edn, 1998)

H. J. Storing (ed.), *The Anti-Federalist: Writings by the Opponents of the Constitution* (Chicago, 1985)

Chapter Nine

Magna Carta in the Nineteenth Century

W. Chadwick, *King John of England; a History and Vindication, Based on the Original Authorities* (London, 1865)

B. Curwen, *Magna Charta. With An Introduction Containing the History of its Rise and Completion, etc* (London, 1810)

J. Greene, *A Lecture on the Magna Charta. With an Appendix Containing a Translation of the Entire Charter* (Bury St Edmunds, 1850)

R. Guha, *Gandhi Before India* (New Delhi, 2013)

A. Hassall, *Magna Charta: the Church and English Freedom*, Oxford House Papers, 6 (London, 1886)

J. C. Holt, *Magna Carta* (Cambridge, 1965)

H. J. M. Johnston, *The Voyage of the Komagata Maru: the Sikh Challenge to Canada's Colour Bar* (Delhi, 1979)

R. B. Kennard, *The Declaration of the King's Supremacy the Magna Charta of the English Churchman's Freedom: A Sermon* (London, 1854)

H. E. Malden (ed.), *Magna Carta Commemoration Essays* (London, 1917)

P. McHugh, *The Maori Magna Carta: New Zealand Law and the Treaty of Waitangi* (Auckland, 1991)

R. McWilliam, *The Tichborne Claimant: A Victorian Sensation* (London, 2007)

J. R. Miller, *Compact, Contract, Covenant: Aboriginal Treaty-Making in Canada* (Toronto, 2009), ch. 3

E. Shepherd Creasy, *The Textbook of the Constitution: Magna Charta, the Petition of Right, and the Bill of Rights: with Historical Comments, and Remarks on the Present Political Emergencies* (London, 1848)

R. Turner, *Magna Carta through the Ages* (London, 2003), ch. 7

Chapter Ten

From World War to World Heritage: Magna Carta in the Twentieth Century

C. Breay, *Magna Carta: Manuscripts and Myths* (London, 2002)

H. E. Malden (ed.), *Magna Carta Commemoration Essays* (London, 1917)

A. Pallister, *Magna Carta: The Heritage of Liberty* (Oxford, 1971)

N. Vincent, *The Magna Carta* (Sotheby's Sale Catalogue, New York, 18 December 2007)

———— *Australia's Magna Carta* (Canberra, 2010)

Chapter Eleven

Twenty-First Century Magna Carta

BBC News, 'US and UK Refuse to Sign UN's Communications Treaty', 14 December 2013, available at http://www.bbc.co.uk/news/technology-20717774

A. Black (ed.), *The Eleanor Roosevelt Papers, vol. 1: The Human Rights Years, 1945–1948*, Journal of American History, 95.4 (2009); also available at http:www.gwu.edu/~erpapers/maps/UDHRspeech.htm

W. J. Brennan Jr, 'The Quest to Develop a Jurisprudence of Civil Liberties in Times of Security Crises', *Israel Yearbook of Human Rights*, 18 (1988)

T. Cohen, 'Mandela Undismayed by High Court Setback', *San Francisco Chronicle*, 23 September 1995, at A12

D. Danziger and J. Gillingham, *1215: The Year of Magna Carta* (London, 2003)

'A Guide to the Memos on Torture', *New York Times* (2005), http://www.nytimes.com/ref/international/24MEMO-GUIDE.html

O. Hathaway and S. Shapiro, *Outcasting: Enforcement in Domestic and International Law*, Yale Law Journal, 121.2 (2011)

S. M. Hersh, 'Torture at Abu Ghraib', *The New Yorker*, 10 May 2004

International Committee of the Red Cross, ICRC Report on the Treatment of Fourteen 'High Value Detainees in CIA Custody' (2007), available at http://assets.nybooks.com/media/doc/2010/04/22/icrc-report.pdf

Unicef, Convention on the Rights of the Child, http://www.unicef.org/crc/

United Nations Treaty Collection, http://treaties.un.org/Pages/Treaties.aspx?id=4&subid=A&lang=en

Index